Houghton Mifflin

Circle Time and Practice

Student Book

- Circle Time
- Practice
- Looking Ahead Activities

Visit Education Place®
www.eduplace.com/kids

HOUGHTON MIFFLIN BOSTON

Printed in the U.S.A.

ISBN-10: 0-618-97348-6
ISBN-13: 978-0-618-97348-4

1 2 3 4 5 6 7 8 9 VH 16 15 14 13 12 11 10 09 08 07

Name ______________________ Date ____________

Circle Time

Problem of the Day

TAKS Objective 1 TEKS 2.6C

Use cubes. Make a pattern like this one:

Number Sense

TAKS Objective 1 TEKS 2.1B

Match the numbers to the words.

0	nine
1	seven
2	five
3	two
4	four
5	eight
6	six
7	one
8	three
9	zero

Number of the Day

TAKS Objective 1 TEKS 2.1A

2

Name some things that come in twos.

____

Numerical Fluency

TAKS Objective 1 TEKS 1.1A

Compare. Circle the correct words.

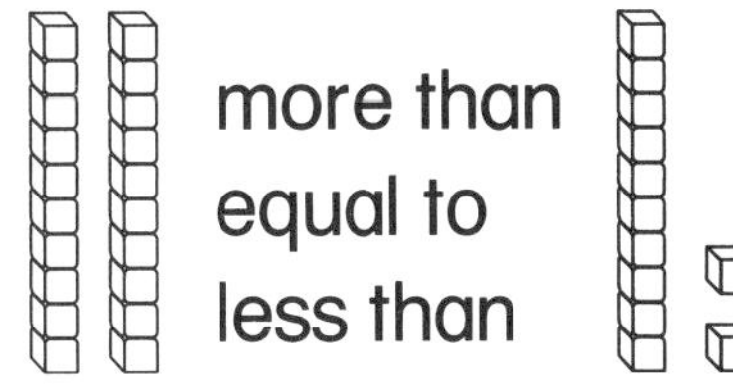

Name ______________________ Date ____________

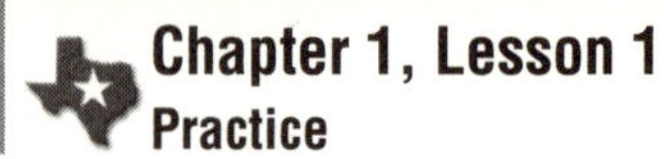

Find a Pattern

TAKS Objective 2
TEKS 2.6C

Draw or write to show the three shapes that come next in each pattern.

1. Marta saw this pattern on beads.

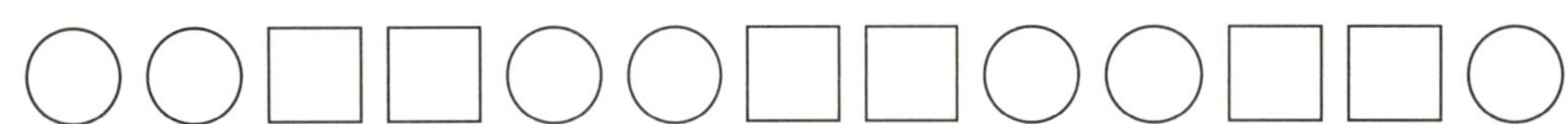

2. Herman saw this pattern on a hat.

3. Lupe saw this pattern on a rug.

Draw the missing part.

4. Charles saw these shapes on a belt.

5. Pam saw this pattern on a scarf.

6. Ari saw this pattern on a necktie.

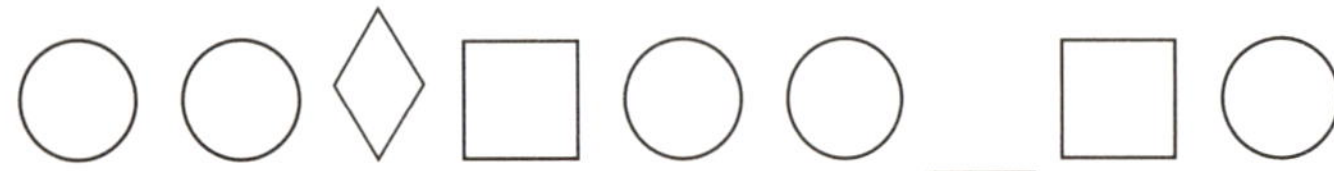

Math Journal **Writing and Reasoning** How do you know which shapes make the pattern unit in Exercise 5?

____

____

Name ______________________ Date ____________

Circle Time

Problem of the Day

TAKS Objective 1 TEKS 2.6C

Take three colors of cubes. Make a repeating pattern.

Number Sense

TAKS Objective 1 TEKS 2.1B

Match the numbers to the words.

10	eleven
11	ten
12	nineteen
13	thirteen
14	fifteen
15	fourteen
16	seventeen
17	sixteen
18	eighteen
19	twelve

Word of the Day

TAKS Objective 1 TEKS 2.1C

between

Name two numbers between 1 and 10. Which number is greater?

Numerical Fluency

TAKS Objective 1 TEKS 1.1B

Use and . Compare.

76 ◯ 69

Growing Patterns

TAKS Objective 2
TEKS 2.6C

**Draw the picture to continue the pattern.
Write the numbers.**

1. ______

2.
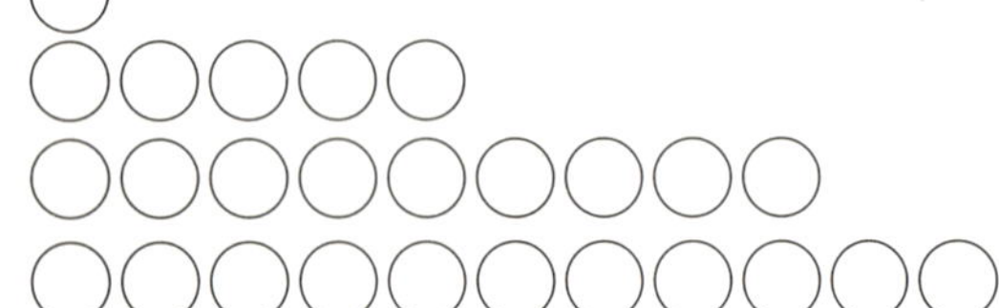
______

3. ______

4.

______

Writing and Reasoning How can you describe the growing pattern in Exercise 3?

____

Circle Time

Problem of the Day

TAKS Objective 1 TEKS 2.6C

Describe the pattern. What number comes next?

2, 4, 6, 8,

Patterns

TAKS Objective 1 TEKS 2.6C

Take two colors of cubes. Make a repeating pattern.

Number of the Day

TAKS Objective 1 TEKS 2.1C

I come just after 5. I come just before 7. What am I?

Numerical Fluency

TAKS Objective 1 TEKS 1.1D

Count the number of circles.

Then write the number three ways.

in words:

with digits:

with ten sticks and ones cubes:

Name ______________________ Date ____________

Show Patterns Another Way

TAKS Objective 6
TEKS 2.12C

You can show a pattern in another way.
Look for the pattern. Then solve.

1. Austin made this pattern on the art easel. Show Austin's pattern using numbers. ____ ____ ____ ____ ____ ____

2. Marilyn drew these shapes on the board. Use colors to show Marilyn's pattern in another way.

____ ____ ____ ____
____ ____ ____ ____
____

3. Show Ted's pattern of cubes using numbers.

____ ____ ____
____ ____ ____
____ ____ ____

4. Peggy started this pattern on the playground. Draw what should come next in Peggy's pattern.

Writing and Reasoning Tell how you could use sound to make the same kind of pattern in Exercise 2.

____

____

Circle Time

Problem of the Day

TAKS Objective 1 TEKS 2.12C

Sally has this pattern on her skirt.

Show what comes next in the pattern.

Patterns

TAKS Objective 1 TEKS 2.6C

Write the numbers to continue the pattern.

1, 3, 5, 7, _____, _____, _____

Calendar

TAKS Objective 1 TEKS 2.3A

What is the date that is one week, or 7 days, from today?

Numerical Fluency

TAKS Objective 1 TEKS 1.2A

Circle the picture that shows a whole separated into 3 equal parts.

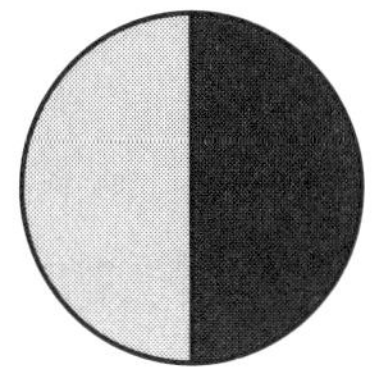 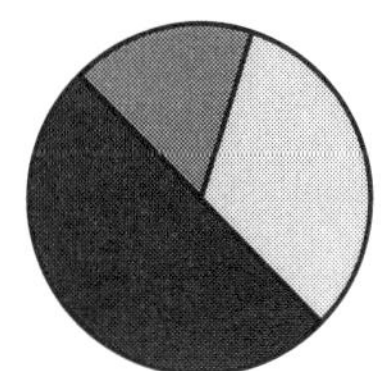 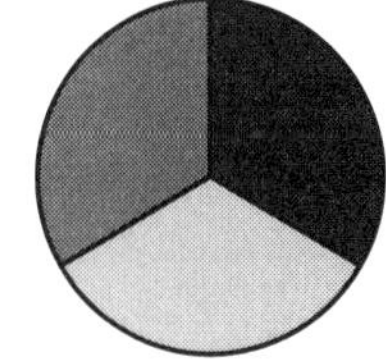

Number Patterns

TAKS Objective 6
TEKS 2.5A

Use the hundred chart.

1	2	3	4	5	6	7	8	9	10
11	12	13	14	15	16	17	18	19	20
21	22	23	24	25	26	27	28	29	30
31	32	33	34	35	36	37	38	39	40
41	42	43	44	45	46	47	48	49	50
51	52	53	54	55	56	57	58	59	60
61	62	63	64	65	66	67	68	69	70
71	72	73	74	75	76	77	78	79	80
81	82	83	84	85	86	87	88	89	90
91	92	93	94	95	96	97	98	99	100

1. Count by 3s.
Shade in the numbers.

2. Count by 6s.
Put an X on the numbers.

**Follow the pattern. Write the missing numbers.
Use the hundred chart if you need help.**

3. 4, 8, 12, 16, 20, _____, 28, 32, _____

4. 32, 34, 36, 38, _____, _____, 44, 46, _____, 50

5. 18, 24, 30, _____, 42, 48, _____, 60

6. Circle the group of numbers that does not follow a pattern.

A. 15, 20, 25, 30, 35
B. 67, 68, 69, 70, 71
C. 33, 36, 39, 42, 45
D. 20, 24, 27, 32, 36

Math Journal **Writing and Reasoning** What patterns do you see in the hundred chart you used for Exercises 1 and 2?

____

____

Circle Time

Problem of the Day

TAKS Objective 1 TEKS 2.5A

Circle the group of numbers that does not follow a pattern.

A 1, 2, 3, 4, 5, 6

B 10, 20, 30, 40, 50

C 1, 3, 2, 4, 1, 6

D 15, 25, 35, 45, 55

Measurement

TAKS Objective 1 TEKS 2.9A

Make a train using 10 connecting cubes. Find an object that is longer than your train.

Number of the Day

TAKS Objective 1 TEKS 2.1C

Say the number that is one more and the number that is one less than:

5, ______, ______

9, ______, ______

14, ______, ______

Numerical Fluency

TAKS Objective 1 TEKS 1.2B

What part of the pennies show heads?

______ pennies show heads out of ______ pennies

What fraction shows this? ______

Name ______________________ Date ____________

Tens and Ones to 100

TAKS Objective 1
TEKS 2.1B

Write the tens and ones.
Write the numbers.

1. 4 tens 5 ones

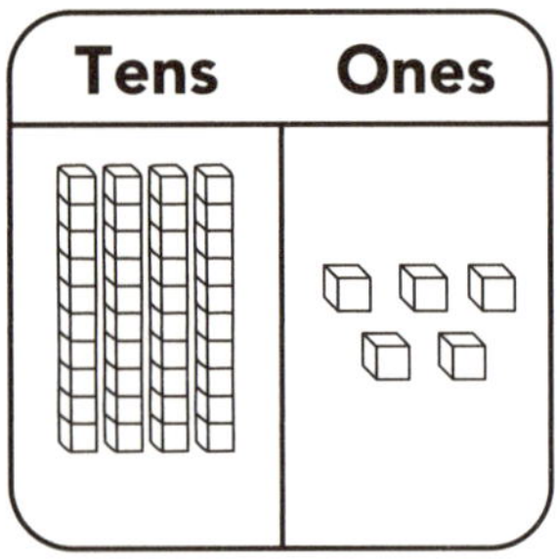

Tens	Ones

_____ forty-five

2. 9 tens 2 ones

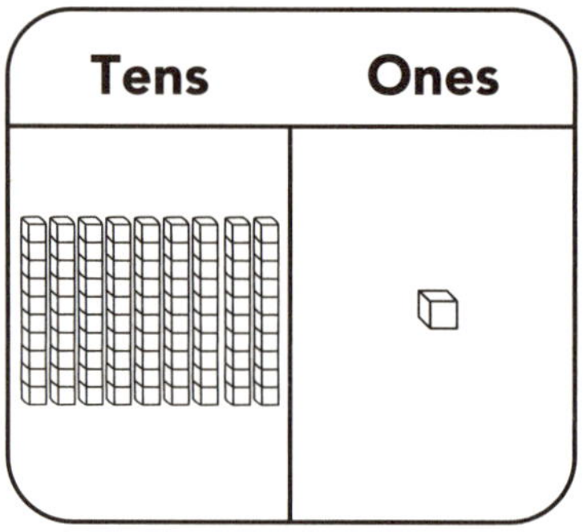

Tens	Ones

_____ ninety-two

3. 5 tens 3 ones

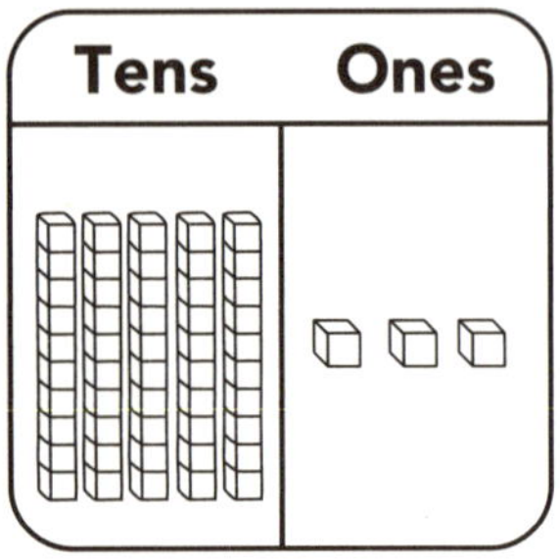

Tens	Ones

_____ fifty-three

4. 7 tens 0 ones

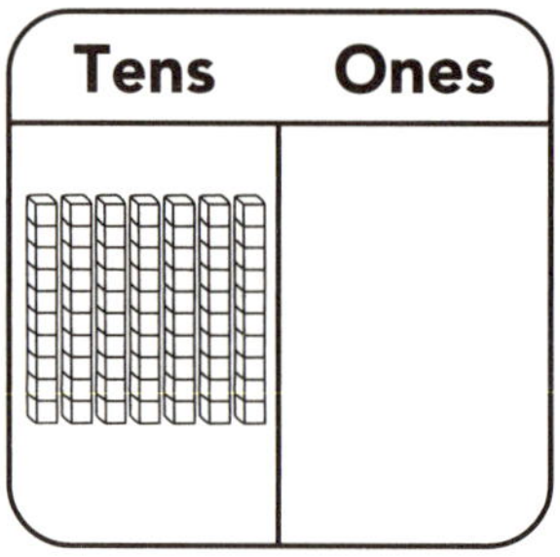

Tens	Ones

_____ seventy

5. 2 tens 6 ones

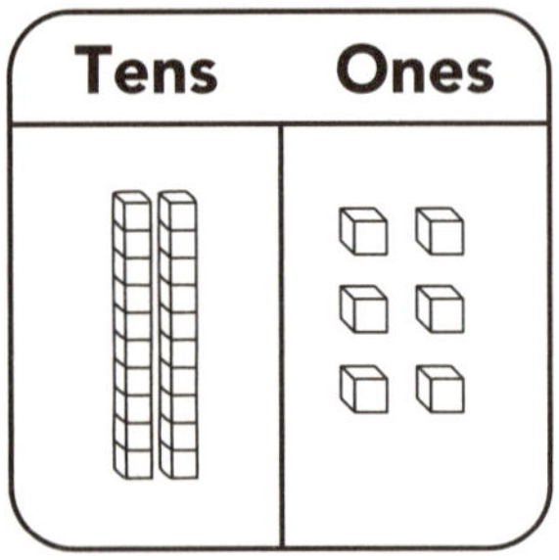

Tens	Ones

_____ twenty-six

6. 1 ten 8 ones

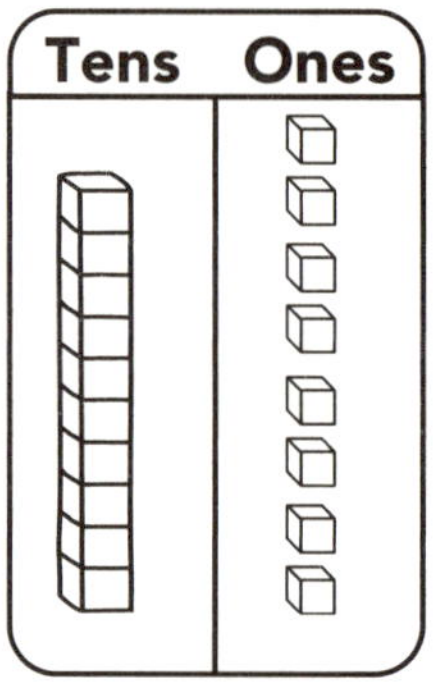

Tens	Ones

_____ eighteen

Math Journal **Writing and Reasoning** Tom sees the words eighty-six in a story he is reading. How would he write this number? How could he draw this number quickly?

____

Circle Time

Problem of the Day

TAKS Objective 1 TEKS 2.1B

Beth and Sean are each thinking of a number. Beth's number has 7 tens and 2 ones. Sean's number has 1 ten and 8 ones. What are their numbers?

Patterns

TAKS Objective 1 TEKS 2.12C

Roger has this pattern on his belt.

 ______

Show what comes next in the pattern.

Calendar

TAKS Objective 1 TEKS 2.1B

Look at a calendar. How many dates this month end in 0?

Numerical Fluency

TAKS Objective 1 TEKS 2.1A

Draw quick pictures to show the following numbers.

and

23 41

Use Place Value

TAKS Objective 1
TEKS 2.1B

Complete the chart.

Remember
To find the value of a digit, find the value of its place.

	Count how many.	Write the tens and ones.	Write the value of each digit.	Write the number.
1.		___ tens ___ ones	___ + ___	___
2.		___ tens ___ ones	___ + ___	___

Circle the value of the underlined digit.

3. 67 (6 underlined) 60 6	**4.** 98 (8 underlined) 80 8	**5.** 23 (2 underlined) 20 2
6. 44 (first 4 underlined) 40 4	**7.** 85 (8 underlined) 80 8	**8.** 71 (1 underlined) 10 1

Solve.

9. I have fewer ones than tens. The value of my tens is 20.
What two numbers can I be? ________

Math Journal **Writing and Reasoning** How would you write a number that has 4 tens and 6 ones? How would you write a number that has 6 tens and 4 ones? What do you notice about the numbers?

____

____

Circle Time

Problem of the Day

TAKS Objective 1 TEKS 2.1B

There are 4 shelves. There are 10 books on each shelf. There are also 5 books on the table. How would you write the total number of books in tens and ones?

______ tens ______ ones

Geometry

TAKS Objective 1 TEKS 1.6B

Draw a circle, a triangle, and a square on your whiteboard.

Word of the Day

TAKS Objective 1 TEKS 2.1A

tens

Find objects in the classroom that can be grouped in tens. Make groups and count how many tens there are.

Facts Practice

TAKS Objective 1 TEKS 1.3B

Use Workmat 2 and counters to subtract the following.

1. 6 – 3 = ______
2. 8 – 5 = ______
3. 7 – 2 = ______
4. 3 – 2 = ______

Different Ways to Show a Number

TAKS Objective 1
TEKS 2.1A

Circle two ways to show the number.

1. 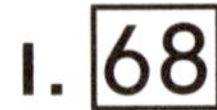

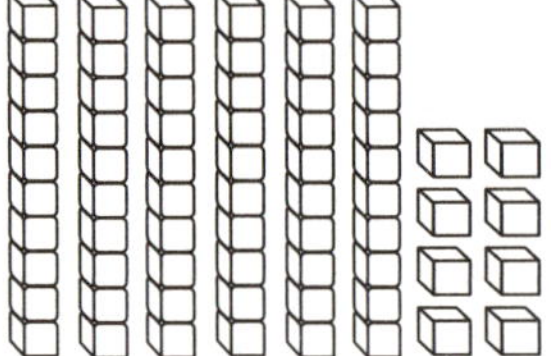

8 tens 6 ones

60 + 8

---

2. 31

30 + 1

1 ten 3 ones

---

3. 57

5 tens 7 ones

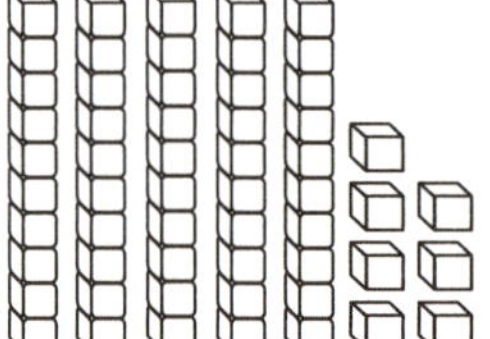

5 + 70

---

4. 14

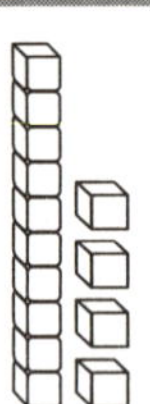

10 + 4

---

5. 26

20 + 6

20 + 60

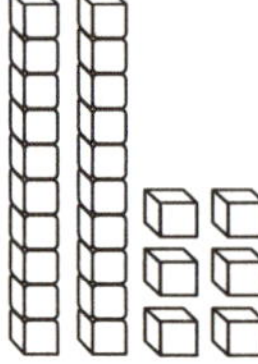

---

6. 72

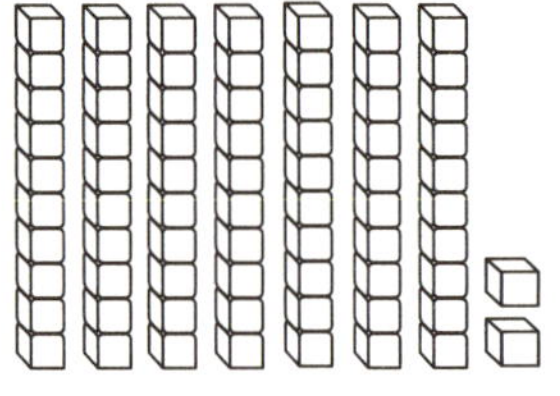

7 tens 2 ones

2 tens 7 ones

Writing and Reasoning What is wrong with showing the number 29 as 20 tens and 9 ones?

____

____

Circle Time

Problem of the Day

TAKS Objective 1 TEKS 2.1A

Martin draws a picture with 10 ducks, 10 geese, and 6 swans.

How many birds does he draw? What is another way to show the number of birds?

____

____

Patterns

TAKS Objective 1 TEKS 2.6C

Write the numbers to continue the pattern.

12, 10, 8, 6, ______, ______, ______

Number of the Day

TAKS Objective 1 TEKS 2.1B

I am a number with 1 ten and 4 ones.
What number am I?

Numerical Fluency

TAKS Objective 1 TEKS 1.1A

Name the number shown by each model.

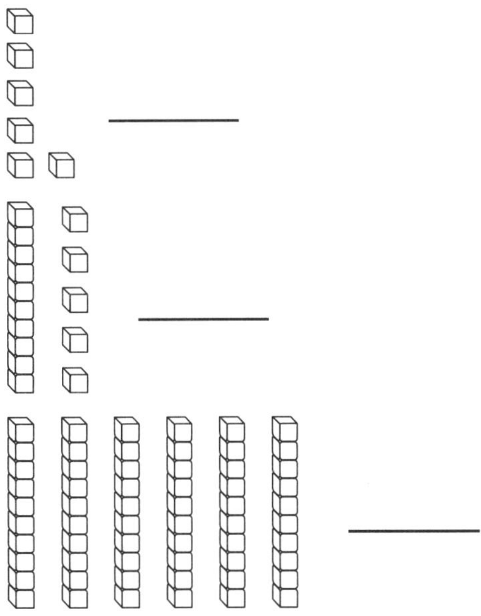

Order Numbers on a Number Line

TAKS Objective 3
TEKS 2.8

Use the number line below.
Complete the sentence.

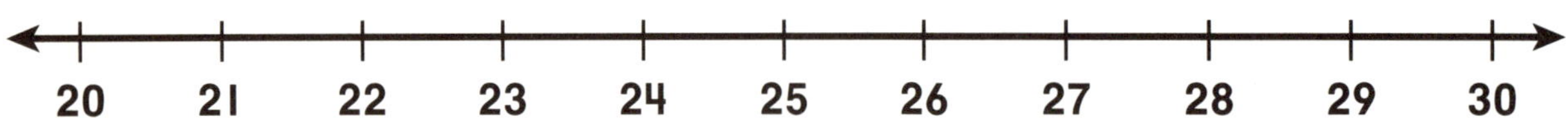

1. _____ is just before 25.
2. 26 is just after _____.
3. 29 is one less than _____.
4. _____ is one more than 27.
5. 23 is just after _____.
6. _____ is just before 22.

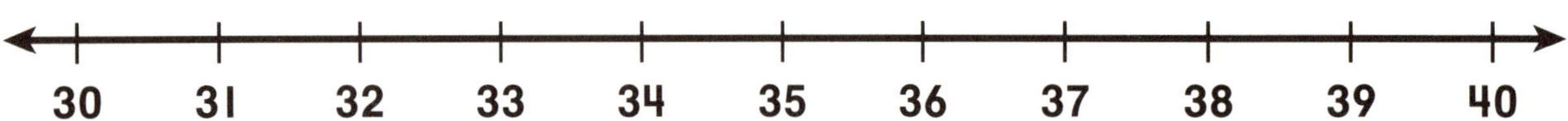

Write the missing numbers.

7. 33, 34, _____, _____, 37
8. 36, 35, _____, 33, _____

Math Journal **Writing and Reasoning** Marsha has ticket number 29. The winning ticket number is just after her ticket number. How do you know what the winning ticket number is?

____

____

Circle Time

Problem of the Day

TAKS Objective 1 TEKS 2.8

What number could be represented by the point on the number line?

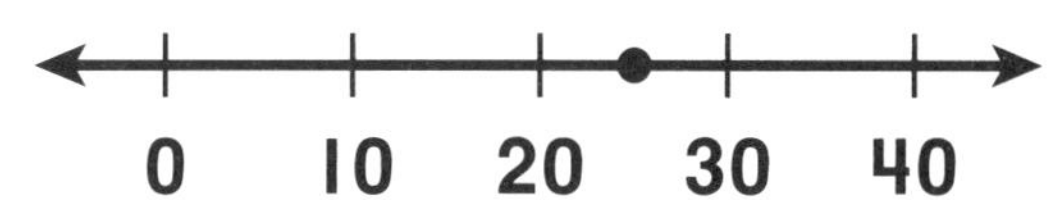

____

____

Patterns

TAKS Objective 1 TEKS 2.6C

Use cubes. Make a pattern like this one:

Word of the Day

TAKS Objective 1 TEKS 2.1B

digit

What digit is in the tens place in 32?
What digit is in the ones place in 32?

Numerical Fluency

TAKS Objective 1 TEKS 1.1B

Model 83 with [tens rod] and [ones cube].

Find a Pattern

TAKS Objectives 2, 6
TEKS 2.12C, 2.6B

Sometimes you can look for a pattern to solve problems.
Look for the pattern.
Complete the table to solve.

1. Each dog eats 3 bones. How many bones will 5 dogs eat?

Dogs	1	2	3	4	5
Bones	3	6	9		

Hint: Think.
What numbers do I already know?

_______ bones

2. Each pencil costs 5 cents. How much do 6 pencils cost?

Pencils	1	2	3	4	5	6
Cents	5	10	15			

Hint: Think.
What is the pattern?

_______ cents

3. There are 2 blue birds in each cage. How many blue birds are in 5 cages?

Cage	1	2	3	4	5
Blue Birds	2	4	6		

_______ blue birds

4. There are 5 cards in every package of collectible cards. How many cards are there in 5 packages?

	1	2	3	4	5
Cards	5	10	15		

_______ cards

Math Journal **Writing and Reasoning** What is the pattern in the table in Exercise 1?

____

Name ______________________ Date ____________

Circle Time

Problem of the Day

TAKS Objective 1 TEKS 2.6B

5 children go to a library. Each child takes out 2 books. How many books do the children take out in all?

Patterns

TAKS Objective 1 TEKS 2.5A

Complete the patterns.

18, 20, 22, 24, ______, ______, ______

1, 3, 5, 1, 3, 5, ______, ______, ______

Word of the Day

TAKS Objective 1 TEKS 2.6C

growing pattern

Draw an example of a growing pattern.

Numerical Fluency

TAKS Objective 1 TEKS 2.1B

Write the number of tens and ones in each number.

74 ______ tens ______ ones

56 ______ tens ______ ones

38 ______ tens ______ ones

20 ______ tens ______ ones

Name ______________________ Date ____________

Compare Two-Digit Numbers

TAKS Objective 1
TEKS 2.1C

Write the numbers.
Compare the numbers using greater than, less than, or equal to.

1.

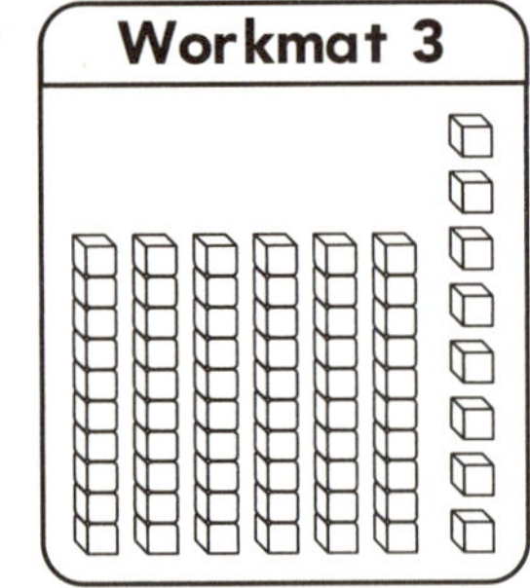

Workmat 3

____ ________________ ____

2.

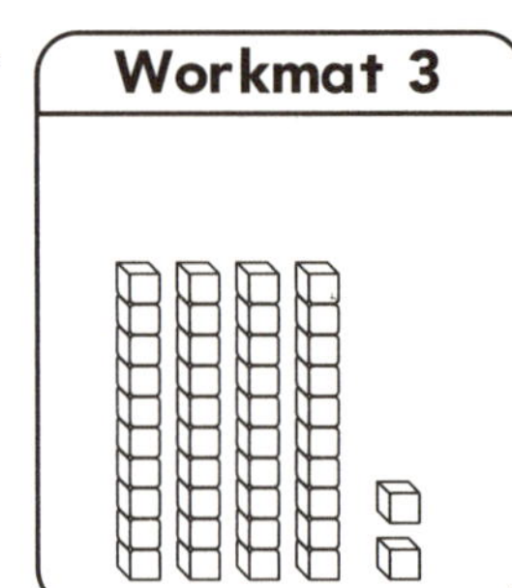

Workmat 3

____ ________________ ____

3.

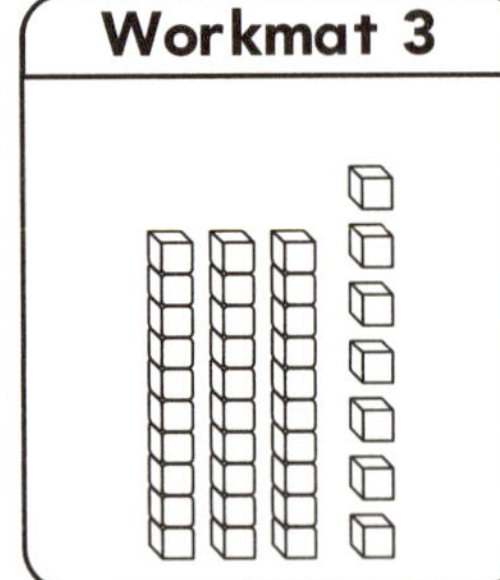

Workmat 3

____ ________________ ____

4.

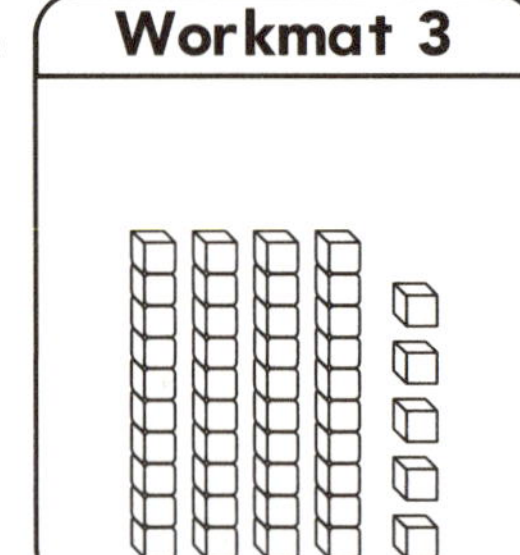

Workmat 3

____ ________________ ____

Writing and Reasoning Mitch has 6 tens cubes and 8 ones cubes. Tim has 68 ones. What do you know about their number of cubes?

____

Circle Time

Problem of the Day

TAKS Objective 1 TEKS 2.1C

Seth has 3 tens and 8 ones. Fong has 5 tens and 2 ones. Who has the greater number? How do you know?

Number Sense

TAKS Objective 1 TEKS 2.1A

Show the number 93 using place value blocks.

Calendar

TAKS Objective 1 TEKS 2.1B

What is the date today? How many tens and ones are in that number?

Numerical Fluency

TAKS Objective 1 TEKS 1.2A

Look at the picture.

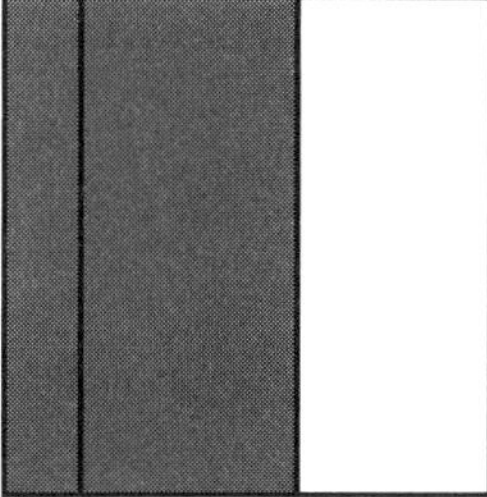

Are the parts equal? ______

Name ______________________ Date ____________

Use Symbols to Compare Numbers

TAKS Objective 1
TEKS 2.1C

Remember
First compare the tens.
Then compare the ones.

Write >, <, or =.

1. 52 ◯ 23	2. 81 ◯ 96	3. 25 ◯ 32
4. 32 ◯ 12	5. 50 ◯ 70	6. 48 ◯ 27
7. 61 ◯ 72	8. 85 ◯ 85	9. 94 ◯ 99
10. 93 ◯ 63	11. 30 ◯ 39	12. 18 ◯ 25
13. 52 ◯ 52	14. 75 ◯ 71	15. 56 ◯ 46
16. 91 ◯ 90	17. 28 ◯ 28	18. 45 ◯ 51
19. 37 ◯ 33	20. 65 ◯ 64	21. 10 ◯ 20

Writing and Reasoning How do you know when two numbers are equal?

____

____

Circle Time

Problem of the Day

TAKS Objective 1 TEKS 2.1C

Miguel brings 3 balls and 4 cars to the school. Andrew brings 6 balls and 2 cars. Whose toy total is greater—Andrew's or Miguel's?

Number Sense

TAKS Objective 1 TEKS 2.1C

Write >, <, or =.

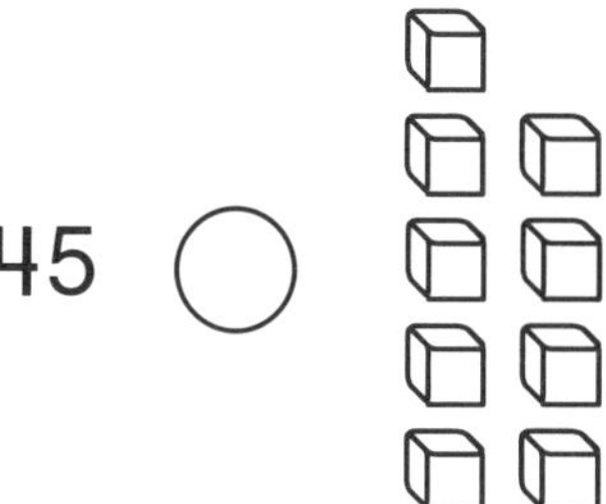

Number of the Day

TAKS Objective 1 TEKS 2.1A

36

Use your place value blocks to model 36.

Numerical Fluency

TAKS Objective 1 TEKS 1.2B

What part of the shapes is circles?

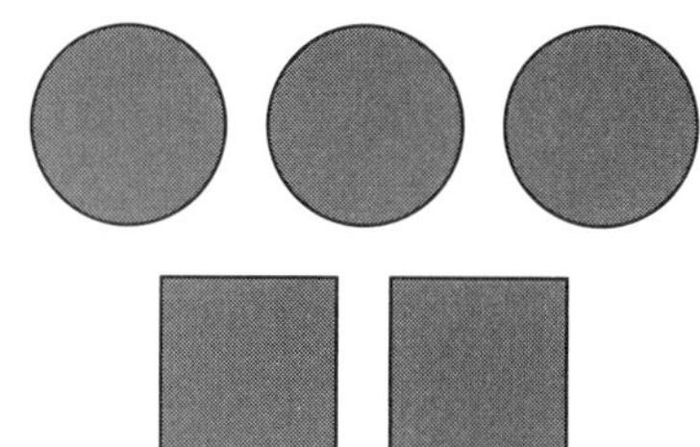

______ circles out of ______ shapes. What fraction

shows this? ______

Order Numbers with Models

TAKS Objective 1
TEKS 2.1C

Write the numbers in order from least to greatest.

1. 39, 30, 33

___ ___ ___

2. 53, 56, 46

___ ___ ___

3. 48, 68, 52

___ ___ ___

4. 57, 93, 91

___ ___ ___

5. 31, 25, 29

___ ___ ___

6. 49, 53, 42

___ ___ ___

Order the numbers from greatest to least.

7. 74, 67, 76

___ ___ ___

8. 38, 49, 41

___ ___ ___

9. 24, 47, 42

___ ___ ___

10. 17, 19, 16

___ ___ ___

11. 81, 79, 86

___ ___ ___

12. 72, 76, 74

___ ___ ___

Writing and Reasoning How are the numbers not in order in the group of numbers in Exercise 9?

___

___

___

Circle Time

Problem of the Day

TAKS Objective 1 TEKS 2.1C

Sania reads 75 pages. Kelly reads 59 pages. Maria reads 95 pages. Who read the greatest number of pages?

Operations

TAKS Objective 1 TEKS 2.3A

Use Workmat 2 and counters to subtract the following.

8 – 3 = ______

4 – 1 = ______

6 – 6 = ______

4 – 2 = ______

Number of the Day

TAKS Objective 1 TEKS 2.1B

100

How many ones make a 100?
How many tens?

Facts Practice

TAKS Objective 1 TEKS 1.3A

Write the number sentence that shows how many circles are not crossed-out.

______ ◯ ______ = ______

Order Numbers

TAKS Objective 1
TEKS 2.1C

Write the numbers in order from least to greatest.

1. 25, 19, 27

___ ___ ___

2. 34, 31, 41

___ ___ ___

3. 46, 38, 35

___ ___ ___

4. 56, 52, 55

___ ___ ___

5. 27, 38, 46

___ ___ ___

6. 45, 42, 25

___ ___ ___

Write the numbers in order from greatest to least.

7. 73, 93, 72

___ ___ ___

8. 64, 48, 84

___ ___ ___

9. 51, 84, 87

___ ___ ___

10. 46, 48, 49

___ ___ ___

11. 15, 51, 50

___ ___ ___

12. 35, 38, 58

___ ___ ___

Math Journal **Writing and Reasoning** Describe how you decide the greatest number in a series of numbers.

___

___

___

Circle Time

Problem of the Day

TAKS Objective 1 TEKS 2.1C

I am a number between 45 and 55. I have 0 ones.
What number am I?

Number Sense

TAKS Objective 1 TEKS 2.1C

Circle the one that is true. Use place value blocks and Workmat 3 to help if you wish.

A 65 is greater than 56

B 65 is less than 56

C 65 is equal to 56

Word of the Day

TAKS Objective 1 TEKS 2.1C

number line

Use a number line to solve this riddle:
I come just after 7.
I am 2 less than 10.
What number am I?

Facts Practice

TAKS Objective 1 TEKS 1.3B

Use Workmat 2 and counters to add the following.

3 + 0 = ______

4 + 1 = ______

6 + 6 = ______

7 + 3 = ______

Too Much Information

TAKS Objective 1, 6
TEKS 2.12A, 2.1C

Cross out the information you do not need. Then solve.

1. Marvin the Great pulled 12 birds out of his hat. Then he pulled 6 flowers out of his hat. After that, he pulled 6 rabbits out of his hat. Did he pull out more rabbits or more birds?

   He pulled more ________ out of his hat.

2. The Owls won 7 blue ribbons, 8 red ribbons, and 5 green ribbons. The Magic won 4 blue ribbons. Which team won more blue ribbons?

   ________ won more blue ribbons.

3. Lilly has 8 toy horses and 7 teddy bears. Marla has 2 toy horses. Becky has 5 toy horses. Who has the most toy horses?

   ________ has the most toy horses.

4. The swim team collected 75 dollars. It took them 2 weeks to collect it. The track team collected 45 dollars. Which team collected more money?

   The ________ team collected more money.

Writing and Reasoning What does the question ask you to compare in Exercise 3?

____

Name ______________________ Date ____________

Circle Time

Problem of the Day

TAKS Objective 1 TEKS 2.12A

The gift shop sold 45 postcards and 39 posters. Did the shop sell more postcards or posters?

Number Sense

TAKS Objective 1 TEKS 2.1A

Circle a way to show the number.

40

A

B

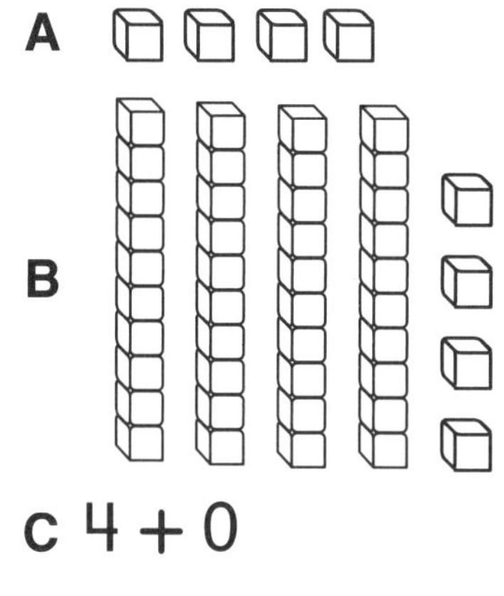

C $4 + 0$

D $40 + 0$

Word of the Day

TAKS Objective 1 TEKS 2.1C

greater than

There are 12 books on the table. Write a number greater than 12.

Numerical Fluency

TAKS Objective 1 TEKS 2.1A

Show the number using expanded form.

30

Turn-Around Addition Facts

TAKS Objective 1
TEKS 2.3A

Draw to show. Write the answer.

1. 4 + 2 = ______ 2 + 4 = ______

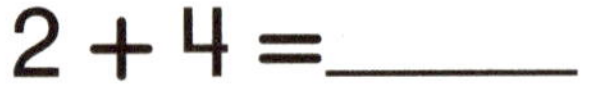

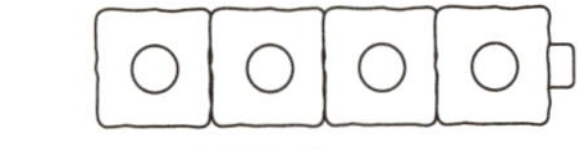

2. 3 + 5 = ______ 5 + 3 = ______

3. 6 + 1 = ______ 1 + 6 = ______

4. 3 + 6 = ______ 6 + 3 = ______

Math Journal **Writing and Reasoning** What 2 number sentences does this picture show?

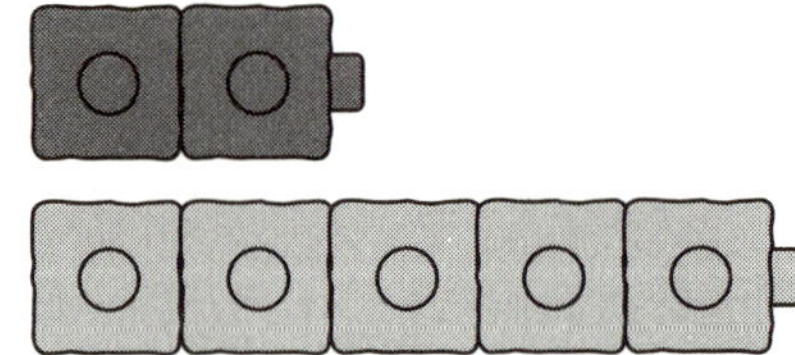

____

Circle Time

Problem of the Day

TAKS Objective 1 TEKS 2.3A

Jake has 3 dogs and 5 cats. Julie has 5 dogs and 3 cats. How many pets does each have?

Number Sense

TAKS Objective 1 TEKS 2.1A

Write the numbers in order from greatest to least.

55 37 75 39

Calendar

TAKS Objective 1 TEKS 2.3A

What day is 3 days after today?

Numerical Fluency

TAKS Objective 1 TEKS 2.1B

Count how many.

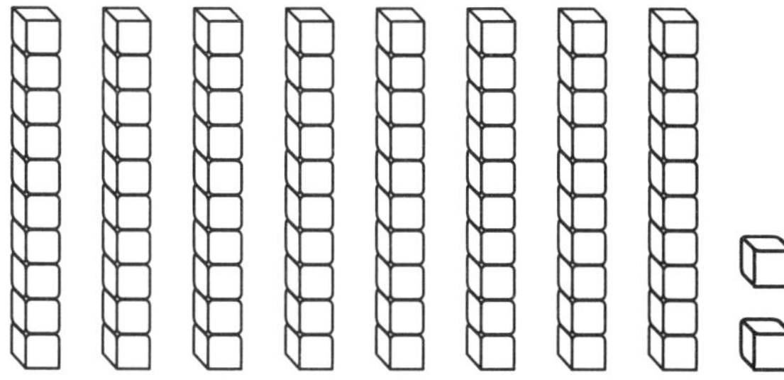

Write the tens and ones.

_______ tens and _______ ones

Write the value.

_______ + _______

Write the number. _______

Hands On: Fact Families

TAKS Objective 1
TEKS 2.3A

Use chart and connecting cubes.
Write the fact families.

1. 5, 2, 7

___ + ___ = ___ ___ + ___ = ___

___ − ___ = ___ ___ − ___ = ___

Whole	
Part	Part

2. 3, 7, 10

___ + ___ = ___ ___ + ___ = ___

___ − ___ = ___ ___ − ___ = ___

Whole	
Part	Part

3. 5, 1, 6

___ + ___ = ___ ___ + ___ = ___

___ − ___ = ___ ___ − ___ = ___

Whole	
Part	Part

4. 4, 3, 7

___ + ___ = ___ ___ + ___ = ___

___ − ___ = ___ ___ − ___ = ___

Whole	
Part	Part

Math Journal

Writing and Reasoning Which number is missing that completes the fact family?

______, 4, 6

Now write the fact family for these numbers.

____________ ____________ ____________ ____________

Circle Time

Problem of the Day

TAKS Objective 1 TEKS 2.3A

Use connecting cubes. Write the facts family.

_____ + _____ = _____

_____ + _____ = _____

_____ − _____ = _____

_____ − _____ = _____

Workmat 2

Whole	
9 cubes	
Part	Part
3 cubes	6 cubes

Number Sense

TAKS Objective 1 TEKS 2.1C

Write the numbers in order from least to greatest.

70 52 90 54

___ ___ ___ ___

Number of the Day

TAKS Objective 1 TEKS 2.5A

5

Circle the numbers with 5 in the ones place on your hundred chart.

Numerical Fluency

TAKS Objective 1 TEKS 2.1C

Write >, <, or =.

38 ◯ 23

Add and Subtract 0 and 1

TAKS Objective 1
TEKS 2.3A

Add or subtract.

1.  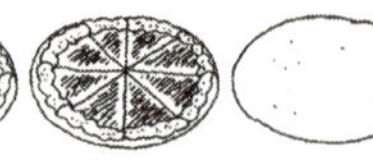

$3 + 0 =$ ______

2. 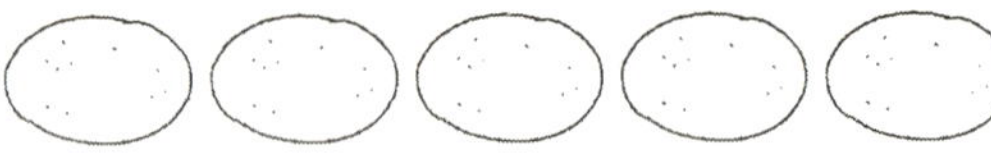

$5 - 1 =$ ______

3. $8 + 0 =$ ______

4. $6 + 1 =$ ______

5. $7 - 1 =$ ______

6. $2 - 1 =$ ______

7. $0 + 0 =$ ______

8. $4 - 0 =$ ______

Writing and Reasoning What is $5 - 0$? How do you know?

____

____

Circle Time

Problem of the Day

TAKS Objective 1 TEKS 2.3A

Carlos has some stickers. Jenny gave him 1 more sticker. Now Carlos has 8 stickers. How many stickers did Carlos start with?

Patterns

TAKS Objective 1 TEKS 2.6C

Take three colors of cubes. Make a repeating pattern.

Word of the Day

TAKS Objective 1 TEKS 2.3A

sum

Circle the sum in the following number sentences:

$5 + 1 = 6$

$2 + 8 = 10$

$3 + 4 = 7$

Numerical Fluency

TAKS Objective 1 TEKS 2.1B

Count how many.

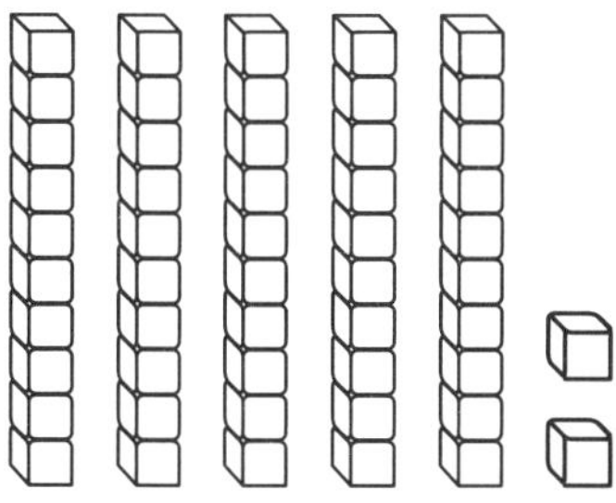

Write the tens and ones.

______ tens and ______ ones

Write the value. ______ + ______

Write the number. ______

Name ______________________ Date ____________

Add Three Numbers

TAKS Objective 1
TEKS 2.3B

Add.

1. $4 + 2 + 1 =$ ____

2. $3 + 0 + 5 =$ ____

3. $6 + 2 + 1 =$ ____

4. $8 + 2 + 0 =$ ____

5. $\begin{array}{r} 2 \\ 0 \\ +\ 6 \\ \hline \end{array}$

6. $\begin{array}{r} 7 \\ 1 \\ +\ 1 \\ \hline \end{array}$

7. $\begin{array}{r} 1 \\ 0 \\ +\ 3 \\ \hline \end{array}$

8. $\begin{array}{r} 3 \\ 2 \\ +\ 4 \\ \hline \end{array}$

Math Journal **Writing and Reasoning** Carlos has 6 blue cars, 2 red cars, and 1 green car. Explain how you find how many cars he has altogether.

____

____

____

Circle Time

Problem of the Day

TAKS Objective 1 TEKS 2.3A

Carrie is two years older than José. José is one year younger than Lin. Lin is 5 years old. What is the sum of the three ages?

Number Sense

TAKS Objective 1 TEKS 2.1C

Write the numbers in order from greatest to least.

75 57 95 59

___ ___ ___ ___

Calendar

TAKS Objective 1 TEKS 2.3A

Find a pair of numbers on the calendar with a sum of 7.

Numerical Fluency

TAKS Objective 1 TEKS 2.1C

Write >, <, or =.

86 ◯ 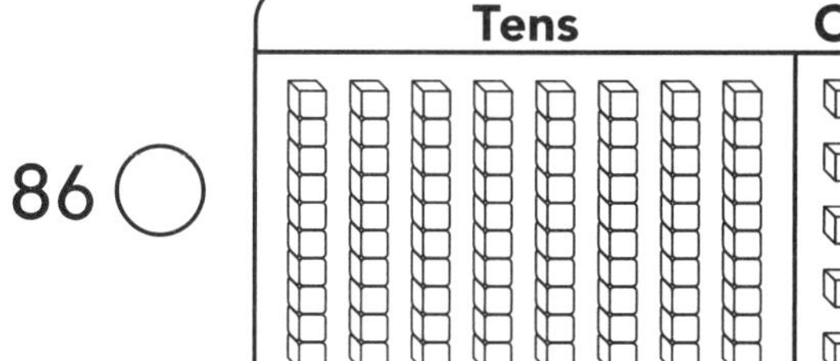

Name ______________________ Date ____________

Problem Solving: Act It Out

TAKS Objective 6
TEKS 2.3A, 2.12B

Solve.

You may use counters if you wish.

1. Jan's team scored 9 runs. Jim's team scored 7 runs. How many runs were scored in all?

   __________ runs

2. Daniel counts 15 stars in the sky. Eva counts 6. How many more stars does Daniel count than Eva?

   __________ stars

3. Esta solved 6 problems on the front of her paper. She solved 5 more problems on the back side of the paper. How many problems did Esta solve altogether?

   __________ problems

4. Zach has 9 pencils. Michelle has 5 pencils. How many more pencils does Zach have?

   __________ pencils

Writing and Reasoning How do the counters help you solve the problem?

____

____

Name ______________________ Date ____________

Circle Time

Problem of the Day

TAKS Objective 1 TEKS 2.3A

There are 8 girls and 7 boys in the puppet club. How many children belong to the puppet club?

Patterns

TAKS Objective 1 TEKS 2.6C

Take three colors of cubes. Make a repeating pattern.

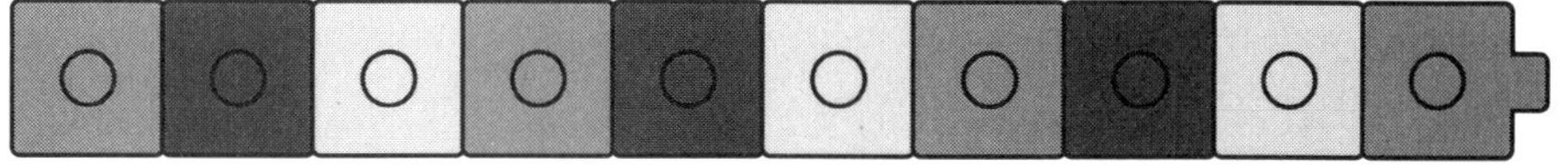

____

____

Number of the Day

TAKS Objective 1 TEKS 2.5A

0

Circle all the numbers with 0 in the ones place on your hundred chart.

Numerical Fluency

TAKS Objective 1 TEKS 2.1B

Count how many.

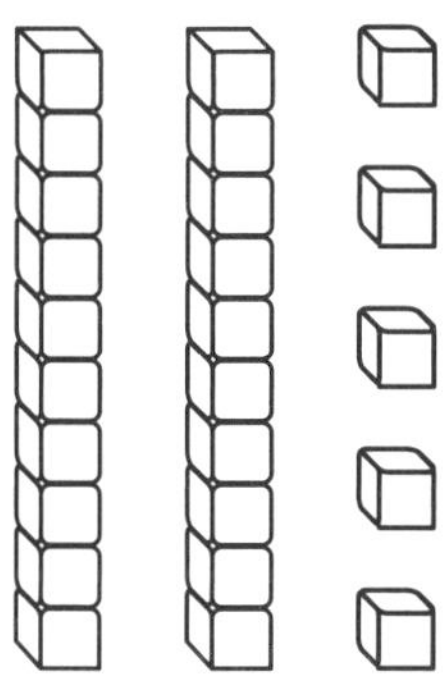

Write the tens and ones.

______ tens and ______ ones

Write the value. ______ + ______

Write the number. ______

Name ______________________ Date ____________

Add 10, Subtract 10

TAKS Objective 1
TEKS 2.3A

Use Workmat 1 with ●.
Add or Subtract.

1. 14 − 10 = ____

2. 3 + 10 = ____

3. 1 + 10 = ____

4. 10 − 4 = ____

5. $\begin{array}{r} 10 \\ +8 \\ \hline \end{array}$

6. $\begin{array}{r} 12 \\ -10 \\ \hline \end{array}$

7. $\begin{array}{r} 19 \\ -10 \\ \hline \end{array}$

8. $\begin{array}{r} 7 \\ +10 \\ \hline \end{array}$

Math Journal **Writing and Reasoning** Complete the number sentence. Write a story to go with it.

10 + ____ = 14

____

Name ______________________ Date ____________

Circle Time

Problem of the Day

TAKS Objective 1 TEKS 2.3A

John has 14 stamps. Josie has 10 stamps. Who has more stamps? ________ How many more?

Operations

TAKS Objective 1 TEKS 2.3A

There are 7 girls and 9 boys in the theater club. How many children are in the theater club?

Word of the Day

TAKS Objective 1 TEKS 2.6C

repeating pattern

Draw an example of a repeating pattern.

Numerical Fluency

TAKS Objective 1 TEKS 2.1C

Circle the choice that is true. Use place value blocks and Workmat 3 to help if you wish.

A 95 is less than 73

B 95 > 97

C 95 is equal to 73

Make 10 to Add

TAKS Objective 1
TEKS 2.3A

Use ●.
Add.

1. $\begin{array}{r} 9 \\ +\ 2 \\ \hline \end{array}$

2. $\begin{array}{r} 8 \\ +\ 4 \\ \hline \end{array}$

3. $\begin{array}{r} 3 \\ +\ 9 \\ \hline \end{array}$

4. $\begin{array}{r} 9 \\ +\ 6 \\ \hline \end{array}$

5. $\begin{array}{r} 6 \\ +\ 8 \\ \hline \end{array}$

6. $\begin{array}{r} 9 \\ +\ 4 \\ \hline \end{array}$

Use ●.
Complete each addition sentence.

7. 10 + ____ = 15

   9 + ____ = 15

   ____ + 7 = 15

   7 + 8 = ____

8. 10 + 6 = ____

   9 + ____ = 16

   8 + ____ = 16

   7 + 9 = ____

Writing and Reasoning How does making 10 help you add 8 + 7?

____

____

Name ______________________ Date ____________

Circle Time

Problem of the Day

TAKS Objective 1 TEKS 2.3A

Use Workmat 1 with

Suvir has 9 books. Rosie has 9 more than Suvir. How many books does Rosie have?

Number Sense

TAKS Objective 1 TEKS 2.12A

The souvenir shop sold 40 postcards and 29 bumper stickers. Did the shop sell more postcards or bumper stickers?

Word of the Day

TAKS Objective 1 TEKS 2.5C

number sentences

Use the numbers 3, 4, and 7 to write four different number sentences.

Numerical Fluency

TAKS Objective 1 TEKS 2.1B

Count how many.

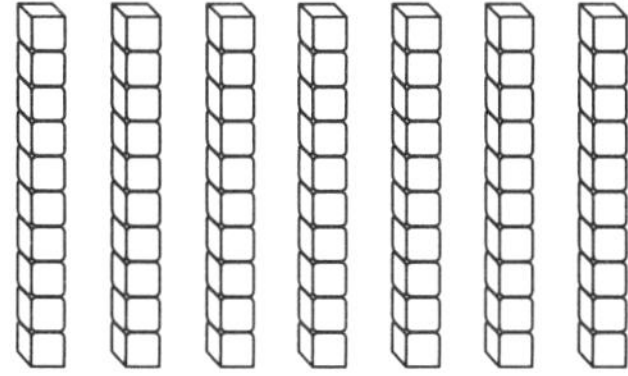

Write the tens and ones.

_______ tens and _______ ones

Write the value. _______ + _______

Write the number. _______

Name ______________________ Date ____________

Subtraction Facts to 18

TAKS Objective 1
TEKS 2.3A

Add. Then subtract.

1. 

$6 + 5 =$ ____

____ $- 6 = 5$

2.

$9 + 3 =$ ____

____ $- 9 = 3$

3. $7 + 7 =$ ____

____ $- 7 = 7$

4. $2 + 8 =$ ____

____ $- 2 = 8$

5. $7 + 5 =$ ____

____ $- 7 = 5$

Add. Then circle the subtraction fact that is related to the addition fact.

6. $6 + 8 =$ ____

$16 - 8 = 8$

$14 - 6 = 8$

$12 - 6 = 6$

7. $9 + 4 =$ ____

$13 - 9 = 4$

$12 - 8 = 4$

$11 - 4 = 7$

Math Journal **Writing and Reasoning** What is one addition fact and one related subtraction fact that matches this picture?

____

____

Circle Time

Problem of the Day

TAKS Objective 1 TEKS 2.3A

Carla has 15 roses. 8 are red and the rest are white.
How many white roses does Carla have?

Number Sense

TAKS Objective 1 TEKS 2.1B

Count how many.

Write the tens and ones in 48.

_____ tens and _____ ones

Write the value. _____ + _____

Write the number. _____

Number of the Day

TAKS Objective 1 TEKS 2.1A

46

Show the number 46 using place value blocks.

Numerical Fluency

TAKS Objective 1 TEKS 2.1A

Circle a way to show the number. 50

A 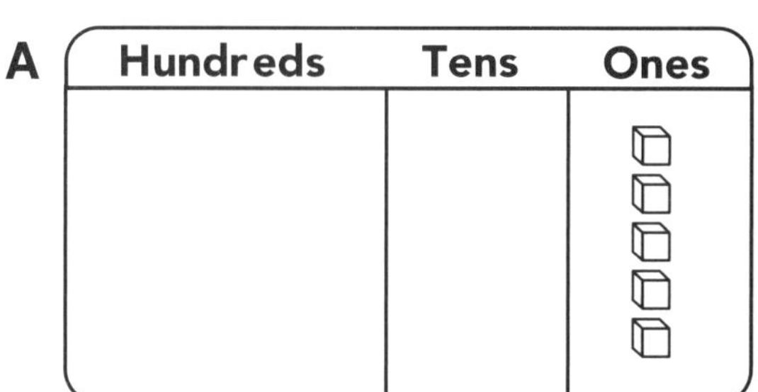

C 5 + 0

B 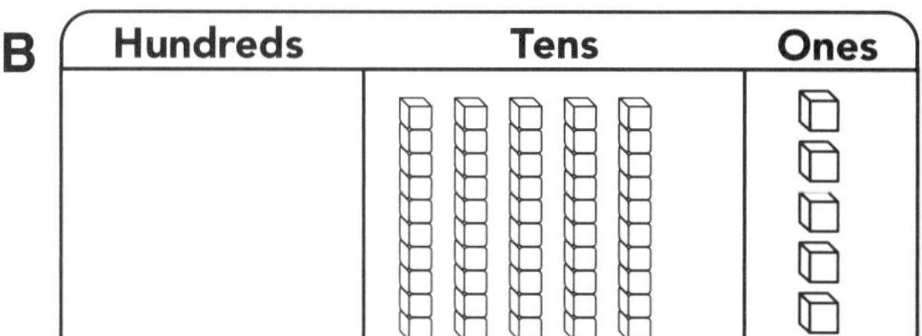

D 50 + 0

Fact Families to 18

TAKS Objective 1
TEKS 2.3A

Use Workmat 2 and counters.

Complete the number sentences for the fact family.

1.

Whole	
16	
Part	Part
7	9

$16 - \_\_\_ = 7$ $16 - 7 = \_\_\_$

$\_\_\_ + 7 = 16$ $7 + \_\_\_ = 16$

2.

Whole	
13	
Part	Part
8	5

$8 + 5 = \_\_\_$ $13 - 8 = \_\_\_$

$5 + \_\_\_ = 13$ $13 - \_\_\_ = 8$

3.

Whole	
15	
Part	Part
8	7

$8 + 7 = \_\_\_$ $15 - 7 = \_\_\_$

$7 + \_\_\_ = 15$ $15 - \_\_\_ = 7$

4. $4 + 7 = \_\_\_$

$7 + 4 = \_\_\_$

$11 - \_\_\_ = 4$

$11 - 4 = \_\_\_$

5. $9 + 3 = \_\_\_$

$3 + \_\_\_ = 12$

$12 - 9 = \_\_\_$

$12 - \_\_\_ = 9$

6. $7 + \_\_\_ = 14$

$14 - 7 = \_\_\_$

7. $\_\_\_ + 5 = 10$

$10 - \_\_\_ = 5$

Math Journal **Writing and Reasoning** Write a fact family using the numbers 5, 6, and 11. How do you know you have included all the related facts?

____

____

Circle Time

Problem of the Day

TAKS Objective 1 TEKS 2.3A

Write a fact family using the numbers
3, 8, 11.

_____ + _____ = _____

_____ + _____ = _____

_____ − _____ = _____

_____ − _____ = _____

Patterns

TAKS Objective 1 TEKS 2.6C

Write the numbers to continue the pattern.

2, 4, 6, 8, _____, _____, _____

Number of the Day

TAKS Objective 1 TEKS 2.7A

4

Find objects in your classroom that have 4 sides.

Numerical Fluency

TAKS Objective 1 TEKS 2.1C

Circle the choice that is true. Use place value blocks and Workmat 3 to help if you wish.

A $46 > 97$

B $46 < 97$

C $46 = 97$

Draw a Picture

TAKS Objective 1
TEKS 2.3A

Draw a picture to solve.

1. There are 8 children in the relay race. There are 2 fewer children in the sack race. How many children are in both races?

   _____ children

2. Tina makes 5 prizes. Tom makes the same number of prizes as Tina. Tony makes 2 more prizes than Tina. How many prizes do they make in all?

   _____ prizes

3. Travis wins 5 prizes. Mary wins 2 fewer prizes than Travis. Rob wins 1 more prize than Mary. How many prizes did they win in all?

   _____ prizes

4. 6 children in the egg race drop their eggs. Four more children than the number who dropped their eggs are still in the race. How many children started the egg race?

   _____ children

Math Journal **Writing and Reasoning** How can you find the number of children who are still in the egg race?

____

Circle Time

Problem of the Day
TAKS Objective 1 TEKS 2.3A

Roger has 4 crayons. Mary has two more than Roger. How many crayons do they have in all?

Number Sense
TAKS Objective 1 TEKS 2.1C

Write >, <, or =

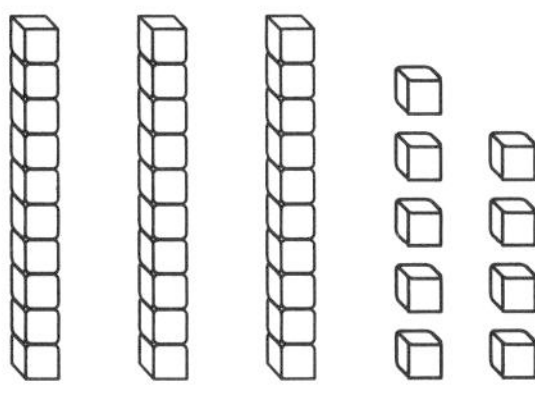

◯ 53

Word of the Day
TAKS Objective 1 TEKS 2.3A

difference

Circle the difference in the following number sentences:

$5 - 1 = 4$

$8 - 2 = 6$

$4 - 0 = 4$

Numerical Fluency
TAKS Objective 1 TEKS 2.1B

Model with [tens rod] and [unit cube]. Write the numbers.

1. $4 + 90 =$ ______

2. $90 + 6 =$ ______

Doubles and Doubles Plus One

TAKS Objective 1
TEKS 2.3A

Doubles and doubles-plus-one facts can help you find other sums. Write the doubles and doubles-plus-one sum.

1. 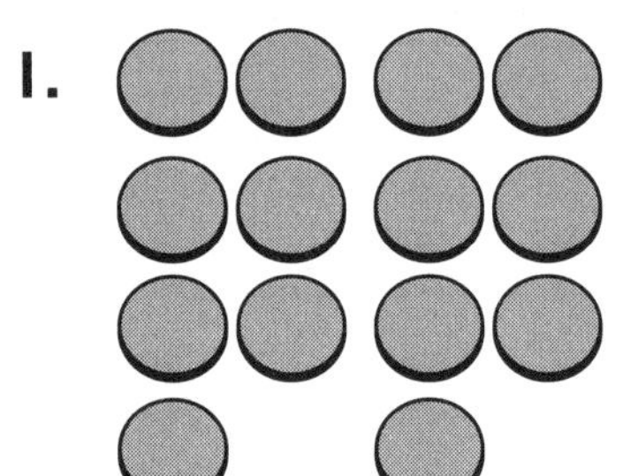

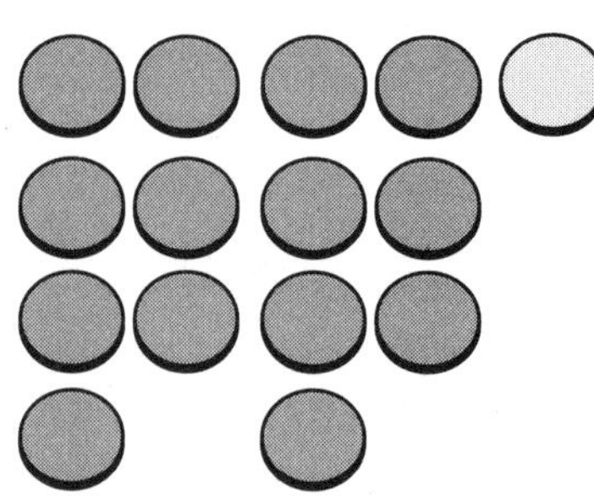

$7 + 7 =$ _____ $8 + 7 =$ _____ $7 + 8 =$ _____

2. $3 + 3 =$ _____ $4 + 3 =$ _____ $3 + 4 =$ _____

3. $6 + 6 =$ _____ $7 + 6 =$ _____ $6 + 7 =$ _____

4. $8 + 8 =$ _____ $9 + 8 =$ _____ $8 + 9 =$ _____

5. Write a doubles and doubles-plus-one number sentence using $1 + 1$.

___ + ___ = ___ ___ + ___ = ___ ___ + ___ = ___

Math Journal **Writing and Reasoning** What do you know about the sum of the doubles-plus-one fact?

____

____

Name ____________________ Date __________

Circle Time

Problem of the Day

TAKS Objective 1 TEKS 2.3A

Tasha has 8 pieces of sea glass. So does Carl. Carl finds another piece of sea glass. How many pieces do they have in all?

Operations

TAKS Objective 1 TEKS 2.3A

There are 10 boys and 4 girls on the soccer team. How many children are on the soccer team?

Calendar

TAKS Objective 1 TEKS 2.3A

Use the calendar to solve this problem: Your library book is due one week from today. What day and date is it due?

Numerical Fluency

TAKS Objective 1 TEKS 2.1C

Circle the choice that is true. Use place value blocks and Workmat 3 to help if you wish.

A $65 > 71$

B $65 < 71$

C $65 = 71$

Count On and Count Back

TAKS Objective 1
TEKS 2.3A

Add or subtract.
Use the number line to count on or count back.

Remember!
The equal sign = means "is the same as".

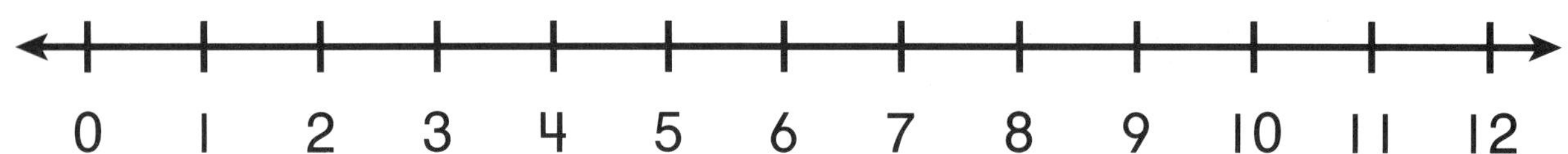

1. $3 + 7 =$ ______ 2. $5 + 2 =$ ______ 3. $11 - 1 =$ ______

4. $6 + 2 =$ ______ 5. ______ $= 6 + 0$ 6. ______ $= 6 - 3$

7. $7 - 3 =$ ______ 8. ______ $= 9 - 2$ 9. $9 + 3 =$ ______

10. ______ $= 10 - 2$ 11. $11 + 1 =$ ______ 12. ______ $= 6 - 2$

13. $\begin{array}{r} 8 \\ -2 \\ \hline \end{array}$ 14. $\begin{array}{r} 5 \\ +3 \\ \hline \end{array}$ 15. $\begin{array}{r} 8 \\ -0 \\ \hline \end{array}$ 16. $\begin{array}{r} 9 \\ +1 \\ \hline \end{array}$ 17. $\begin{array}{r} 10 \\ -3 \\ \hline \end{array}$ 18. $\begin{array}{r} 9 \\ +0 \\ \hline \end{array}$

Math Journal **Writing and Reasoning** When you add by counting on, which addend is it easiest to start with? Explain your answer.

____

____

Circle Time

Problem of the Day

TAKS Objective 1 TEKS 2.3A

Louis bakes 12 muffins. He gives 3 muffins to his sister.
How many muffins does he have now?

Use the number line to solve the problem.

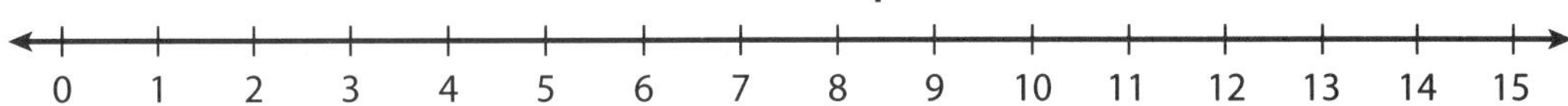

Number Sense

TAKS Objective 1 TEKS 2.1B

Count how many.

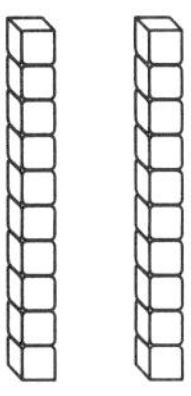

Write the tens and ones.

______ tens and ______ ones

Write the value. ______ + ______

Write the number. ______

Number of the Day

TAKS Objective 1 TEKS 2.6C

4

Make a growing pattern using the number 4.

Numerical Fluency

TAKS Objective 1 TEKS 2.1B

Model with place value blocks.
Write the numbers.

1. $2 + 30 =$ ______ **2.** $3 + 20 =$ ______

Name ____________________ Date ____________

Different Ways to Add

TAKS Objective 1
TEKS 2.3A

Add.

1. $\begin{array}{r} 4 \\ +2 \\ \hline 6 \end{array}$

2. $\begin{array}{r} 8 \\ +3 \\ \hline 11 \end{array}$

3. $\begin{array}{r} 2 \\ +7 \\ \hline 9 \end{array}$

Ways to Add

- Mental math
- Hundred chart
- Counters
- Paper and pencil
- Number line

4. $\begin{array}{r} 6 \\ +2 \\ \hline \end{array}$

5. $\begin{array}{r} 8 \\ +1 \\ \hline \end{array}$

6. $\begin{array}{r} 4 \\ +8 \\ \hline \end{array}$

7. $\begin{array}{r} 8 \\ +7 \\ \hline \end{array}$

8. $\begin{array}{r} 4 \\ +6 \\ \hline \end{array}$

9. $\begin{array}{r} 8 \\ +0 \\ \hline \end{array}$

10. $\begin{array}{r} 9 \\ +3 \\ \hline \end{array}$

11. $\begin{array}{r} 8 \\ +8 \\ \hline \end{array}$

12. $\begin{array}{r} 6 \\ +9 \\ \hline \end{array}$

13. $\begin{array}{r} 5 \\ +5 \\ \hline \end{array}$

14. $\begin{array}{r} 8 \\ +9 \\ \hline \end{array}$

15. $\begin{array}{r} 4 \\ +3 \\ \hline \end{array}$

16. $\begin{array}{r} 1 \\ +4 \\ \hline \end{array}$

17. $\begin{array}{r} 0 \\ +5 \\ \hline \end{array}$

18. $\begin{array}{r} 6 \\ +7 \\ \hline \end{array}$

Math Journal

Writing and Reasoning What way would you choose to add $9 + 4 + 1$? What is the sum?

____

____

Circle Time

Problem of the Day

TAKS Objective 1 TEKS 2.3A

Didi brings 5 leaves for a science lesson. Mel brings 1 less leaf than Didi. How many leaves do they bring in all?

Number Sense

TAKS Objective 1 TEKS 2.1B

Complete the table.

Write the Number	Write a Quick Picture	Write the tens and ones

Word of the Day

TAKS Objective 1 TEKS 2.3A

Doubles

Write a doubles fact for each of the following.

2

4

3

6

Numerical Fluency

TAKS Objective 1 TEKS 2.1A

Write the number shown by the model.

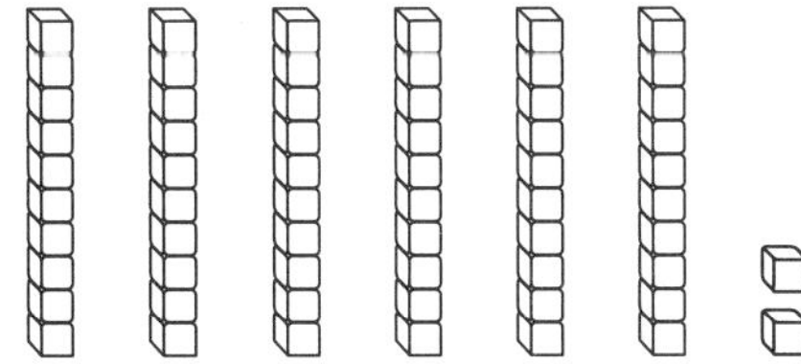

Different Ways to Subtract

TAKS Objective 1
TEKS 2.3A

Subtract.

1. $6 - 3 = 3$	2. $14 - 7 = 7$	3. $9 - 3 = 6$	**Ways to Subtract** mental math hundred chart counters paper and pencil number line

4. $11 - 6$
5. $4 - 0$
6. $12 - 8$
7. $3 - 3$
8. $8 - 7$
9. $5 - 3$
10. $18 - 9$
11. $10 - 5$
12. $6 - 5$
13. $14 - 6$
14. $10 - 7$
15. $14 - 5$
16. $9 - 9$
17. $12 - 6$
18. $13 - 4$

Writing and Reasoning Write the subtraction number sentence shown by this number line. How did you know what number to start with? How do you know the answer?

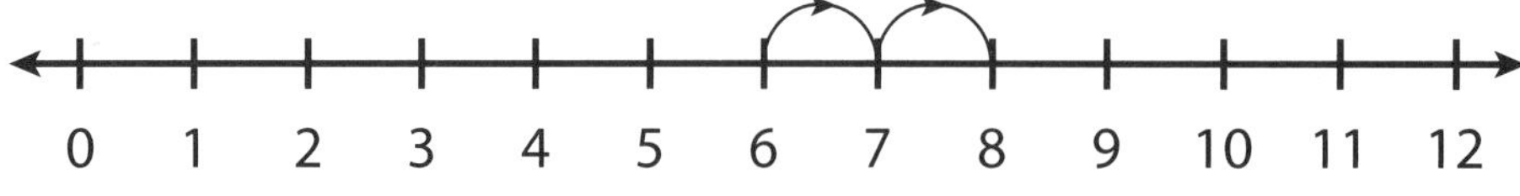

____

____

____

Circle Time

Problem of the Day

TAKS Objective 1 TEKS 2.3A

Fiona picks 8 pink flowers and 5 yellow flowers.
How many more pink flowers than yellow flowers does she pick?

Operations

TAKS Objective 1 TEKS 2.3A

$7 + 5 + 3 =$ ______

$8 + 2 + 4 =$ ______

$6 + 0 + 4 =$ ______

Word of the Day

TAKS Objective 1 TEKS 2.5C

fact family

Use the numbers 5, 6, and 11 to write a fact family.

Numerical Fluency

TAKS Objective 1 TEKS 2.1C

Circle the choice that is true. Use base-ten blocks and Workmat 3 to help if you wish.

A $75 < 57$

B $75 > 57$

C $75 = 57$

Choose the Operation

TAKS Objective 6
TEKS 2.12B

Choose the operation.
Then write a number sentence to solve.

Draw or write to explain.

1. Martha works 8 problems. Then she works 6 more. How many problems does Martha work?

   ____ + ____ = ____ problems

2. Kendra buys 9 toy windmills. 3 of them are broken. How many are not broken?

   ____ − ____ = ____ toy windmills

3. Jean writes 3 short stories. Bev writes 6 short stories. How many more stories does Bev write than Jean ?

   ____ − ____ = ____ stories

4. Tom has 7 marbles in one bag and 4 marbles in another bag. How many marbles does Tom have in the two bags?

   ____ + ____ = ____ marbles

Writing and Reasoning How did you know what operation to use in Exercise 4?

____

____

Circle Time

Problem of the Day

TAKS Objective 1 TEKS 2.12B

Last week it rained 3 days. How many days did it not rain last week?

Number Sense

TAKS Objective 1 TEKS 2.12A

There are 17 girls and 21 boys on the school band. Are there more boys or girls on the school band?

Word of the Day

TAKS Objective 1 TEKS 2.5C

subtraction facts

Name two subtraction facts related to the addition fact $3 + 6 = 9$.

Facts Practice

TAKS Objective 1 TEKS 2.3A

Use connecting cubes to model. Draw to show. Write the answer.

$9 + 3 =$ ______

$3 + 9 =$ ______

Take a Survey

TAKS Objective 6
TEKS 2.13A

Sarah took a survey of her classmates.
Tim took a survey of his classmates.

Sarah's Class	
Favorite color	**Tally Marks**
Blue	|||
Red	𝍸 |
Green	|
Orange	
Yellow	||

Tim's Class	
Favorite color	**Tally Marks**
Blue	||||
Red	𝍸 |
Green	
Orange	||
Yellow	||

Use the data in the charts to answer the questions.

1. Which color is the favorite in both classes?

   ____

2. In whose class did more children choose blue?

   ____

3. Which colors are liked by the same number of children?

   ____

4. Which color is liked by the fewest children?

   ____

5. How many children altogether like red?

   ______________ children

6. How many children did Tim survey?

   ____

Math Journal **Writing and Reasoning** Maria and Andrew see these tally marks 𝍸 |. Maria says they show 6. Andrew says they show 4. Who is right and why?

____

____

Name ______________________ Date ____________

Circle Time

Problem of the Day

TAKS Objective 1 TEKS 2.13A

This is the result of the class survey.

Favorite Day of the Week	
Monday	||
Saturday	卌 ||
Sunday	卌 |

How many students took part in the survey?

Patterns

TAKS Objective 1 TEKS 2.6B

Lisa is planting carrots. She put 3 carrot plants in each pot. How many carrot plants does Lisa need for 5 pots?

Pots	1	2	3	4	5
Carrot Plants	3	6	9		

Calendar

TAKS Objective 1 TEKS 2.1B

Find two dates on the calendar. They should have the same number in the ones place.

Facts Practice

TAKS Objective 1 TEKS 2.3A

Use connecting cubes to model. Draw to show. Write the answer.

$6 + 5 =$ ______

$5 + 6 =$ ______

Name ______________________ Date ____________

Make a Picture Graph

TAKS Objective 5
TEKS 2.11A

The table shows what games the children like to play during recess.

Recess Games			
Simon Says	Jump rope	Catch	Soccer
||||	~~||||~~ |||	~~||||~~ |	~~||||~~ ~~||||~~ ||

1. Use the table to make a picture graph.

   Draw 1 ☺ for every 2 children.

Recess Games

Simon Says	
Jump rope	
Catch	
Soccer	

Key: Each ☺ stands for 2 children.

Use the information in the picture graph to answer the question.

2. How many more children like playing soccer than Simon Says?

   ______ more children

3. If 4 more children say they like catch best, how many ☺ will you add to the picture graph?

   ______ more ☺

Math Journal **Writing and Reasoning** If each ☆ stands for 2 children, what number does ☆ ☆ ☆ stand for?

How do you know?

____

Name ______________________ Date ____________

Circle Time

Problem of the Day

TAKS Objective 1 TEKS 2.11A

Each ○ in a picture graph stands for 2 children.
How many children does ○ ○ stand for?

Operations

TAKS Objective 1 TEKS 2.3A

Use Workmat 1 with counters.
Add or subtract.

$$\begin{array}{r} 18 \\ -8 \\ \hline \end{array} \qquad \begin{array}{r} 10 \\ +8 \\ \hline \end{array}$$

Word of the Day

TAKS Objective 1 TEKS 2.11A

tally marks

Use tally marks to show the number of girls in your class.

Facts Practice

TAKS Objective 1 TEKS 2.3A

Use Workmat 1 with counters.
Add or subtract.

$6 + 8 =$ _____

$8 + 6 =$ _____

$14 - 6 =$ _____

$14 - 8 =$ _____

Read a Picture Graph

TAKS Objective 5
TEKS 2.11B

This picture graph shows where the class would like to go on a field trip.

Remember The key tells how many each symbol stands for.

Field Trip Favorites	
Museum	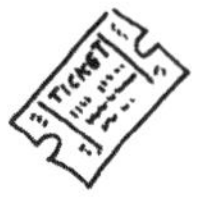 🎟
Library	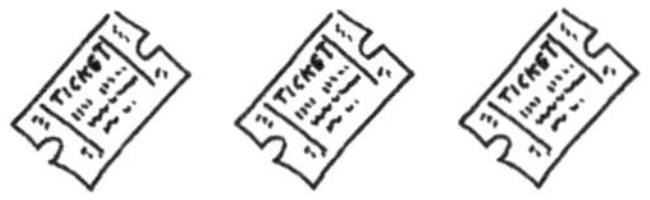 🎟 🎟 🎟
Farm	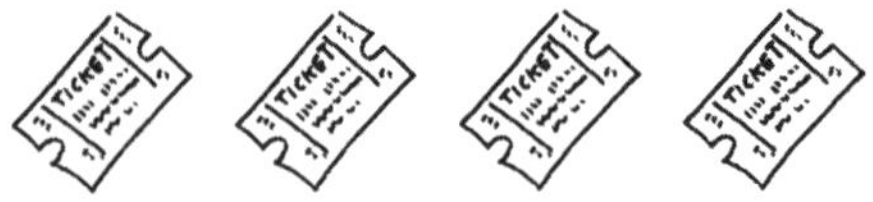 🎟 🎟 🎟 🎟
Theater	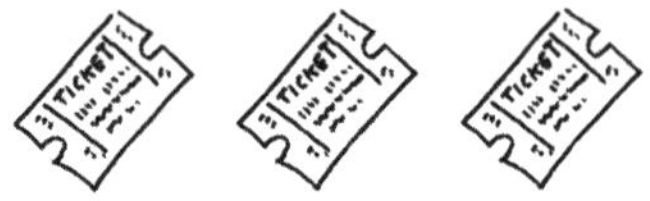 🎟 🎟 🎟

Key: Each 🎟 **stands for** 2 **children.**

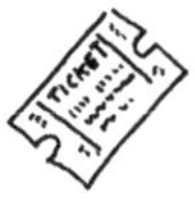

Use the information in the picture graph to answer the question.

1. How many children want to go to the library?

   _______ children

2. How many children want to go to the farm?

   _______ children

3. How many fewer children want to go to the theater than the farm?

   _______ children

4. How many more children want to go to the farm than the museum?

   _______ children

Math Journal **Writing and Reasoning** How did you count the total number of children in the class using the picture graph?

____

Name ______________________ Date ____________

Circle Time

Problem of the Day

TAKS Objective 1 TEKS 2.11B

School Field Trip

zoo	☆ ☆ ☆
beach	☆ ☆ ☆ ☆ ☆
museum	☆

Key: Each ☆ stands for 2 students

How many more students voted for the beach than the zoo?

Number Sense

TAKS Objective 1 TEKS 2.1C

Write >, <, or =.

41 ◯ 37

Number of the Day

TAKS Objective 1 TEKS 2.1A, 2.1B

21

Show the number 21 using words and pictures.

Facts Practice

TAKS Objective 1 TEKS 2.3A

Add.

$\begin{array}{r} 8 \\ +8 \\ \hline \end{array}$ $\begin{array}{r} 9 \\ +5 \\ \hline \end{array}$ $\begin{array}{r} 4 \\ +7 \\ \hline \end{array}$

Name ______________________ Date ____________

Make and Read Bar-Type Graphs

TAKS Objective 5
TEKS 2.11A, 2.11B

Make a bar graph from the data below.

1. Miguel sells school supplies. He sold 1 backpack. He sold 2 more books than backpacks. He sold 4 more T-shirts than backpacks.

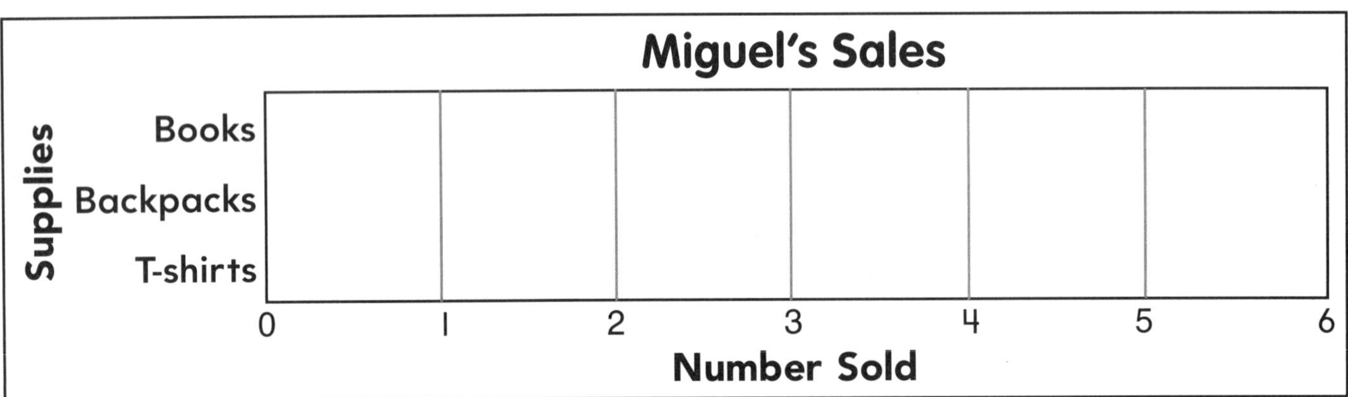

Use the data in the graph to answer the questions.

2. How many books did Miguel sell?

   ______ books

3. How many T-shirts did Miguel sell?

   ______ T-shirts

4. What did Miguel sell the fewest of?

   ____

5. What is the total number of school supplies Miguel sold?

   ______

Writing and Reasoning Each colored box on a bar graph stands for 2 children. How many boxes must be colored to show 6 children? How do you know?

____

Circle Time

Problem of the Day

TAKS Objective 1 TEKS 2.11A

School Field Trip

zoo	☆ ☆ ☆
beach	☆ ☆ ☆ ☆ ☆
museum	☆

Key: Each ☆ stands for 2 students

Fill the graph below to show the same results as the picture graph.

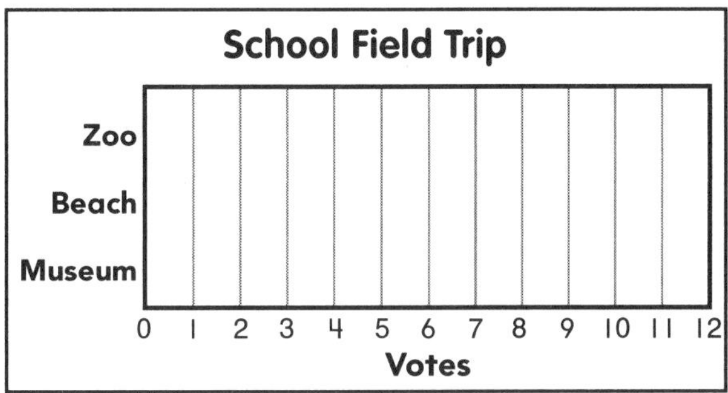

Operations

TAKS Objective 1 TEKS 2.3A

Add or subtract.

$9 + 0 =$ ______

$9 - 0 =$ ______

Number of the Day

TAKS Objective 1 TEKS 2.1A

15

Throughout the day, find ways to use the number 15. For example, you may see 15 pencils or take 15 steps.

Facts Practice

TAKS Objective 1 TEKS 2.3A

Write the facts family for 8, 3, 11.

Use a Graph

TAKS Objective 5
TEKS 2.11B, 2.12B

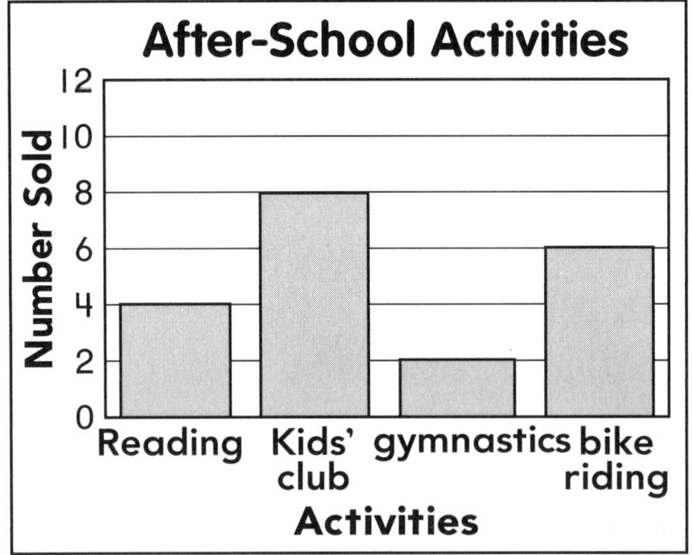

Use the data in the graph to solve.

Draw or write to explain.

1. How many children read? ______ children

2. How many children altogether do bike riding and gymnastics? ______ children

3. How many more children are in the kids' club than read? ______ children

4. Which activity do children do the least? ____________

Math Journal **Writing and Reasoning** Justin makes a bar-type graph. He shows 9 children like soccer, 4 children like hockey, and 3 children like skating. Which sport will have the longest bar and how do you know?

____

____

Name ______________________ Date ____________

Circle Time

Problem of the Day

TAKS Objective 1 TEKS 2.11B

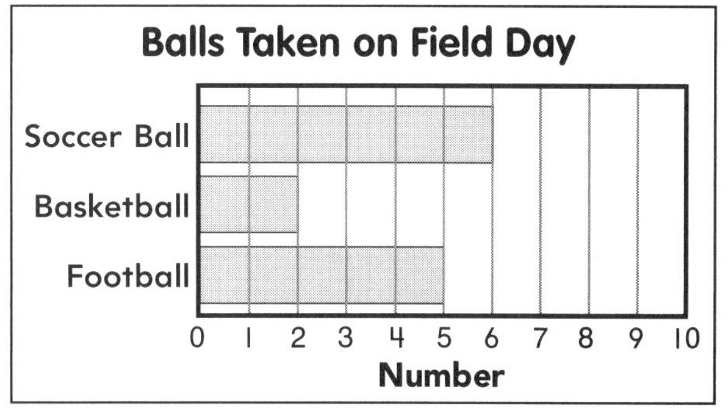

How many more soccer balls were taken on the field day than basketballs?

Patterns

TAKS Objective 1 TEKS 2.6B

The grocery store is giving 2 free strawberries to each customer. How many strawberries does the store needs for 6 customers?

Customers	1	2	3	4	5	6
Strawberries	2	4	6			

Word of the Day

TAKS Objective 1 TEKS 2.11A

picture graph

What does a picture graph look like?

Facts Practice

TAKS Objective 1 TEKS 2.3A

Model with connecting cubes. Add.

$3 + 1 + 1 =$ _____

$$\begin{array}{r} 3 \\ 1 \\ +\ 1 \\ \hline \end{array}$$

Name ____________________ Date ____________

Hands On: More Likely and Less Likely

TAKS Objective 5
TEKS 2.11C

You can tell if an event is more likely or less likely to happen.

1. 7 red cubes and 5 blue cubes are in a bag. How likely are you to pick a red cube rather than a blue cube?

   more likely   less likely

2. 3 red cubes and 9 blue cubes are in a bag. How likely are you to pick a red cube rather than a blue cube?

   more likely   less likely

3. Place 7 red cubes and 5 blue cubes in a bag. Pick one cube from a bag. Record the color. Return the cube to the bag.

Color	Times Picked (10 picks in all)
Red	
Blue	

4. Place 3 red cubes and 9 blue cubes in a bag. Pick one cube from a bag. Record the color. Return the cube to the bag.

Color	Times Picked (10 picks in all)
Red	
Blue	

Math Journal **Writing and Reasoning** What did you expect the results of Exercise 4 to be? Are the results what you would expect?

____

____

Name ______________________ Date ____________

Circle Time

Problem of the Day

TAKS Objective 1 TEKS 2.11C

There are 5 red cubes and 3 blue cubes in a bag. How likely are you to pick a red cube rather than a blue cube?

Data

TAKS Objective 1 TEKS 2.11A

This is the result of the class survey.

Favorite Day of the Week	
Monday	II
Saturday	𝍸 II
Sunday	𝍸 I

How many more students prefer Saturday to Sunday?

Number of the Day

TAKS Objective 1 TEKS 2.1A

12

Show different ways to model 12 using place value blocks.

Facts Practice

TAKS Objective 1 TEKS 2.3A

Add.

$$\begin{array}{r} 8 \\ 2 \\ +6 \\ \hline \end{array} \qquad \begin{array}{r} 9 \\ 7 \\ +1 \\ \hline \end{array} \qquad \begin{array}{r} 12 \\ 3 \\ +3 \\ \hline \end{array}$$

Hands On: Use a Spinner

TAKS Objective 5
TEKS 2.11C

Use the spinner.

1. Predict the color the spinner will land on most often. ____________

2. Use a paper clip and pencil. Spin 15 times. Record your spins.

   Which color did you land on most often?

   ____

   ____

Color	Tally
White	
Gray	
Black	

3. Use three colors to color the parts of this spinner. Use blue to color the part the spinner would land on most often.

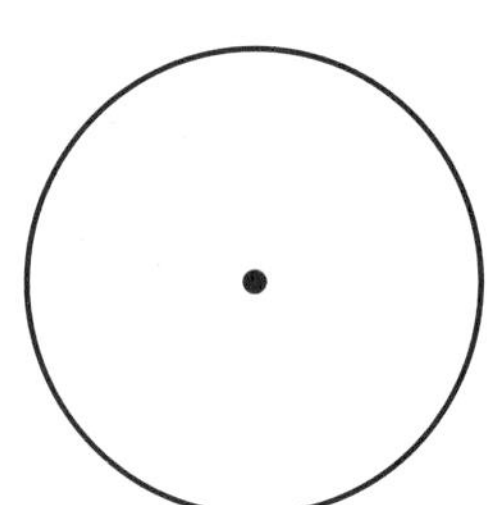

Writing and Reasoning May spins this spinner 10 times. Which number do you think she will spin most often?

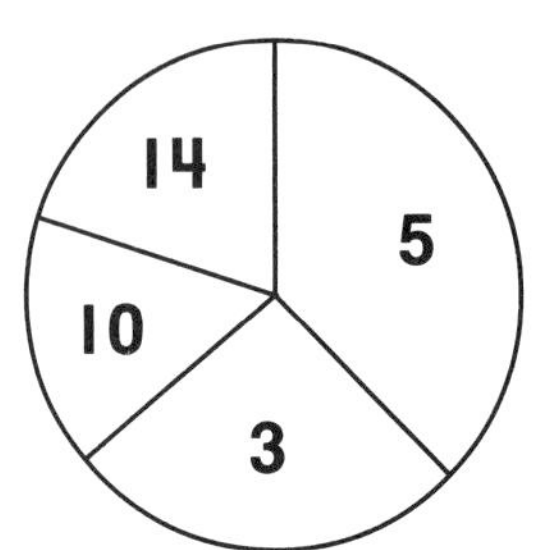

____

____

Circle Time

Problem of the Day

TAKS Objective 1 TEKS 2.11C

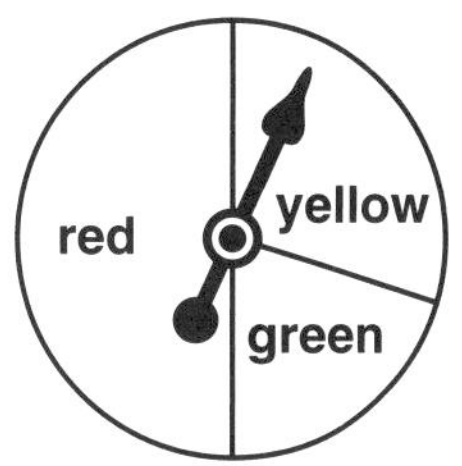

Predict the color that the spinner will land most often.

Data

TAKS Objective 1 TEKS 2.11A

School Field Trip

zoo	☆ ☆ ☆ ☆
beach	☆ ☆ ☆ ☆ ☆ ☆
museum	☆ ☆ ☆

Key: Each ☆ stands for 2 students

Fill the graph below to show the same results.

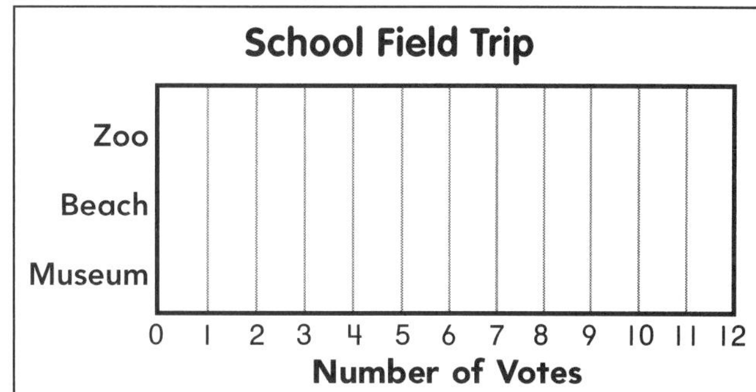

Calendar

TAKS Objective 1 TEKS 2.1C

Find the dates in which the tens digit is less than the ones digit.

Facts Practice

TAKS Objective 1 TEKS 2.3A

Subtract.

$7 - 1 =$ ____ $7 - 0 =$ ____ $7 - 7 =$ ____

Hands On: Graph Outcomes

TAKS Objective 5
TEKS 2.11C

Place 8 striped cubes, 3 white cubes and 5 gray cubes in the bag. Pick a cube and draw an X in the row for that color. Return the cube to the bag. Repeat this 10 times.

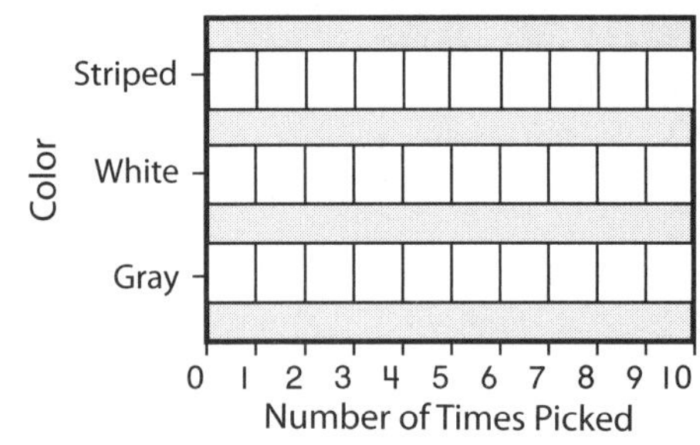

1. Which color has the biggest bar on your graph?

____

2. Which color has the smallest bar on your graph?

____

Color the sections of the spinner using 3 colors. Label the graph. Take turns using a pencil and paper clip to spin. Spin 10 times. Fill in the graph with your results.

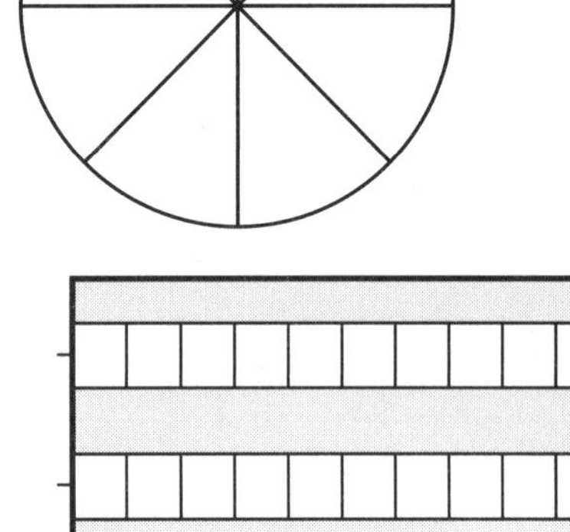

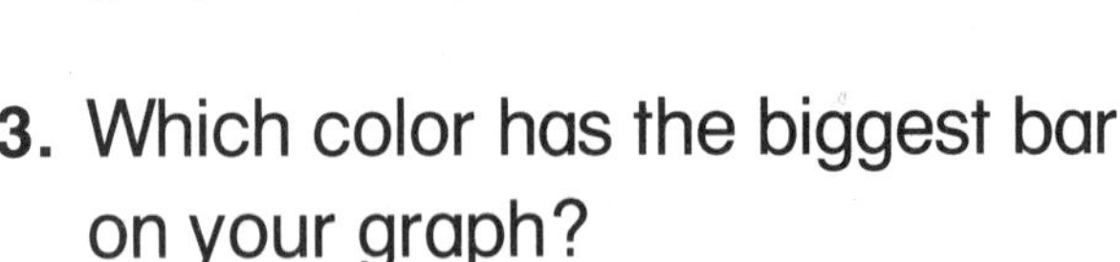

3. Which color has the biggest bar on your graph?

____

Color

0 1 2 3 4 5 6 7 8 9 10

Number of Times Spun

4. Which color has the smallest bar on your graph?

____

Writing and Reasoning If you do the experiment again in Exercise 2, what would you expect the results on the graph to look like?

____

Circle Time

Problem of the Day

TAKS Objective 1 TEKS 2.11A

Tom has 6 red buttons and 3 blue buttons in a bag. He draws a button from a bag 10 times and records the results. Tom creates a bar-type graph to show the results.

Which color is likely to have the longest bar?

Geometry

TAKS Objective 1 TEKS 1.6C

Use 6 triangle pattern blocks. Make the shape shown.

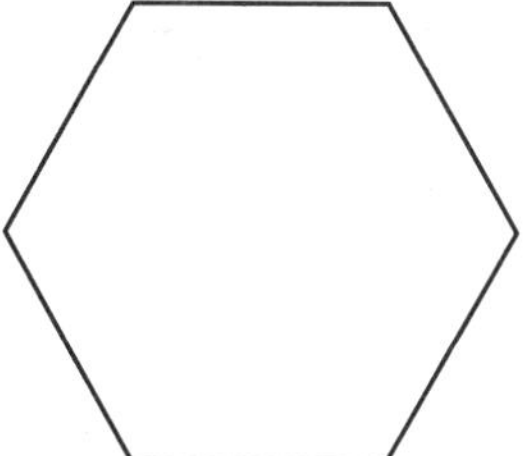

Word of the Day

TAKS Objective 1 TEKS 2.1C

$<$, $>$, $=$

Use $<$, $>$, or $=$ to compare the number of boys and girls in your class.

Facts Practice

TAKS Objective 1 TEKS 2.3A

Add or subtract.

$8 + 4 =$

$8 - 4 =$

$6 + 6 =$

$6 - 6 =$

Use Data to Predict

TAKS Objective 5
TEKS 2.11B

Carolyn makes this bar-type graph that shows coins collected for the book drive this week.

1. What does the bar graph show?

_______ coins on Monday.

_______ coins on Tuesday.

_______ coins on Wednesday.

_______ coins on Thursday.

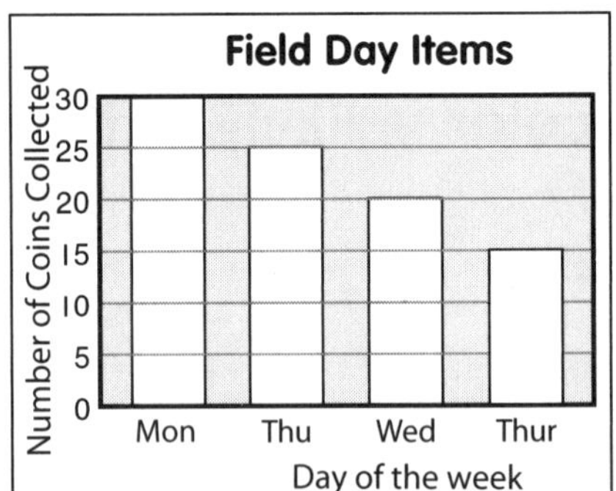

2. What is the pattern?

____

____

____

3. If the pattern continues, will there be more coins collected on Friday or on Saturday? _______

4. How many coins were collected in total on Wednesday and Thursday? _______

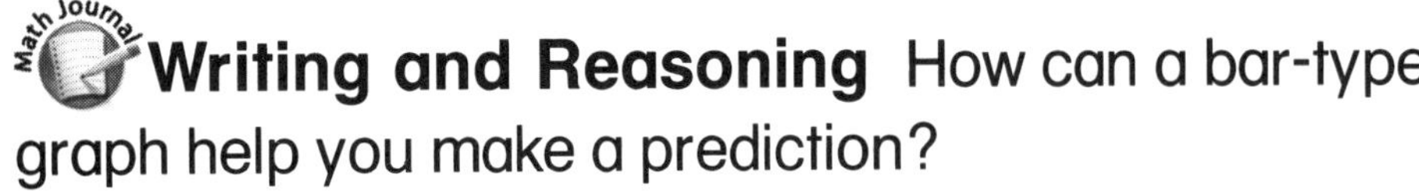

Writing and Reasoning How can a bar-type graph help you make a prediction?

____

Circle Time

Problem of the Day

TAKS Objective 1 TEKS 2.11B

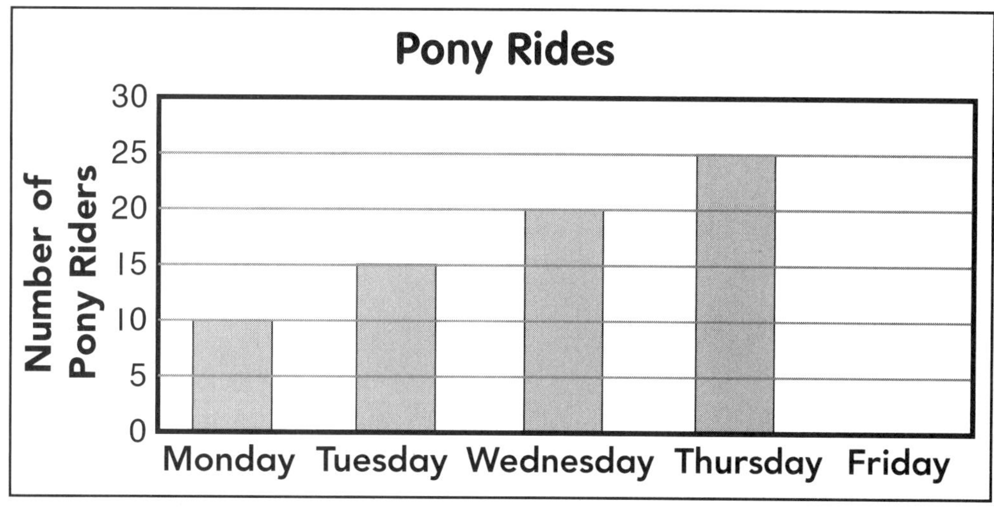

What is the pattern shown in the graph?

How many riders do you predict for Friday?

Probability

TAKS Objective 1 TEKS 2.11C

8 blue cubes and 5 yellow cubes are in a bag. How likely are you to pick a blue cube instead of a yellow cube?

Number of the Day

TAKS Objective 1 TEKS 2.5A

3

Find a pattern on the hundred chart using the number 3.

Facts Practice

TAKS Objective 1 TEKS 2.3A

Subtract.

12 − 5 = _____ 7 − 5 = _____ 5 − 2 = _____

Problem Solving: Act it Out

TAKS Objective 6
TEKS 2.11C, 2.12C

Act it out to solve.

Shanna put 9 gray cubes in a bag.
Teddy put 4 white cubes in the same bag.

1. Which color cube is more likely to be pulled from the bag? ________
2. Which color cube is less likely to be pulled from the bag? ________

Shelly plays a game with this spinner.

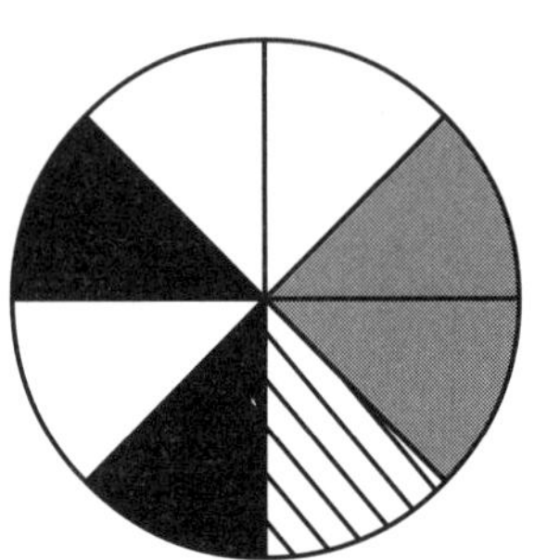

3. Which color is she least likely to land on? ________
4. Which color is she most likely to land on? ________

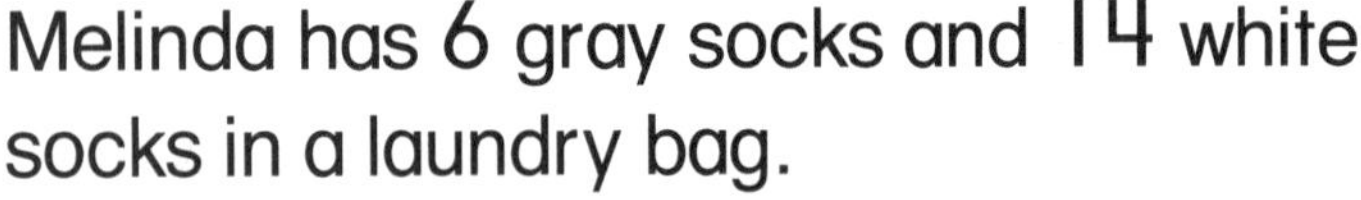

Melinda has 6 gray socks and 14 white socks in a laundry bag.

5. Which color sock is Melinda more likely to pull from the laundry bag? ________
6. Melinda takes 8 white socks out of the bag. Now which color sock is Melinda more likely to pull from the bag? ________________________

____

Writing and Reasoning Is your prediction always right? Explain.

____

____

____

Circle Time

Problem of the Day

TAKS Objective 1 TEKS 2.11C

Sandra spun this spinner several times.
What color is the spinner most likely to land on?

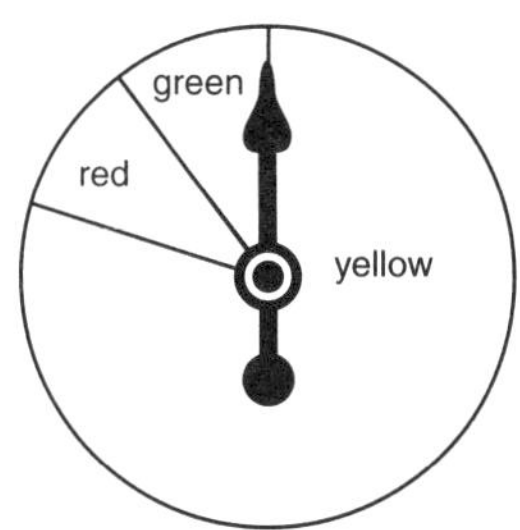

Operations

TAKS Objective 1 TEKS 2.3A

Anna has 5 crayons. Pedro has two fewer than Anna.
How many crayons do they have in all?

Number of the Day

TAKS Objective 1 TEKS 2.1B

57

Name the number 57 as many ways as you can.

Facts Practice

TAKS Objective 1 TEKS 2.3A

Use connecting cubes to model. Draw to show. Write the answer.

1 + 3 = ____

3 + 1 = ____

Name ______________________ Date ______________

Mental Math: Add Tens

TAKS Objective 1
TEKS 2.3A, 2.3B

Complete the addition sentences.
Use a basic fact to help.

1. 2 tens + 6 tens = _____ tens

   _____ + _____ = _____

2. 5 tens + 3 tens = _____ tens

   _____ + _____ = _____

3. 3 tens + 4 tens = _____ tens

   _____ + _____ = _____

4. 1 ten + 1 ten = _____ tens

   _____ + _____ = _____

5. 7 tens + 1 ten = _____ tens

   _____ + _____ = _____

6. 3 tens + 6 tens = _____ tens

   _____ + _____ = _____

7. 4 tens + 2 tens = _____ tens

   _____ + _____ = _____

8. 1 ten + 8 tens = _____ tens

   _____ + _____ = _____

Math Journal **Writing and Reasoning** Paul used the basic fact 6 + 2 to help him find the sum of 20 + 60. Sharon used the fact 2 + 6. Who is right and why?

____

____

____

Name ______________________ Date ____________

Circle Time

Problem of the Day

TAKS Objective 1 TEKS 2.3B

Chen puts 10 marbles in each bag. He fills 6 bags with blue marbles and 2 bags with red marbles. How many marbles does Chen have?

Geometry

TAKS Objective 1 TEKS 2.8

What number could be represented by the point on the number line?

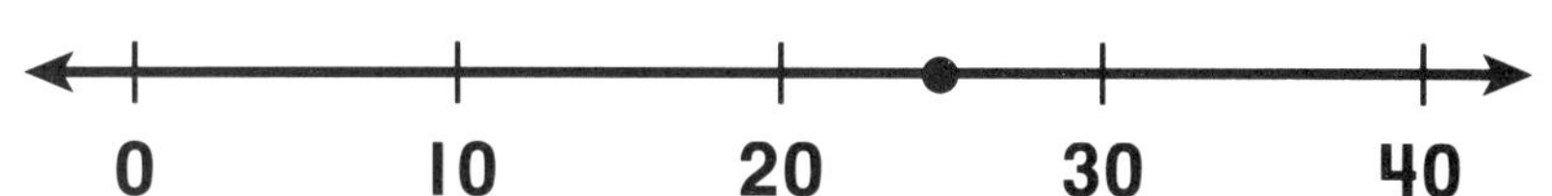

Words of the Day

TAKS Objective 1 TEKS 2.11C

likely, less likely

Use the words *likely* and *less likely* to describe something during your school day.

Facts Practice

TAKS Objective 1 TEKS 2.3A

Use connecting cubes. Write the fact family for 1, 9, 10.

Whole	
Part	Part

Name ______________________ Date ____________

Count on Tens to Add

TAKS Objective 1
TEKS 2.3B

Use the hundred chart.
Add.

1	2	3	4	5	6	7	8	9	10
11	12	13	14	15	16	17	18	19	20
21	22	23	24	25	26	27	28	29	30
31	32	33	34	35	36	37	38	39	40
41	42	43	44	45	46	47	48	49	50
51	52	53	54	55	56	57	58	59	60
61	62	63	64	65	66	67	68	69	70
71	72	73	74	75	76	77	78	79	80
81	82	83	84	85	86	87	88	89	90
91	92	93	94	95	96	97	98	99	100

1. $27 + 30 =$ 57

2. $10 + 16 =$ ______

3. $43 + 30 =$ ______

4. $50 + 21 =$ ______

5. $11 + 40$

6. $20 + 32$

7. $79 + 10$

8. $50 + 14$

9. $27 + 70$

10. $18 + 60$

11. $30 + 29$

12. $80 + 12$

Writing and Reasoning How can you use the hundred chart to count on tens to add?

____

____

Circle Time

Problem of the Day

TAKS Objective 1 TEKS 2.3B

Shawna puts 29 stamps on one page. She puts 40 stamps on another page. How many stamps does Shawna have altogether?

Operation

TAKS Objective 1 TEKS 2.12B

Last week it snowed 5 days. How many days did it not snow last week?

Calendar Activity

TAKS Objective 1 TEKS 2.3B

Find the date that is ten days from today.

Numerical Fluency

TAKS Objective 1 TEKS 2.1B

Model with place value blocks. Write the numbers.

1. $7 + 80 =$ ____
2. $40 + 4 =$ ____

Write a Number Sentence

TAKS Objective 6
TEKS 2.12C, 2.13B

Write the number sentence. Then solve.

	Draw or write to explain.
1. Paul counts 12 frogs on a large lily pad. He counts 20 frogs on a log. How many frogs did Paul count? _____ + _____ = _____	_____ frogs
2. 10 ducks are swimming on the pond. 15 geese fly to the pond. Now how many birds are on the pond? _____ + _____ = _____	_____ birds
3. In the pond Ricky counts 28 catfish and 20 perch. How many fish does Ricky count? _____ + _____ = _____	_____ fish

Writing and Reasoning Explain how you found your answer for Exercise 3.

____

____

Name ______________________ Date ____________

Circle Time

Problem of the Day

TAKS Objective 1 TEKS 2.12C

There are 17 children and 30 adults in the bus.
How many are in the bus?

Data

TAKS Objective 1 TEKS 2.11B

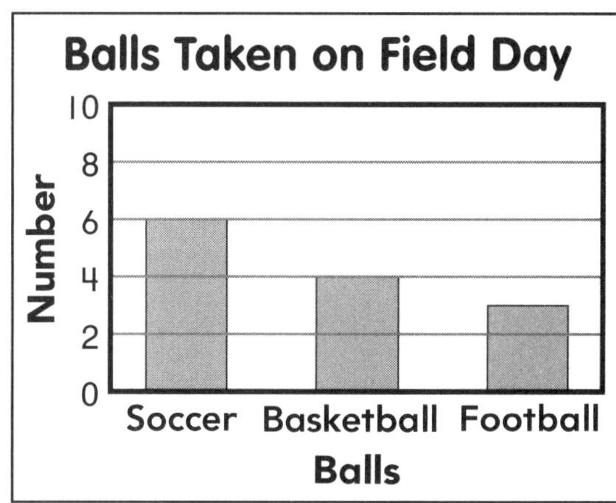

How many more soccer balls were taken on the field day than footballs?

Number of the Day

TAKS Objective 1 TEKS 2.1B

84

What is the value of 8 in 84?
What is the value of 4?

Numerical Fluency

TAKS Objective 1 TEKS 2.1C

Circle the choice that is true. Use place value blocks and Workmat 3 to help if you wish.

A $80 + 8 < 80 + 9$ **B** $80 + 8 > 80 + 9$ **C** $80 + 8 = 80 + 9$

Hands On: Regroup Ones as Tens

TAKS Objective 1
TEKS 2.3B, 2.3C

Use Workmat 3 with [ten rod] and [unit cube].

Write the tens and ones.
Regroup. Write the number.

1.

_____ tens _____ ones → _____ tens _____ ones [ ]

2. 6 tens 10 ones → Regroup → _____ tens _____ ones [ ]

3. 5 tens 14 ones → Regroup → _____ tens _____ ones [ ]

4. 1 tens 19 ones → Regroup → _____ tens _____ ones [ ]

5. 7 tens 13 ones → Regroup → _____ tens _____ ones [ ]

6. 2 tens 11 ones → Regroup → _____ tens _____ ones [ ]

Math Journal **Writing and Reasoning** How many tens are there after you regroup 2 tens and 18 ones? Explain how you decided.

____

____

Circle Time

Problem of the Day
TAKS Objective 1 TEKS 2.3B

Rena has 37 books. The shelves in her room can hold ten books each. How many shelves can she fill with books? How many books will be left over?

Operations
TAKS Objective 1 TEKS 2.3A

There are 6 sail boats and 5 row boats on the lake. How many boats are on the lake?

Word of the Day
TAKS Objective 1 TEKS 2.3B

number sentences

Write 5 number sentences using the number 15.

Facts Practice
TAKS Objective 1 TEKS 2.3A

Model with connecting cubes.
Add.

1. $3 + 0 + 5 =$ ____
2. $6 + 0 =$ ____
3. $8 + 1 =$ ____
4. $10 + 0 =$ ____

Name ______________________ Date ____________

Hands On: Decide When to Regroup

TAKS Objective 1
TEKS 2.3B, 2.3C

Use Workmat 3 with [ten rod] and [unit cube].

Show both numbers.	Add the ones. How many tens and ones are there?	Do you need to regroup?	What is the sum?
1. 24 + 6	_____ tens _____ ones	Yes No	
2. 51 + 4	_____ tens _____ ones	Yes No	
3. 47 + 5	_____ tens _____ ones	Yes No	
4. 63 + 7	_____ tens _____ ones	Yes No	
5. 38 + 6	_____ tens _____ ones	Yes No	
6. 59 + 7	_____ tens _____ ones	Yes No	
7. 26 + 3	_____ tens _____ ones	Yes No	
8. 38 + 9	_____ tens _____ones	Yes No	

Math Journal **Writing and Reasoning** Does the addition sentence 12 + 9 need to have the ones regrouped? Tell why or why not.

____

____

Circle Time

Problem of the Day

TAKS Objective 1 TEKS 2.3B

Circle the exercises where you need to regroup to add. Solve to find the sum.

1. 72 + 8
2. 34 + 2
3. 56 + 5

Operations

TAKS Objective 1 TEKS 2.3A

Add. Then subtract.

8 + 5 = _____

13 − 5 = _____

13 − 8 = _____

Number of the Day

TAKS Objective 1 TEKS 2.6A

3

How many wheels do 3 tricycles have?

Numerical Fluency

TAKS Objective 1 TEKS 2.3A

Count how many.

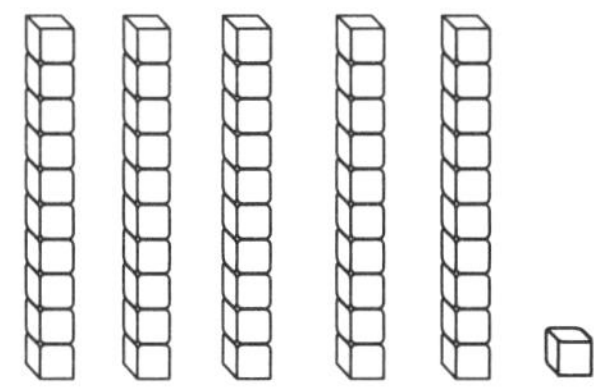

Write the tens and ones.

_____ tens and _____ ones

Write the value. _____ + _____

Write the number. _____

Name ______________________ Date ____________

Hands On: Add One-Digit Numbers to Two-Digit Numbers

TAKS Objective 1
TEKS 2.3B, 2.3C

Remember
Regroup when you have ten or more ones.

Use charts with [ten block] and [one cube]. Add.

1.

	Tens	Ones
	☐	
	4	3
+		9
	☐	☐

2.

	Tens	Ones
	☐	
	3	8
+		4
	☐	☐

3.

	Tens	Ones
	☐	
		7
+	2	6
	☐	☐

4.

	Tens	Ones
	☐	
	5	6
+		4
	☐	☐

5.

	Tens	Ones
	☐	
		8
+	2	7
	☐	☐

6.

	Tens	Ones
	☐	
	6	2
+		5
	☐	☐

7.

	Tens	Ones
	☐	
	7	0
+		8
	☐	☐

8.

	Tens	Ones
	☐	
	1	5
+		7
	☐	☐

Math Journal

Writing and Reasoning Why is there not a 1 in the ☐ in Exercise 6?

____

____

Circle Time

Problem of the Day

TAKS Objective 1 TEKS 2.3B

Ruth scored 83 points in a game. Todd scored 75 points and then another 4 points in the same game. Who scored more points?

Explain how you know.

Data

TAKS Objective 1 TEKS 2.11A

This is the result of the class survey.

Favorite Activity	
Reading	||
Sports	卌 ||
Talking	卌	

How many more students prefer sports to reading?

Word of the Day

TAKS Objective 1 TEKS 2.3A

related facts

Name 2 related facts for $12 + 4 = 16$

Numerical Fluency

TAKS Objective 1 TEKS 2.1C

Write the numbers in order from least to greatest.

171 133 702 113

_____ _____ _____ _____

Add Two-Digit Numbers

TAKS Objective 1
TEKS 2.3B, 2.3C

Remember
When you regroup, record in the tens column.

Use charts with [ten rod] and [unit cube]. Add.

1.

	Tens	Ones
	□	
	3	6
+	2	7
	□	□

2.

	Tens	Ones
	□	
		9
+	3	7
	□	□

3.

	Tens	Ones
	□	
	4	5
+	1	5
	□	□

4.

	Tens	Ones
	□	
	4	7
+	2	9
	□	□

5.

	Tens	Ones
	□	
	5	8
+		4
	□	□

6.

	Tens	Ones
	□	
	2	7
+	5	2
	□	□

7. $\begin{array}{r} 9 \\ +\ 38 \\ \hline \end{array}$

8. $\begin{array}{r} 63 \\ +\ 18 \\ \hline \end{array}$

9. $\begin{array}{r} 42 \\ +\ 30 \\ \hline \end{array}$

Math Journal **Writing and Reasoning** When you add 47 + 15, tell how you know how many tens are in the sum.

____

____

Circle Time

Problem of the Day

TAKS Objective 1 TEKS 2.3B

Tara has 6 more beads than Ethan. Aisha has twice as many beads as Ethan. Ethan has 5 beads. How many beads do Tara and Aisha have altogether?

Operations

TAKS Objective 1 TEKS 2.3B

Add.

$$\begin{array}{r} 60 \\ +13 \\ \hline \end{array} \qquad \begin{array}{r} 53 \\ +18 \\ \hline \end{array} \qquad \begin{array}{r} 23 \\ +17 \\ \hline \end{array}$$

Calendar

TAKS Objective 1 TEKS 2.3B

Write a number sentence to show how many days are between the 12th and 15th of this month.

Numerical Fluency

TAKS Objective 1 TEKS 2.1C

Write >, <, or =.

86 ◯ 81

46 ◯ 64

17 ◯ 17

31 ◯ 63

Rewrite to Add

TAKS Objective 1
TEKS 2.3C

Remember
When you rewrite the addends, line up the ones.

Rewrite the addends. Add.

1. 16 + 54

	Tens	Ones
	1	6
+	5	4
	7	0

2. 62 + 33

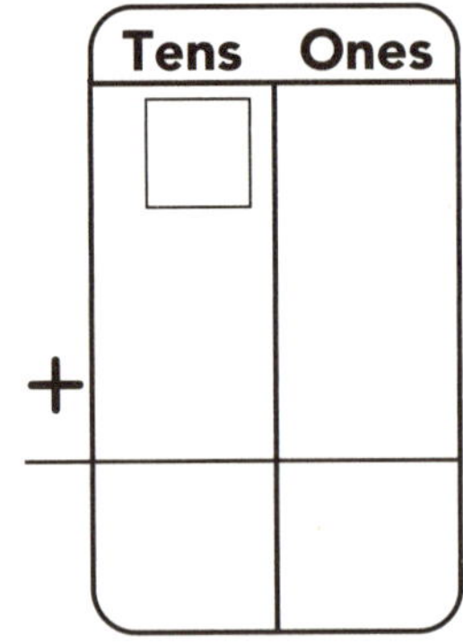

3. 79 + 3

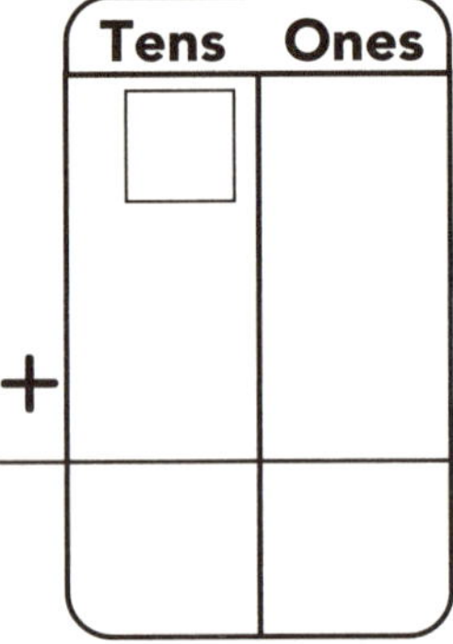

4. 46 + 48

	Tens	Ones
+		

5. 27 + 16

	Tens	Ones
+		

6. 17 + 29

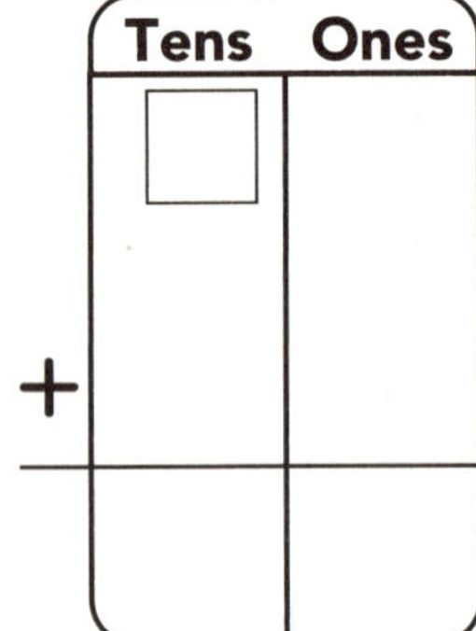

Writing and Reasoning Pat and Saul add 6 + 38. Pat gets a sum of 44. Saul gets a sum of 98. Who is right and why?

____

____

Circle Time

Problem of the Day

TAKS Objective 1 TEKS 2.3C

Tony has a tank with 46 fish. He also has a bowl with 6 fish. How many fish does Tony have?

Rewrite in vertical form to solve.

Patterns

TAKS Objective 1 TEKS 2.11B

What is the pattern?

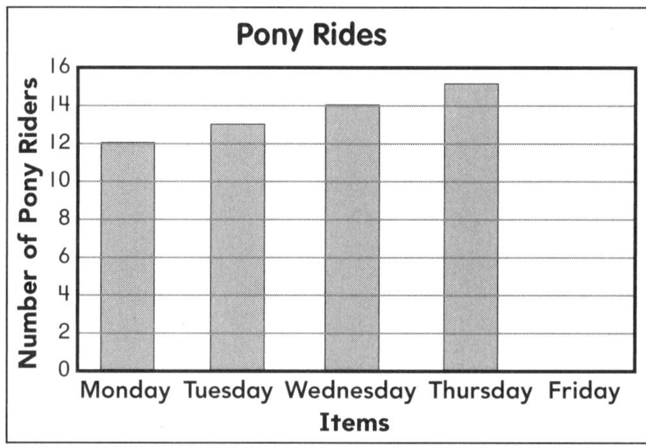

How many riders do you predict for Friday?

Word of the Day

TAKS Objective 1 TEKS 2.3A

doubles facts

List all doubles facts that have a sum of 10 or less.

Facts Practice

TAKS Objective 1 TEKS 2.3A

Use Workmat 1 with counters. Add or subtract.

$2 + 4 =$ ______ $4 + 2 =$ ______

$6 - 2 =$ ______ $6 - 4 =$ ______

Choose a Way to Add

TAKS Objective 1
TEKS 2.12D, 2.14

Choose a way to add. Add.
Explain the way you find the sum.

1. 42 + 20

2. 50 + 7

3. 39 + 26

4. 84 + 10

5. 40 + 9

6. 68 + 17

Writing and Reasoning Why is it helpful to know different ways to add?

____

____

Name ______________________ Date ____________

Circle Time

Problem of the Day

TAKS Objective 1 TEKS 2.3C

Choose a way to add. Add. Explain the way you found the sum.

37 + 43 = ______

Operations

TAKS Objective 1 TEKS 2.3A

Sarah has 12 comic books. Tehasha has three fewer than Sarah. How many comic books does Tehasha have?

Number of the Day

TAKS Objective 1 TEKS 2.1B

50

How many tens are there in 50?

Numerical Fluency

TAKS Objective 1 TEKS 2.3B

Show the tens and ones. Regroup. Write the number.

80 + 11

______ tens ______ ones

Regroup

______ tens ______ ones

Number: ______

Guess and Check

TAKS Objective 1
TEKS 2.12C, 2.13B

Use guess and check to solve.

	Draw or write to explain.
1. Mrs. Tucker needs 55 buttons for some button dolls that she is making. Which jars should she buy? ______ and ______	
2. The button store sold 58 buttons to the High Street Elementary School. Which two jars of buttons did the school buy? ______ and ______	
3. Mr. Richards needs 70 buttons for an art project. Which two jars of buttons should Mr. Richards buy? ______ and ______	

Math Journal **Writing and Reasoning** How can you use place value to help you guess and check for Exercise 3?

____

____

Name ______________________ Date ____________

Circle Time

Problem of the Day

TAKS Objective 1 TEKS 2.12C

Laura used two of these stamps for 57¢ of postage on her letter.

A

B

C

Which two stamps did Laura use?

Number Sense

TAKS Objective 1 TEKS 2.8

What number is best represented by the point on the number line?

Number of the Day

TAKS Objective 1 TEKS 2.1A

63

Show the number 63 using place value blocks.

Facts Practice

TAKS Objective 1 TEKS 2.3A

Use connecting cubes. Write the facts family for 8, 9, 17.

_____ + _____ = _____

_____ + _____ = _____

_____ − _____ = _____

_____ − _____ = _____

Whole

Part | Part

Name ____________________ Date ____________

Different Names for Numbers

TAKS Objective 1
TEKS 2.3A

Break apart the number.
Write different ways to name the number.

1. 4

2. 9

3. 5

4. 10

5. 6

6. 8

Writing and Reasoning What number does 3 + 4 name? What is another name for that number?

Name ______________________ Date ____________

Circle Time

Problem of the Day

TAKS Objective 1 TEKS 2.3A

Rosa has 5 roses. Karim has 12 flowers. He has 4 daisies and the rest are roses. Jennifer has 8 roses. Which two children have the same number of roses?

Operations

TAKS Objective 1 TEKS 2.3A

Subtract.

$$\begin{array}{r} 18 \\ -7 \\ \hline \end{array}$$

18 − 7 = ______

Words of the Day

TAKS Objective 1 TEKS 2.9A

guess, check

Guess how many paper clips long your desk is.
Then check by measuring with paper clips.

Facts Practice

TAKS Objective 1 TEKS 2.3A

Use connecting cubes. Write the facts family for 7, 8, 15.

_____ + _____ = _____

_____ + _____ = _____

_____ − _____ = _____

_____ − _____ = _____

Whole	
(15 cubes)	
Part	Part
(7 cubes)	(8 cubes)

Name ______________________ Date ____________

TAKS Objective 1
TEKS 2.3A, 2.3B

Make Tens

Make tens to solve.

1. 36 + 7

36 + ____ + ____

____ + ____

____

2. 69 + 5

69 + ____ + ____

____ + ____

____

3. 37 + 8

37 + ____ + ____

____ + ____

____

4. 58 + 6

58 + ____ + ____

____ + ____

____

5. 26 + 7

26 + ____ + ____

____ + ____

____

6. 78 + 9

78 + ____ + ____

____ + ____

____

Math Journal

Writing and Reasoning How would you break apart 8 when you add 27 + 8? Explain your answer.

____

Name ______________________ Date ____________

Circle Time

Problem of the Day

TAKS Objective 1 TEKS 2.3B

Robert has 19 stamps. His sister gives him 17 more stamps. Robert places 20 stamps in an album. How many stamps are left over?

How many stamps does he have altogether?

Operations

TAKS Objective 1 TEKS 2.3A

Add.

$$\begin{array}{r} 11 \\ +\ 6 \\ \hline \end{array}$$

11 + 6 = ______

Calendar Activity

TAKS Objective 1 TEKS 2.1B

How many tens are there in today's date?
How many ones?

Facts Practice

TAKS Objective 1 TEKS 2.3A

Use connecting cubes. Write the facts family for 2, 7, 9.

______ + ______ = ______

______ + ______ = ______

______ − ______ = ______

______ − ______ = ______

Name ______________________ Date ____________

TAKS Objective 1
TEKS 2.3B

Compatible Numbers

Use numbers that add together easily to find a close answer.

1. 28 + 39 is about ______
2. 33 + 31 is about ______
3. 47 + 32 is about ______
4. 39 + 37 is about ______
5. 31 + 43 is about ______
6. 21 + 28 is about ______
7. 42 + 48 is about ______
8. 28 + 39 is about ______

Math Journal

Writing and Reasoning Write a number sentence that is about the same amount as 30 + 30.

______ + ______ = ______

Circle Time

Problem of the Day

TAKS Objective 1 TEKS 2.3B

Raul drove his truck 28 miles on Monday. Shari drives her truck 22 miles further than Raul. How many miles did Shari drive?

Probability

TAKS Objective 1 TEKS 2.11C

Rhonda has a bag with 3 green cubes and 8 red cubes. How likely is it that she will pick a red cube instead of a green cube?

Word of the Day

TAKS Objective 1 TEKS 2.3B

addends

Circle the addends in $4 + 5 = 9$.

Facts Practice

TAKS Objective 1 TEKS 2.3B

Add.

$10 + 20 =$ ______

$15 + 15 =$ ______

$15 + 25 =$ ______

$14 + 26 =$ ______

Name ______________________ Date ____________

Use Mental Math with Addition

TAKS Objective 1
TEKS 2.3B

Add using mental math.

1. 43 + 43 = 86

   So, 43 + 45 = ______

2. 50 + 50 = 100

   So, 50 + 53 = ______

3. 31 + 35 = ______

4. 15 + 14 = ______

5. 47 + 9 = ______

6. 34 + 35 = ______

7. 44 + 42 = ______

8. 7 + 48 = ______

Math Journal **Writing and Reasoning** Tommy mentally added 25 + 24 and gave a sum of 51. What did he do wrong?

____

____

____

Circle Time

Problem of the Day

TAKS Objective 1 TEKS 2.3B

Gale throws 3 beanbags. On her first throw she scores 20. Then she scores 10 points. On her last throw she scores 10 more points.

What is the sum of her points?

Number Sense

TAKS Objective 1 TEKS 2.1A

Circle a way to show the number.

18

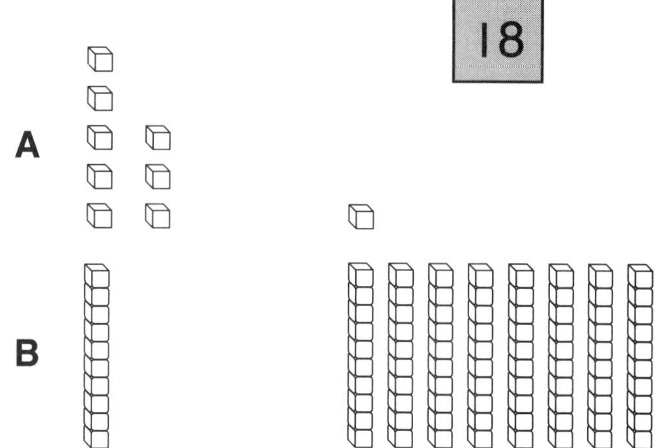

C 1 + 8

D 10 + 8

Word of the Day

TAKS Objective 1 TEKS 2.1A

pattern

Identify a pattern on Workmat 5. Use markers to highlight the pattern.

Numerical Fluency

TAKS Objective 1 TEKS 2.1C

Write >, <, or =.

85 ◯ 50 + 8

Name _______________ Date ________

Choose a Method

TAKS Objectives 1, 6
TEKS 2.3B, 2.12C

Choose a method to solve.	Draw or write to explain.
1. Max sees 21 parrots. Emily sees 12 parrots. How many parrots do they see in all? ______ parrots	
2. The snapping turtle measures 28 inches long. The Texas tortoise measures 9 inches long. How much longer is the snapping turtle than the Texas tortoise? ______ inches	
3. A tiger jumps 14 feet and then runs 42 feet. How far does the tiger go? ______ feet	

Math Journal **Writing and Reasoning** What strategy did you use to solve Problem 1?

____

____

____

Name ______________________ Date __________

Circle Time

Problem of the Day

TAKS Objective 1 TEKS 2.3B

There are 19 adult and 11 baby armadillos at the zoo. Write a number sentence to tell how many armadillos there are in all.

_____ ◯ _____ = _____

Operations

TAKS Objective 1 TEKS 2.3B

Add.

48 + 42 = _____

36 + 44 = _____

73 + 17 = _____

Calendar Activity

TAKS Objective 1 TEKS 2.1A

Use place value blocks to model the number that names the date of your birthday.

Numerical Fluency

TAKS Objective 1 TEKS 2.1B

Count how many.

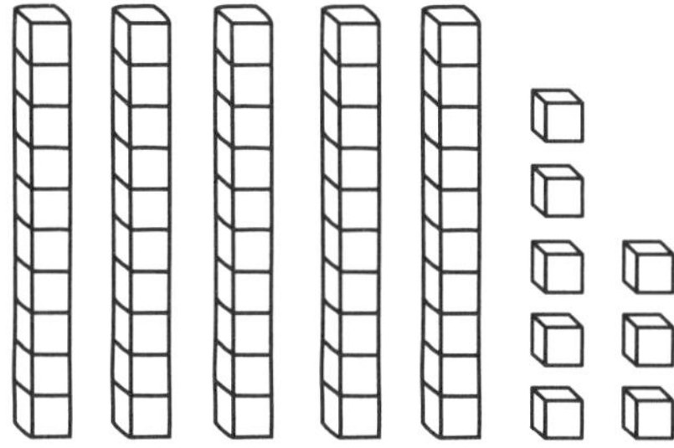

Write the tens and ones.

_____ tens and _____ ones

Write the value.

_____ + _____

Write the number.

_____

Name ______________________ Date ____________

Subtract Tens

TAKS Objective 1
TEKS 2.3B

Complete the subtraction sentences.
Use a basic fact to help.

1. 7 tens − 2 tens = ____ tens ____ − ____ = ____	**2.** 6 tens − 3 tens = ____ tens ____ − ____ = ____
3. 9 tens − 5 tens = ____ tens ____ − ____ = ____	**4.** 4 tens − 1 ten = ____ tens ____ − ____ = ____
5. 8 tens − 6 tens = ____ tens ____ − ____ = ____	**6.** 9 tens − 2 tens = ____ tens ____ − ____ = ____
7. 5 tens − 3 tens = ____ tens ____ − ____ = ____	**8.** 7 tens − 4 tens = ____ tens ____ − ____ = ____

Math Journal **Writing and Reasoning** Sheets of paper come in stacks of ten. Anid has 6 stacks of paper. She gives 3 stacks to her friend. Show how you can find how many sheets of paper Anid has left.

____

____

Circle Time

Problem of the Day

TAKS Objective 1 TEKS 2.3B

Mimi has 70 stickers. She gives Taylor 40 stickers. How many stickers does Mimi have now?

Number Sense

TAKS Objective 1 TEKS 2.8

What number could be represented by the point on the number line?

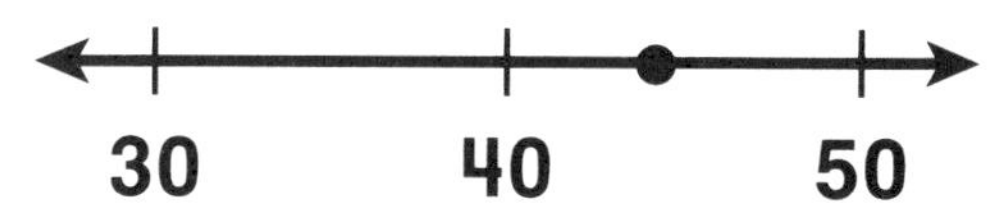

Word of the Day

TAKS Objective 1 TEKS 2.13B

addend, sum

Give an example of addend and sum.

Numerical Fluency

TAKS Objective 1 TEKS 2.1C

Write >, <, or =.

76 ◯ 67

86 ◯ 68

14 ◯ 21

63 ◯ 69

Subtract Tens on a Hundred Chart

TAKS Objectives 1, 2
TEKS 2.5A

Subtract.

1	2	3	4	5	6	7	8	9	10
11	12	13	14	15	16	17	18	19	20
21	22	23	24	25	26	27	28	29	30
31	32	33	34	35	36	37	38	39	40
41	42	43	44	45	46	47	48	49	50
51	52	53	54	55	56	57	58	59	60
61	62	63	64	65	66	67	68	69	70
71	72	73	74	75	76	77	78	79	80
81	82	83	84	85	86	87	88	89	90
91	92	93	94	95	96	97	98	99	100

1. $53 - 20 =$ ____

2. $78 - 30 =$ ____

3. $62 - 10 =$ ____

4. $85 - 30 =$ ____

5. $\begin{array}{r} 57 \\ -30 \\ \hline \end{array}$

6. $\begin{array}{r} 90 \\ -40 \\ \hline \end{array}$

7. $\begin{array}{r} 74 \\ -10 \\ \hline \end{array}$

8. $\begin{array}{r} 61 \\ -20 \\ \hline \end{array}$

Math Journal **Writing and Reasoning** Donna finds 63 shells on the beach. She gave 20 shells to her sister. How can you use the hundred chart to help you find how many shells Donna has left? How many does she have left?

____

____

Circle Time

Problem of the Day

TAKS Objective 1 TEKS 2.5A

Clyde collects 47 shells at the beach. He gives 20 shells to his best friend. How many shells does he have left?

Data

TAKS Objective 1 TEKS 2.11B

School Field Trip

Zoo	☆☆☆☆☆
library	☆☆☆
park	☆☆

☆= 3 students

How many more students voted for the zoo than the library?

Number of the Day

TAKS Objective 1 TEKS 2.3C

25

Find two numbers on the calendar that have a sum of 25.

Facts Practice

TAKS Objective 1 TEKS 2.1A

Subtract.

$$\begin{array}{r} 5 \\ -\ 3 \\ \hline \end{array} \qquad \begin{array}{r} 8 \\ -\ 2 \\ \hline \end{array} \qquad \begin{array}{r} 9 \\ -\ 5 \\ \hline \end{array} \qquad \begin{array}{r} 7 \\ -7 \\ \hline \end{array}$$

Problem Solving: Use Models to Act It Out

TAKS Objectives 1, 6
TEKS 2.3C, 2.12B

Remember:	
Understand	Plan
Solve	Look back

You can solve some problems by acting them out with tens and ones blocks.

Solve.

	Draw or write to explain.
1. Jesse's team scores 10 runs. Lindsay's team scores 23 runs. How many more runs does Lindsay's team score than Jesse's team? ______ runs	
2. Daniel counts 36 stars in the sky. Erin counts 20. How many more stars does Daniel count? ______ stars	
3. Jennifer baked 48 cookies for the bake sale. Tracy baked 30 cookies. How many more cookies did Jennifer bake? ______ cookies	
4. The man at the pet shop sold all but 20 of his 42 canaries. How many canaries did he sell? ______ canaries	

Math Journal **Writing and Reasoning** Which number sentence did you write for Exercise 4 and how did you know which number to write first?

____

____

Circle Time

Problem of the Day

TAKS Objective 1 TEKS 2.3C

Eduardo has 67 baseball cards. 20 are of his favorite team. How many cards are not from Eduardo's favorite team?

Algebraic Thinking

TAKS Objective 1 TEKS 2.3A

Use connecting cubes to model. Draw to show. Write the answer.

$7 + 6 =$ _____ $6 + 7 =$ _____

Why are the answers the same?

Word of the Day

TAKS Objective 1 TEKS 2.6C

pattern

2, 4, 6, 8, ?

Name the missing number and describe the pattern.

Numerical Fluency

TAKS Objective 1 TEKS 2.1C

Write >, <, or =.

62 ◯ 30 + 30

70 ◯ 69 + 3

Name ______________________ Date ____________

Regroup Tens

TAKS Objective 1
TEKS 2.1A, 2.1B

Regroup 1 ten. Write the tens and ones.

1.	73	7 tens 3 ones	Regroup	____ tens ____ ones
2.	57	5 tens 7 ones	Regroup	____ tens ____ ones
3.	65	6 tens 5 ones	Regroup	____ tens ____ ones
4.	86	8 tens 6 ones	Regroup	____ tens ____ ones
5.	49	4 tens 9 ones	Regroup	____ tens ____ ones
6.	54	5 tens 4 ones	Regroup	____ tens ____ ones
7.	92	9 tens 2 ones	Regroup	____ tens ____ ones
8.	70	7 tens 0 ones	Regroup	____ tens ____ ones

Math Journal **Writing and Reasoning** Draw quick pictures to show 23 in 2 ways. Explain the difference between the two pictures.

____

____

____

Circle Time

Problem of the Day

Objective 1 TEKS 2.3C

Julian has 83 stamps. He has an album with 7 pages. He can place 10 stamps on each page. How many stamps can he place in the album? How many stamps are left over?

Time

Objective 1 TEKS 2.10B

What time does the clock show?

Number of the Day

Objective 1 TEKS 2.1B

64

Use place value blocks to model. Show 64 in two different ways.

Facts Practice

Objective 1 TEKS 2.3A

Use connecting cubes. Write the facts family for 7, 10, 17.

_____ + _____ = _____

_____ + _____ = _____

_____ − _____ = _____

_____ − _____ = _____

Name ______________________ Date ____________

Decide When to Regroup

TAKS Objective 1
TEKS 2.3B, 2.3C

	Show the greater number.	Do you need to regroup to subtract?	Subtract the ones. How many tens and ones are left?	What is the difference?
1.	45 – 9	Yes No	____ tens ____ ones	
2.	68 – 3	Yes No	____ tens ____ ones	
3.	72 – 5	Yes No	____ tens ____ ones	
4.	58 – 8	Yes No	____ tens ____ ones	
5.	92 – 4	Yes No	____ tens ____ ones	
6.	36 – 9	Yes No	____ tens ____ ones	
7.	29 – 7	Yes No	____ tens ____ ones	
8.	81 – 5	Yes No	____ tens ____ ones	

Math Journal **Writing and Reasoning** Write a subtraction sentence that needs regrouping.

____

Circle Time

Problem of the Day

TAKS Objective 1 TEKS 2.3C

Donna had 15 toy bugs. She got 9 more. Later she gave 6 of the bugs to her brother. How many toy bugs does Donna have now?

Number Sense

TAKS Objective 1 TEKS 2.1B

Complete the table.

Write the number	Write a Quick Picture	Write the tens and ones
40		
63		

Word of the Day

TAKS Objective 1 TEKS 2.9A

long

Find 3 objects in your classroom that are as long as your foot.

Facts Practice

TAKS Objective 1 TEKS 2.3A

Use connecting cubes. Write the facts family for 3, 6, 9.

_____ + _____ = _____

_____ + _____ = _____

_____ − _____ = _____

_____ − _____ = _____

Name ____________________ Date ____________

Subtract One-Digit Numbers From Two-Digit Numbers

TAKS Objectives 1, 3
TEKS 2.3B, 2.3C

Use ▭ and ▫. Subtract.

1.

	Tens	Ones
	☐	☐
	6	3
−		8

2.

	Tens	Ones
	☐	☐
	4	5
−		6

3.

	Tens	Ones
	☐	☐
	5	7
−		4

4.

	Tens	Ones
	☐	☐
	7	2
−		6

5.

	Tens	Ones
	☐	☐
	8	4
−		9

6.

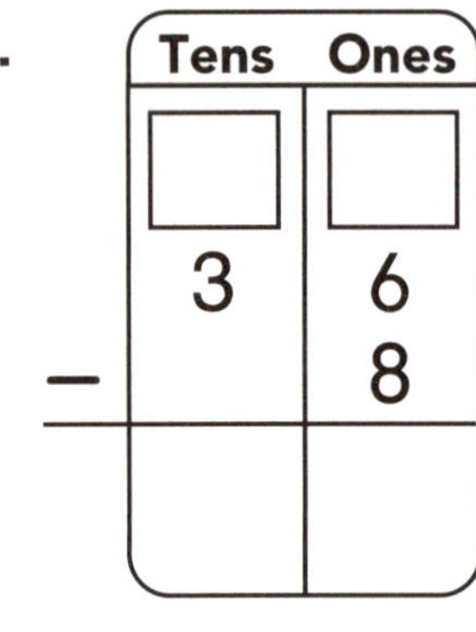

	Tens	Ones
	☐	☐
	3	6
−		8

7.

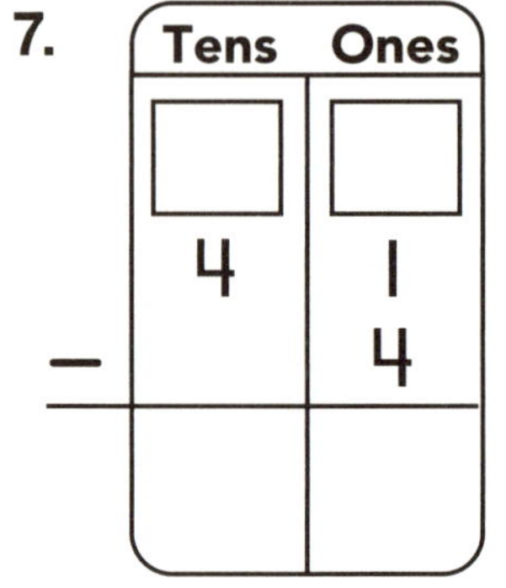

	Tens	Ones
	☐	☐
	4	1
−		4

Math Journal

Writing and Reasoning Why did you write numbers in some of the ☐ and some you did not?

____

____

Name ______________________ Date ____________

Circle Time

Problem of the Day

TAKS Objective 1 TEKS 2.3B

Jean bought 24 balloons for her party. She gives 9 balloons away to her guests. How many balloons does Jean keep?

Data

TAKS Objective 1 TEKS 2.11B

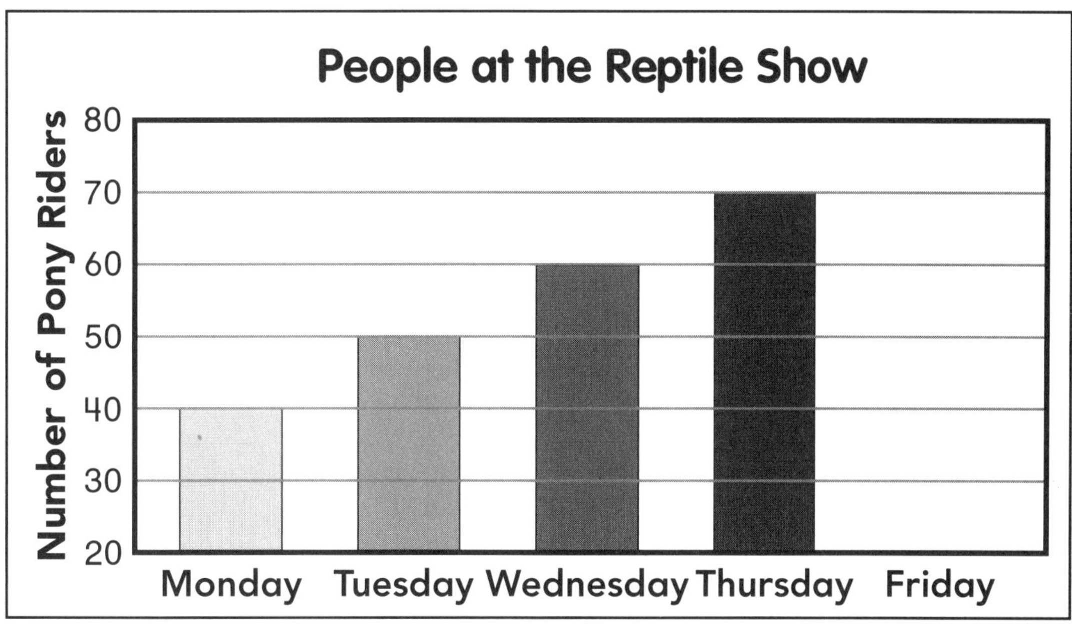

What is the pattern?

How many riders do you predict for Friday?

Number of the Day

TAKS Objective 1 TEKS 2.1A

12

Find the number 12 in your classroom.

Numerical Fluency

TAKS Objective 1 TEKS 2.1B

Model with place value blocks. Write the numbers.

1. $2 + 40 =$ ______
2. $60 + 2 =$ ______

Name ______________________ Date ____________

Subtract Two-Digit Numbers

TAKS Objective 1
TEKS 2.3B, 2.3C

Use [tens block] and [ones cube]. Subtract.

1.

	Tens	Ones
	☐	☐
	5	6
−	2	7

2.

	Tens	Ones
	☐	☐
	3	4
−	1	6

3.

	Tens	Ones
	☐	☐
	7	5
−	3	8

Remember

Record the number of tens and ones when you regroup.

4.

	Tens	Ones
	☐	☐
	6	1
−	4	5

5.

	Tens	Ones
	☐	☐
	4	8
−	1	5

6.

	Tens	Ones
	☐	☐
	7	4
−	3	1

7.

	Tens	Ones
	☐	☐
	8	5
−	3	8

Math Journal

Writing and Reasoning Which of the numbers in the box, when subtracted from 85, gives you a difference with a 0 in the ones place? How do you know?

____

____

10	15	22	34

Circle Time

Problem of the Day

TAKS Objective 1 TEKS 2.3B

Erin has 73 stickers. She gives 24 stickers to her brother. How many stickers does Erin have now?

Operations

TAKS Objective 1 TEKS 2.3B

Use Workmat 3 and place value blocks.
Add.

$24 + 67 =$ ____

Word of the Day

TAKS Objective 1 TEKS 2.12A

before, after

Use the words *before* and *after* to talk about 3 things you do in the morning.

Numerical Fluency

TAKS Objective 1 TEKS 2.1C

Circle the choice that is true.

A $82 > 28$

B $82 < 28$

C $82 = 28$

Name ______________________ Date ____________

Rewrite to Subtract

TAKS Objective 1
TEKS 2.3B, 2.3C

Write the numbers in vertical form. Subtract.

Remember
Line up the ones and then tens.

1. 37 − 19

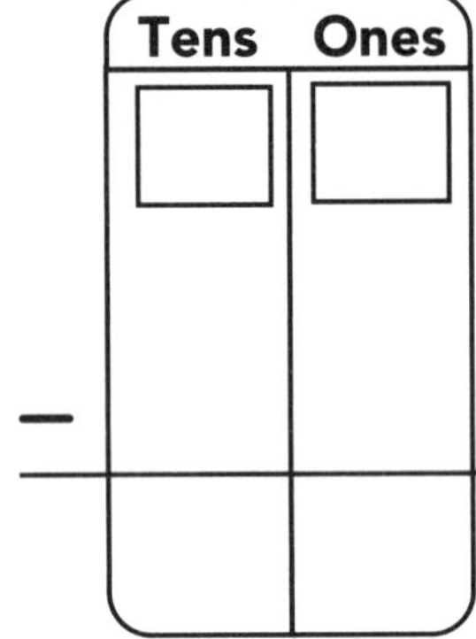

2. 54 − 21

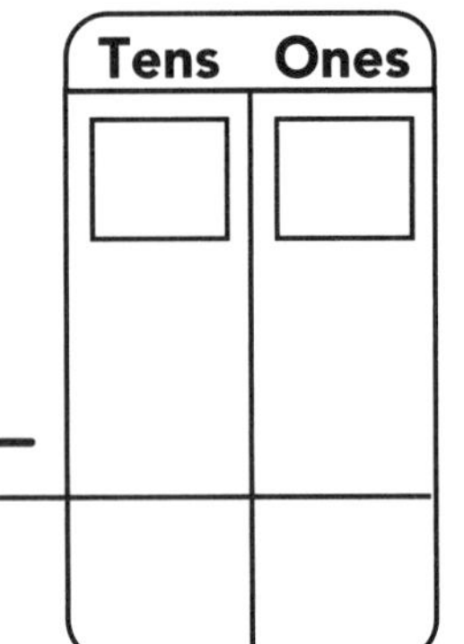

3. 66 − 37

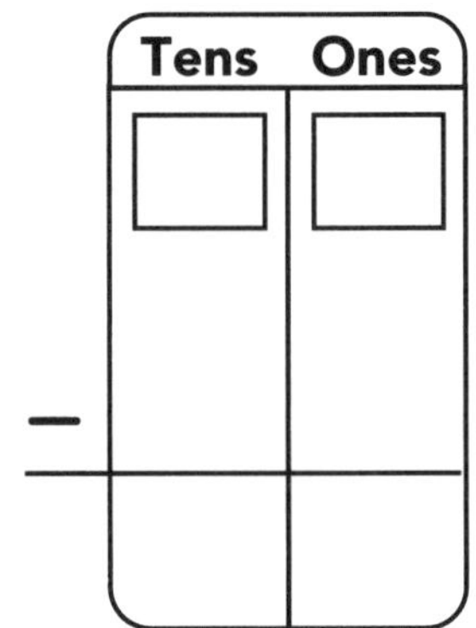

4. 98 − 16

Tens	Ones

5. 50 − 25

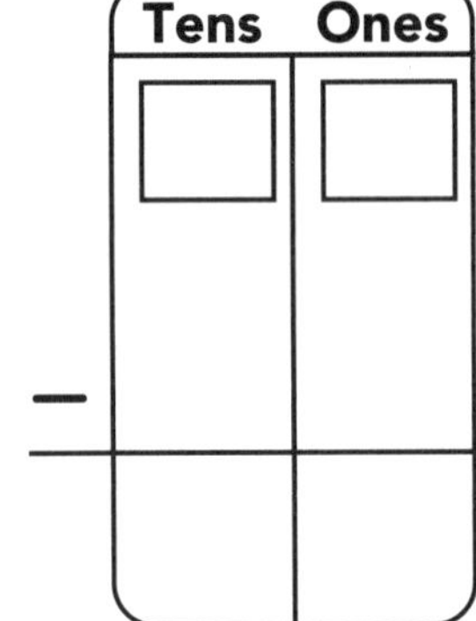

6. 86 − 59

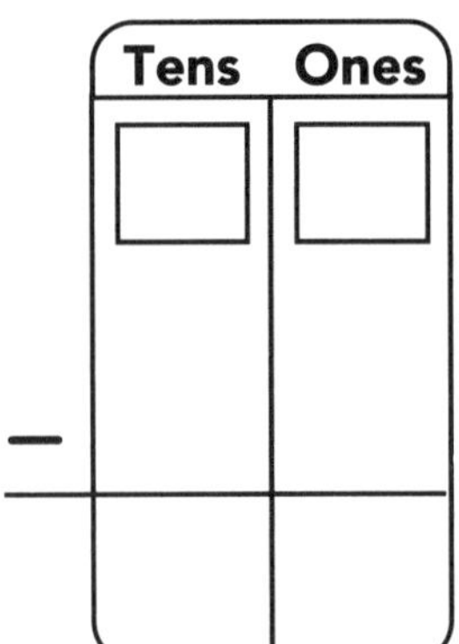

7. 75 − 20

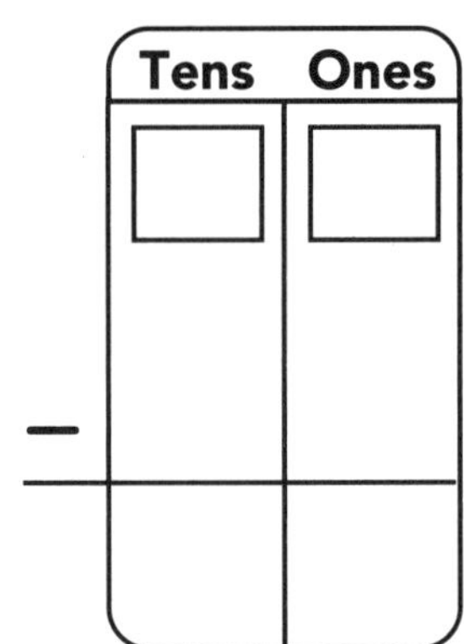

8. 41 − 3

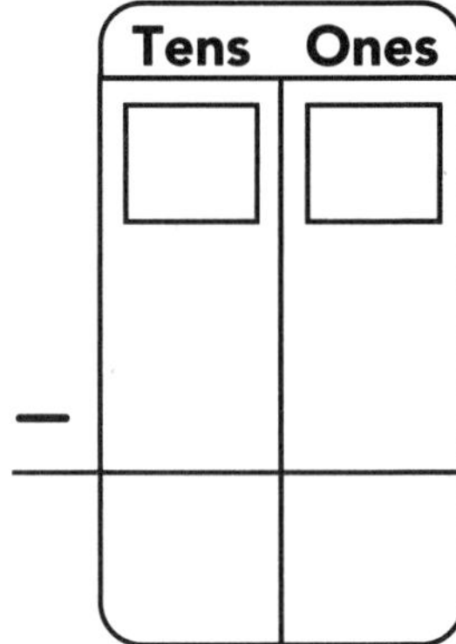

Math Journal **Writing and Reasoning** Sue and Brenda both subtract 53 − 4. Sue finds a difference of 13 and Brenda finds a difference of 49. Who is correct and why?

____

____

Circle Time

Problem of the Day

TAKS Objective 1 TEKS 2.3B

Linda has 52 marbles. She gives some marbles to her brother. Now Linda has 45 marbles. How many marbles did Linda give to her brother?

Operations

TAKS Objective 1 TEKS 2.5A

Use the hundred chart or Workmat 5. Subtract.

$$\begin{array}{r} 97 \\ -70 \\ \hline \end{array}$$

Word of the Day

TAKS Objective 1 TEKS 2.7A

sides

Draw a shape with 3 sides.

Facts Practice

TAKS Objective 1 TEKS 2.3A

Add.

1. $7 + 3 + 8 =$ ______
2. $1 + 5 + 9 =$ ______
3. $8 + 7 + 2 =$ ______

Different Ways to Subtract

TAKS Objective 1
TEKS 2.3B, 2.3C

Choose a way to subtract. Explain how you find the difference.

Different ways to subtract:
mental math
calculator
tens and ones blocks
paper and pencil

1. 56 − 22

2. 60 − 20

3. 64 − 17

4. 94 − 56

Writing and Reasoning Write a subtraction sentence that could be solved easily with mental math. Tell how it would be solved.

Circle Time

Problem of the Day

TAKS Objective 1 TEKS 2.3B

There are 65 people on the bus. 25 people get off at Dover Street. How many people are on the bus now?

Operations

TAKS Objective 1 TEKS 2.3A

There are 9 girls and 9 boys on the playground. How many children are on the playground?

Calendar

TAKS Objective 1 TEKS 2.3C

What would the return date be if you spend the first 15 days of a month visiting a friend and 12 days driving back?

Facts Practice

TAKS Objective 1 TEKS 2.3A

Subtract.

$$\begin{array}{r} 18 \\ -9 \\ \hline \end{array} \qquad \begin{array}{r} 15 \\ -7 \\ \hline \end{array} \qquad \begin{array}{r} 12 \\ -8 \\ \hline \end{array} \qquad \begin{array}{r} 11 \\ -6 \\ \hline \end{array}$$

Name ______________________ Date ____________

Choose the Operation

TAKS Objective 1
TEKS 2.12A, 2.3C, 2.12

Find the parts and whole to solve. Write the answer.

Draw or write to explain.

1. There are 52 children on two soccer teams. 27 children are on Team A. How many children are on Team B?

Whole	
Part	Part

_____ children

2. The second graders invite 22 third graders and 20 first graders to their class play. How many children do they invite?

Whole	
Part	Part

_____ children

3. The art class drew 46 animal postcards and 35 flower postcards. How many postcards did they draw in all?

Whole	
Part	Part

_____ postcards

4. The science class collected 22 sea shells and 10 pieces of sea glass. How many more sea shells than sea glass did they collect?

Whole	
Part	Part

_____ sea shells

Math Journal **Writing and Reasoning** Tell which operation you would use to solve this problem and why: The children blew up 25 yellow balloons and 36 green balloons for the party. How many balloons did they blow up in all?

____

Circle Time

Problem of the Day

TAKS Objective 1 TEKS 2.12A

There are 28 students in the class. 15 are girls. 8 students wear glasses. Write a number sentence to show how many students don't wear glasses.

Algebraic Thinking

TAKS Objective 1 TEKS 2.3A

Use connecting cubes to model. Draw to show.
Write the answer.

$13 + 5 =$ $\qquad$ $5 + 13 =$

Calendar

TAKS Objective 1 TEKS 2.4B

How many complete weeks are there in the month? How many days are in each week?

Numerical Fluency

TAKS Objective 1 TEKS 2.1C

Use >, <, or =.

37 ◯ 73

13 ◯ 10 + 3

89 ◯ 88

Hundreds, Tens, Ones

TAKS Objective 1
TEKS 2.1A, 2.1B

Use , , and .

Show this many.	Write how many hundreds, tens, and ones.	Write the number.
1.	Hundreds / Tens / Ones	______
2.	Hundreds / Tens / Ones	______
3.	Hundreds / Tens / Ones	______

Write the missing numbers.

4. 310, ______, 330, 340, ______, 360, ______,
380, 390, ______

5. 531, 532, ______, ______, 535, ______, 537,
538, ______, 540

Math Journal **Writing and Reasoning** I brush my teeth about ______ (2, 20, 200) times a day. Which is the best answer? Why?

____

____

Circle Time

Problem of the Day

TAKS Objective 1 TEKS 2.1A

There are 100 balloons in each pack. Count to find the number of balloons in 6 packs. How many balloons are in 6 packs?

Operations

TAKS Objective 1 TEKS 2.3A

Write a fact family using the numbers 4, 9, 13.

Number of the Day

TAKS Objective 1 TEKS 2.5C

18

Write 2 related facts using the number 18.

Facts Practice

TAKS Objective 1 TEKS 2.3A

Subtract.

$8 - 5 =$ ___

$12 - 8 =$ ___

$13 - 8 =$ ___

$14 - 7 =$ ___

Name ______________________ Date ____________

Trade Ones and Tens Game

TAKS Objective 1
TEKS 2.1A, 2.1B

Count by hundreds and tens.

Write the number.

1. 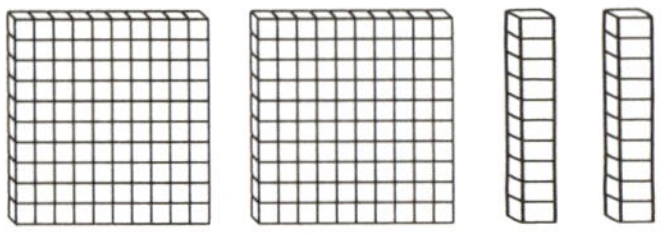 ______ hundreds ______ tens

______

two hundred twenty

2. 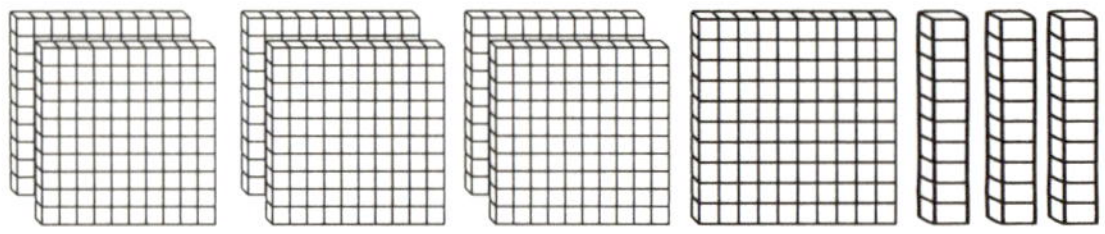 ______ hundreds ______ tens

______

seven hundred thirty

3. 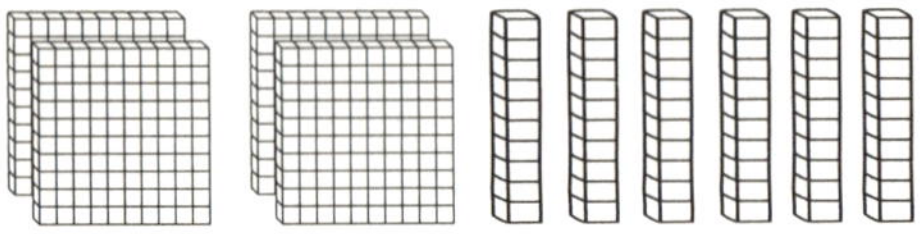 ______ hundreds ______ tens

______

four hundred sixty

4. 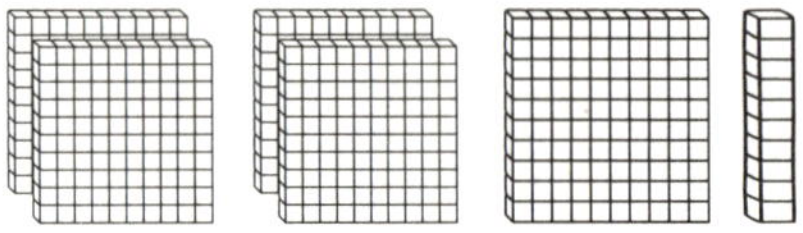 ______ hundreds ______ tens

______

five hundred ten

5. 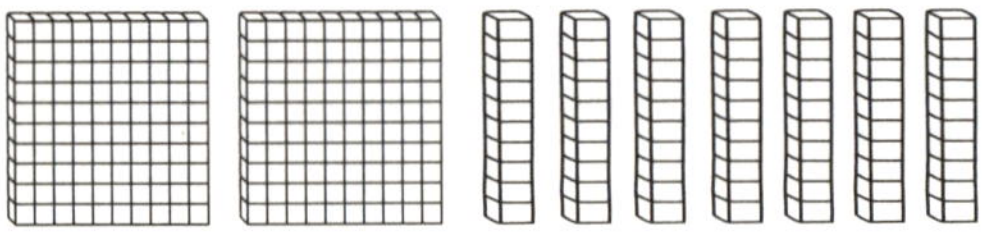 ______ hundreds ______ tens

______

two hundred seventy

6. 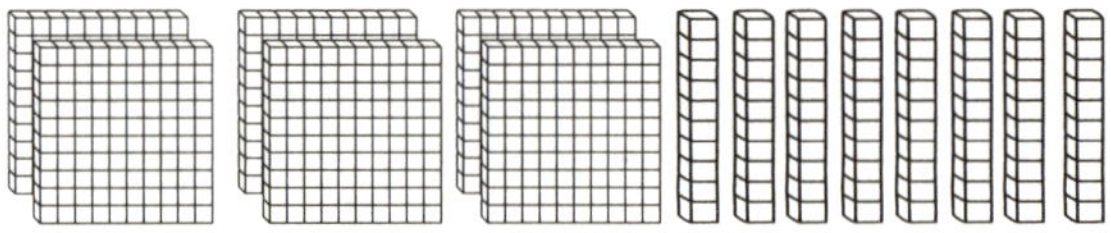 ______ hundreds ______ tens

______

six hundred eighty

Math Journal **Writing and Reasoning** Mary says that 100 more than 759 is 769. James says 100 more than 759 is 859. Who is correct and why?

____

____

Circle Time

Problem of the Day

TAKS Objective 1 TEKS 2.1A

Miranda has 44 chairs. She wants to set the chairs in rows of 10 chairs. How many rows of ten can she set? How many chairs are left over?

Data

TAKS Objective 1 TEKS 2.13A

This is the result of the class survey.

Favorite Subject	
Reading	𝍸 ǁ
Writing	𝍸
Math	ǁǁ

How many students took part in the survey?

Word of the Day

TAKS Objective 1 TEKS 2.2A

half, halves

Fold a piece of paper into two halves. Color one half blue.

Numerical Fluency

TAKS Objective 1 TEKS 2.1C

Use >, <, or =.

89 ◯ 98

67 ◯ 76

45 ◯ 40 + 5

Place Value to 999

TAKS Objective 1
TEKS 2.1B

Write the number.

1. 7 + 40 + 300 ______

2. 9 + 50 + 400 ______

3. 20 + 100 ______

4. 900 + 9 ______

Circle the value of the underlined digit.

5. 1<u>2</u>7 200 20 2

6. <u>6</u>31 600 60 6

7. 50<u>3</u> 300 30 3

8. 2<u>9</u>0 900 90 9

Writing and Reasoning Which is a way to write 264: 4 + 60 + 200 or 200 + 60 + 4?

____

____

Circle Time

Problem of the Day

TAKS Objective 1 TEKS 2.1B

Mr. Cataldo helps to make 542 cookies for the fair. What is the value of the digit 5 in 542?

Data

TAKS Objective 1 TEKS 2.11A

Fill the graph below to show the same results.

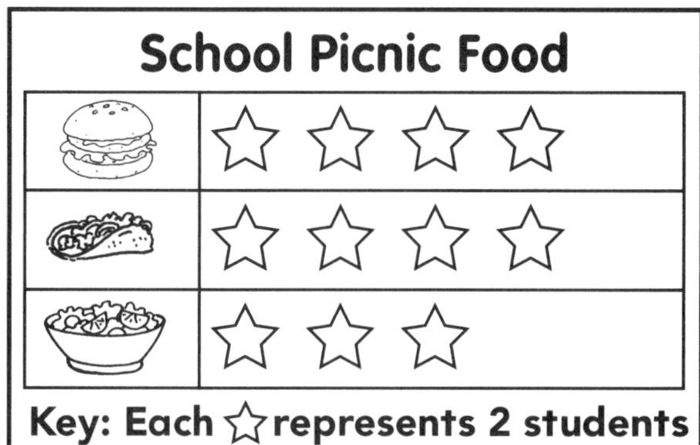

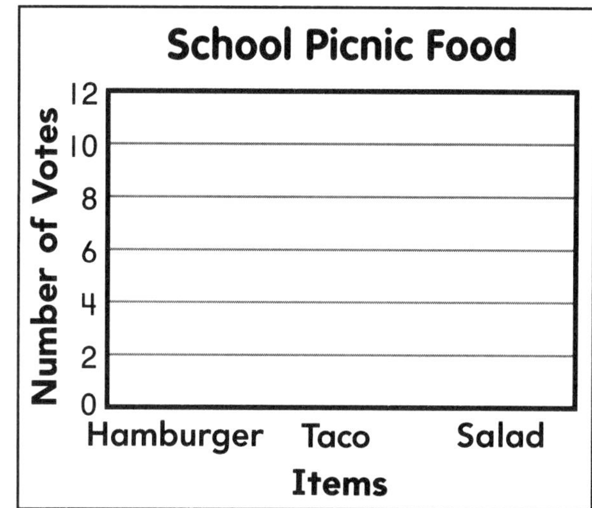

Word of the Day

TAKS Objective 1 TEKS 2.3A

false

Which of these number sentences is false?

2 + 10 = 13; 7 + 7 = 14; 8 + 8 = 16

Numerical Fluency

TAKS Objective 1 TEKS 2.1C

Write the numbers in order from least to greatest.

62 34 61 94

Problem Solving: Find a Pattern

TAKS Objective 1
TEKS 2.12C, 2.6A

Solve. Complete the table and look for a pattern.

1. Carmen reads 8 chapters every night.
How many chapters does she read in 4 nights?

Night	1			
Chapters	8			

_______ chapters

2. The toy factory makes 20 teddy bears a day. How many teddy bears do they make in 5 days?

Day	1				
Teddy Bears	20				

_______ teddy bears

3. Marcus drew 2 pictures each day for a week. How many pictures did he draw in the 7 days?

Day	1						
Pictures	2						

_______ pictures

Math Journal **Writing and Reasoning** How can you describe the pattern in the table in Exercise 3?

____

____

Circle Time

Problem of the Day

TAKS Objective 1 TEKS 2.6A

Each of the 5 guests at Kim's party got 3 party favors. Complete the table and look for a pattern.

Guests	1	2	3	4	5
Party Favor	3	6			

How many party favors did 5 guests receive?

Probability

TAKS Objective 1 TEKS 2.11C

There are 8 green cubes and 3 blue cubes in a bag. How likely are you to pick a blue cube rather than a green cube?

Number of the Day

TAKS Objective 1 TEKS 2.1B

6

What is the value of 6 in these numbers: 16, 64, 467?

Numerical Fluency

TAKS Objective 1 TEKS 2.1A

Circle a way to show the number. 17

A 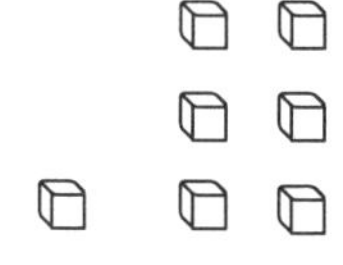

C 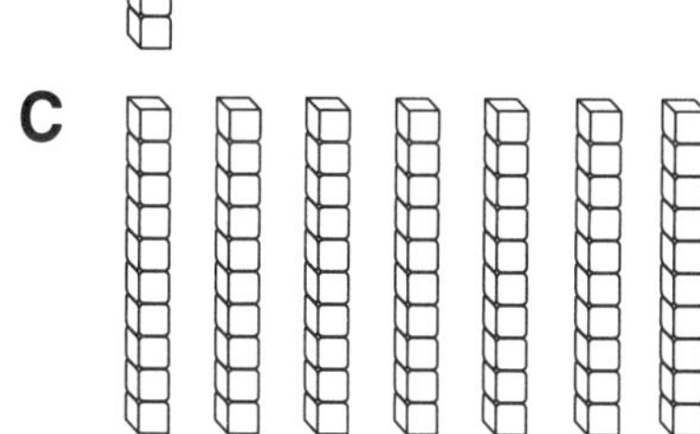

B 1 + 7

D 10 + 7

Name ______________________ Date ____________

Patterns and Place Value

TAKS Objective 2
TEKS 2.5B

1. Increase by 10

Hundreds	Tens	Ones
3	5	2

2. Increase by 100

Hundreds	Tens	Ones
1	4	9

Make a pattern. Increase by 10.

3. 936, ______, ______, ______

4. 803, ______, ______, ______

Make a pattern. Increase by 100.

5. 123, ______, ______, ______

6. 508, ______, ______, ______

Writing and Reasoning Why is there a 0 in the tens place in all the numbers in Exercise 6?

____

____

Name ______________________ Date ____________

Circle Time

Problem of the Day

TAKS Objective 1 TEKS 2.1B

Anna is thinking of a three-digit number. The digit in tens is 0. The digit in the ones place is 5. The digit in hundreds place is the sum of the other two digits. What is Anna's number?

Money

TAKS Objective 1 TEKS 2.12C

Lewis used two of these coins to buy a 30¢ marker.

He did not get any change back. Which two coins did Lewis use?

Word of the Day

TAKS Objective 1 TEKS 2.3A

true

Which of these number sentences is true?

2 + 9 = 13
7 + 8 = 15
6 + 8 = 18

Numerical Fluency

TAKS Objective 1 TEKS 2.1B

Model with place value blocks. Write the numbers.

1. 5 + 00 + 600 =

2. 500 + 00 + 6 =

Before, After, Between

TAKS Objectives 1, 3
TEKS 2.8

Use the number line.

380 381 382 383 384 385 386 387 388 389 390 391 392 393 394 395

Write the number.

Before	Between	After
1. ______, 381	393, ______, 395	386, ______
2. ______, 386	391, ______, 393	389, ______
3. ______, 390	389, ______, 391	391, ______
4. ______, 388	385, ______, 387	380, ______

Write the missing numbers.

5. 101, ____, ____, 104, 105, 106, ____, ____
6. 890, ____, 892, 893, 894, 895, ____, ____
7. 25, 26, ____, 28, ____, ____, 31, 32, ____
8. 364, 365, 366, ____, ____, 369, ____, 371

Math Journal **Writing and Reasoning** Harry is thinking of a number. It is between 184 and 187. What number could it be and why?

____

____

____

Circle Time

Problem of the Day

TAKS Objective 1 TEKS 2.1B

Find a number between 0 and 100. The number has 2 tens and 17 ones. What number is it?

Operations

TAKS Objective 1 TEKS 2.3A

Make 10 to solve.

67 + 18

Number of the Day

TAKS Objective 1 TEKS 2.1A

100

Use place value blocks to show 100.

Numerical Fluency

TAKS Objective 1 TEKS 2.1A

Model with place value blocks. Write the numbers.

1. 8 + 70 + 600 =
2. 800 + 70 + 6 =

Name ____________________ Date __________

Compare Three-Digit Numbers

TAKS Objective 1
TEKS 2.1B, 2.1C

Compare the numbers.
Write >, <, or = in the .

1. 741 ◯ 544
2. 913 ◯ 903
3. 460 ◯ 355
4. 799 ◯ 800
5. 429 ◯ 249
6. 850 ◯ 895
7. 864 ◯ 846
8. 667 ◯ 695
9. 311 ◯ 113

Choose the correct number.

10. 347 > ______ 360 348 345
11. 618 > ______ 620 610 618
12. 545 = ______ 554 504 545
13. 189 < ______ 298 109 180
14. 436 > ______ 439 413 463
15. 296 = ______ 296 269 692

Writing and Reasoning Tell how you know 345 is greater than 337.

____

____

Circle Time

Problem of the Day

TAKS Objective 1 TEKS 2.1C

Amelie has 239 stamps. José has 293 stamps. Who has more stamps?

Operations

TAKS Objective 1 TEKS 2.5A

Use the hundred chart or Workmat 5. Add.

$$\begin{array}{r} 37 \\ +\ 50 \\ \hline \end{array}$$

Calendar Activity

TAKS Objective 1 TEKS 2.13B

Name the days that come before and after Thursday.

Numerical Fluency

TAKS Objective 1 TEKS 2.1B

What is the value of 8 in each of the following numbers?

708 _____

682 _____

808 __________

Name ______________________ Date ____________

Order Three-Digit Numbers

TAKS Objective 1
TEKS 2.1B, 2.1C

Write the numbers in order from least to greatest.

1. 648 700 685 658 ______, ______, ______, ______
2. 900 967 876 970 ______, ______, ______, ______
3. 376 367 637 673 ______, ______, ______, ______

Write the numbers in order from greatest to least.

4. 267 284 270 262 ______, ______, ______, ______
5. 714 670 706 760 ______, ______, ______, ______
6. 480 408 400 488 ______, ______, ______, ______

Math Journal

Writing and Reasoning

Ben's model car traveled 345 feet. Sasha's model car traveled 410 feet. Whose car traveled farther?

__________ car traveled farther.

Draw or write to explain.

Circle Time

Problem of the Day

TAKS Objective 1 TEKS 2.1

Jeff has cards numbered 595, 600, 611, and 99. He puts them in order from the greatest to the least. How does Jeff order the cards?

Algebraic Thinking

TAKS Objective 1 TEKS 2.3A

Add. Then subtract.

$7 + 9 = \_\_\_\_$

$16 - 7 = \_\_\_\_$

$16 - 9 = \_\_\_\_$

Word of the Day

TAKS Objective 1 TEKS 2.4B

equal groups

Draw a picture showing classroom items in equal groups.

Facts Practice

TAKS Objective 1 TEKS 2.3B

Subract.

$\begin{array}{r} 80 \\ -20 \\ \hline \end{array}$ $\begin{array}{r} 80 \\ -18 \\ \hline \end{array}$ $\begin{array}{r} 80 \\ -16 \\ \hline \end{array}$

Name ______________________ Date ____________

Different Ways to Show Numbers

TAKS Objective 1
TEKS 2.1A

Circle another way to show the number.

1. 324	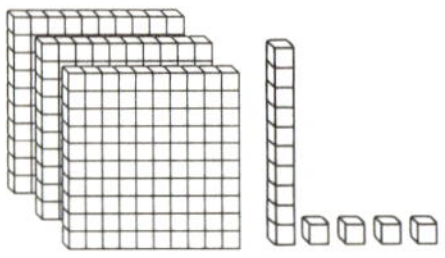	300 + 20 + 4
2. 490	4 hundreds 9 tens	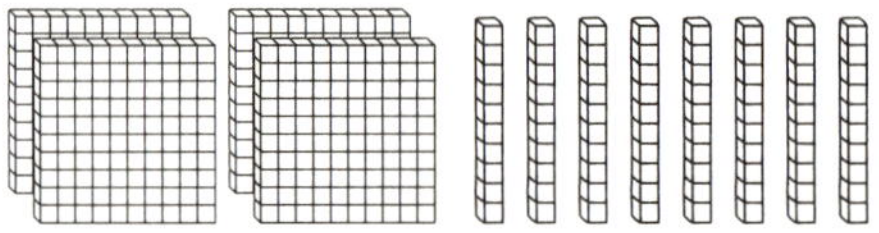
3. 113	100 + 30 + 1	1 hundred 1 ten 3 ones
4. 936	900 + 30 + 6	9 hundreds 6 tens 3 ones

Draw or write to show the number another way.

5. 362

6. 203

Math Journal

Writing and Reasoning Paul has 3 boxes with 100 pencils in each box. He has 4 boxes with 10 pencils in each. He has 1 box with 5 pencils. How can you show how many pencils he has?

____

____

____

Name ______________________ Date __________

Circle Time

Problem of the Day

TAKS Objective 1 TEKS 2.1B

Kina has 4 boxes with 100 cans each. She has 6 boxes with 10 cans each. How many cans are there?

Operations

TAKS Objective 1 TEKS 2.3B

Ilan has 24 toys cars. Mike has 17 more toy cars than Ilan. How many toy cars does Mike have?

Number of the Day

TAKS Objective 1 TEKS 2.5B

126

Find page 126 in three different books.

Facts Practice

TAKS Objective 1 TEKS 2.3A

Add.

11 + 3 = _____

12 + 0 = _____

15 + 5 = _____

17 + 8 = _____

Use a Model

TAKS Objective 6
TEKS 2.12B, 2.1C

Solve. Use the place value model.
The library has 658 books on science topics. There are 660 books on history. Fiction books total 865.

1. Are there more books on science or history at the library?

	Hundreds	Tens	Ones
Science			
History			

____

2. Are there more fiction books or history books at the library?

	Hundreds	Tens	Ones
History			
Fiction			

____

3. What is the order of the number of books in the library from least to greatest?

	Hundreds	Tens	Ones
Science			
History			
Fiction			

____

Math Journal **Writing and Reasoning** How did you know which subject came between the others in Exercise 3?

____

Circle Time

Problem of the Day

TAKS Objective 1 TEKS 2.1C

Pinewood Elementary school has 307 students. Seaside has 310 students and Ohlone has 297 students. Order these numbers from least to greatest.

Probability

TAKS Objective 1 TEKS 2.11C

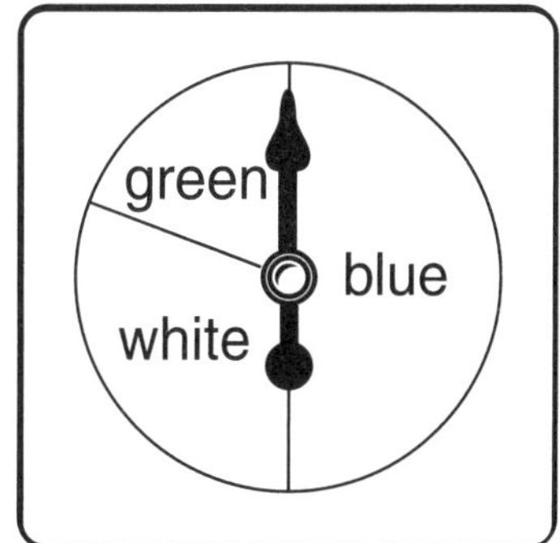

Predict the color that the spinner will land least often.

Word of the Day

TAKS Objective 1 TEKS 2.7A

sides

Draw a shape with 4 sides.

Numerical Fluency

TAKS Objective 1 TEKS 1.3A

Put these two sets of triangles together. Write the number sentence that shows how many in all.

Pennies, Nickels, and Dimes

TAKS Objective 1
TEKS 2.3D

Count the money.

1.    

_____ ¢ _____ ¢ _____ ¢ _____ ¢ _____ ¢ total

2.    

_____ ¢ _____ ¢ _____ ¢ _____ ¢ _____ ¢ total

3.    

_____ ¢ _____ ¢ _____ ¢ _____ ¢ _____ ¢ total

4.    

_____ ¢ _____ ¢ _____ ¢ _____ ¢ _____ ¢ total

Writing and Reasoning Millie and Sue count these coins  . Millie says they total 27¢. Sue says they total 32¢. Who is correct and why?

____

____

Name ______________________ Date ____________

Circle Time

Problem of the Day

TAKS Objective 1 TEKS 2.3D

Jessie has 2 dimes, 1 nickel, and 3 pennies. How much money does she have?

Operations

TAKS Objective 1 TEKS 2.5A

Use the hundred chart or Workmat 5. Subtract.

$$\begin{array}{r} 68 \\ -\,60 \\ \hline \end{array}$$

Word of the Day

TAKS Objective 1 TEKS 2.9D

weigh

Find 3 objects in your classroom that weigh less than your math book.

Facts Practice

TAKS Objective 1 TEKS 1.3B

Add.

1. $15 + 2 =$ ______
2. $14 + 1 =$ ______
3. $3 + 10 =$ ______
4. $12 + 5 =$ ______
5. $0 + 17 =$ ______

Quarters and Half-Dollars

TAKS Objective 1
TEKS 2.3D

Count on to find the value of the coins.

1.   

_______ ¢ _______ ¢ _______ ¢

2.    

_______ ¢ _______ ¢ _______ ¢

3.    

_______ ¢ _______ ¢ _______ ¢

4.    

_______ ¢ _______ ¢ _______ ¢

Math Journal **Writing and Reasoning** Tell how you would count on to find the value of 2 quarters and 1 penny. What is the total?

____

Circle Time

Problem of the Day

TAKS Objective 1 TEKS 2.3D

Maria has 50¢ in her pocket. All her coins are alike. Does she have 2 dimes, 2 quarters, or 2 half-dollars?

Operations

TAKS Objective 1 TEKS 2.3A

Write the doubles and doubles-plus-one sum.

$8 + 8 =$

$8 + 9 =$

$8 + 7 =$

Calendar Activity

TAKS Objective 1 TEKS 2.3B

Write a subtraction problem using today's date.

Facts Practice

TAKS Objective 1 TEKS 2.3A

Subtract.

1. $17 - 7 =$ _____
2. $1 - 1 =$ _____
3. $11 - 10 =$ _____
4. $17 - 2 =$ _____
5. $6 - 2 =$ _____

Name ______________________ Date ____________

Chapter 16 Lesson 3
Practice

Count Coins

TAKS Objective 1
TEKS 2.3D

Count on to find the value of the coins.

1.

______ ¢

2.

______ ¢

3.

______ ¢

4.

______ ¢

5.

______ ¢

6.

______ ¢

Writing and Reasoning Josh has these coins: Amy has these coins: . Who has more money and how do you know?

____

____

Name ______________________ Date ____________

Circle Time

Problem of the Day

TAKS Objective 1 TEKS 2.3D

Keesha has 2 quarters, 1 dime, and 4 pennies. How much money does she have?

Operations

TAKS Objective 1 TEKS 2.3C

Choose a way to add. Add. Explain the way you found the sum.

46 + 48 =

Number of the Day

TAKS Objective 1 TEKS 2.13A

60

Count to 60 by ones, fives, and tens.

Numerical Fluency

TAKS Objective 1 TEKS 2.3B

Use Workmat 3 and [ten-block] and [unit cube].

Add.

8 + 15 =

Name ______________________ Date ____________

One Dollar

TAKS Objective 1
TEKS 2.3D, 2.3E

Write the value of the coins.
Circle the sets of coins that equal one dollar.

1.

____

2.

____

3.

____

4.

____

Find the value of the coins. Circle the correct answer.

5.

less than $1.00

equal to $1.00

Writing and Reasoning How many dimes would you draw to equal one dollar? Explain.

____

____

Circle Time

Problem of the Day

TAKS Objective 1 TEKS 2.3D

Alison earns 25¢ each time she helps with dinner. How much money will she earn if she helps with dinner for 4 nights?

Number Sense

TAKS Objective 1 TEKS 2.3A

Break apart the number. Write different ways to name the number.

5

Word of the Day

TAKS Objective 1 TEKS 2.1C

number line

Draw a number line from 40 to 60.

Numerical Fluency

TAKS Objective 1 TEKS 2.3C

Heather had 25 cubes. She gave 5 away.

What operation do you use to find how many cubes Heather has now?

How many cubes does Heather have now?

Problem Solving: Use Models to Act It Out

TAKS Objectives 1, 6
TEKS 2.3D, 2.1B

Use coins to act out the problem. Solve.

Draw or write to explain.

1. Anna has 4 dimes and 2 nickels. If she loses 1 dime, how much will she have left?

   ____

2. Sasha has 2 quarters and 5 pennies. A snack bar costs 75¢. How much more money does he need to buy a snack bar?

   ____

3. James has 3 dimes, 2 nickels, and 1 penny. He buys a pencil for 35 cents. How much money does he have now?

   ____

4. Sophia bought a drink with 3 quarters and 1 nickel. She received 1 dime and 2 pennies in change. How much did the drink cost?

   ____

5. Alice wants a book that costs 90¢. She has 5 dimes and 1 quarter. How much more does she need?

   ____

Math Journal **Writing and Reasoning** Explain how you found how much more Alice needs to buy the book in problem 6.

____

____

Circle Time

Problem of the Day

TAKS Objective 1 TEKS 2.3D

A toy airplane costs 95¢. Heather has 3 quarters, 2 nickels, and 5 pennies. Does Heather have enough money to buy the toy airplane?

Operations

TAKS Objective 1 TEKS 2.3B

Make 10 to solve.

17 + 18

Number of the Day

TAKS Objective 1 TEKS 2.2A

one fourth

Draw and divide a circle into four equal parts. Shade one fourth of the circle.

Numerical Fluency

TAKS Objective 1 TEKS 2.1B

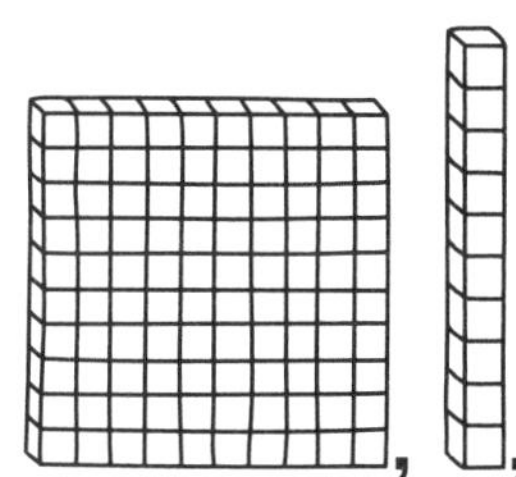

Model with , , and . Write the numbers.

1. 6 + 80 + 600 = __________
2. 600 + 80 + 6 = __________

Name ________________ Date ____________

TAKS Objective 4
TEKS 2.10c

Estimate
1 Second, 1 Minute, 1 Hour

Estimate how many times you can do an activity in one minute. Then do the activity for one minute. Count the number of times you do it.

	Activity	Estimate	Count
1.	Touch your toes		
2.	Tie your shoe		
3.	Count to 20		

Think about the length of the time. Draw or write the things you do that take that long.

4. About 10 seconds

5. About 5 minutes

6. About 1 hour

Math Journal **Writing and Reasoning** Martin says it takes about 20 minutes to eat lunch. Raymond says it takes about 20 seconds to eat lunch. Who is more reasonable and why?

____

____

____

Name ______________________ Date ____________

Circle Time

Problem of the Day

TAKS Objective 1 TEKS 2.10C

About how long does it takes to sneeze? Circle the best answer.

about 1 second

about 1 minute

about 1 hour

Money

TAKS Objective 1 TEKS 2.3D

Circle the set of coins that equal 1 dollar.

Word of the Day

TAKS Objective 1 TEKS 2.4B

pennies

Find 20 pennies and divide them into 2 equal groups.

Numerical Fluency

TAKS Objective 1 TEKS 2.1C

Write >, <, or =.

646 ◯

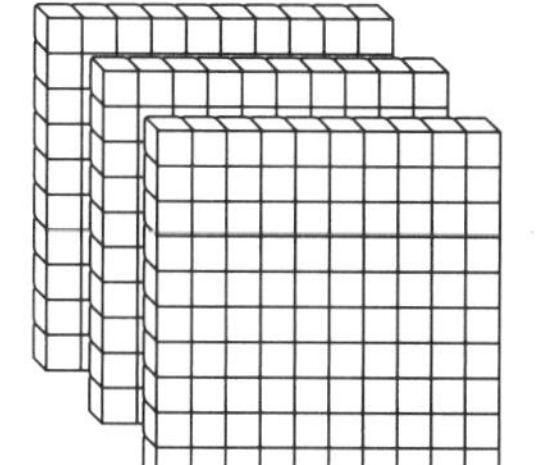
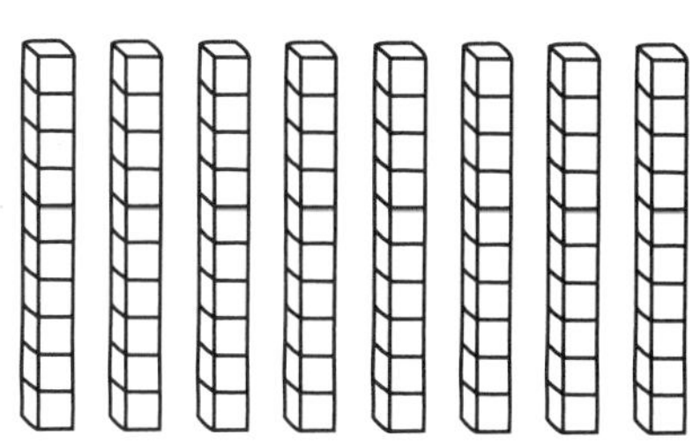

Name ______________________ Date ____________

Time to 15 and 30 Minutes

TAKS Objective 4
TEKS 2.10B

Write the time.

1. 

____

2. 

____

3. 

____

4. 

____

5. 

____

6. 

____

7. 

____

8. 

____

Math Journal **Writing and Reasoning** Max says the clock reads 6:45. Maggie says the clock reads 7:45. Who is correct and how do you know?

____

____

Circle Time

Problem of the Day

TAKS Objective 1 TEKS 2.10B

Write the time.

Operations

TAKS Objective 1 TEKS 2.6B

Each of the 6 visitors to the library borrowed 3 books.
Fill the table.

Visitors	1	2	3	4	5	6
Books	3	6	9			

How many books were borrowed in all?

Number of the Day

TAKS Objective 1 TEKS 2.1A

271

Show the number 271 using place value blocks.

Numerical Fluency

TAKS Objective 1 TEKS 2.1C

Use <, =, or > to compare.

800 + 60 + 4 ◯ 800 + 80 + 2

400 + 20 + 1 ◯ 100 + 40 + 2

Name ______________________ Date ____________

Time to Five Minutes

TAKS Objective 4
TEKS 2.10B

Write the time.

1. 

______

2. 

______

3. 

______

4. 

______

Draw the minute hand to show the time.

5. 

5:45

6. 

11:00

7. 

2:50

8. 

12:10

Math Journal **Writing and Reasoning** Milton is saying these times in a pattern: 7:50, 7:55, 8:00, 8:05. What time comes next and how could you describe the pattern?

____

____

____

Circle Time

Problem of the Day

Objective 1 TEKS 2.10B

Write the time.

Operations

Objective 1 TEKS 2.3A

Add or subtract.

13 + 0 = ______

13 − 0 = ______

13 + 1 = ______

13 − 1 = ______

Calendar Activity

Objective 1 TEKS 2.4A

How many days are in one week? Two weeks?

Numerical Fluency

Objective 1 TEKS 2.1B

Model with 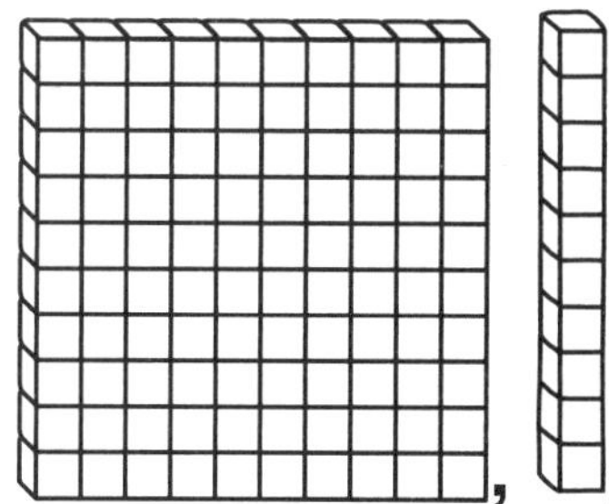**, and ▢. Write the numbers.**

1. 7 + 70 + 200 = ______

2. 700 + 70 + 2 = ______

Name ______________________ Date ____________

Read Fahrenheit Temperature

TAKS Objective 4
TEKS 2.10B

Write the temperature.

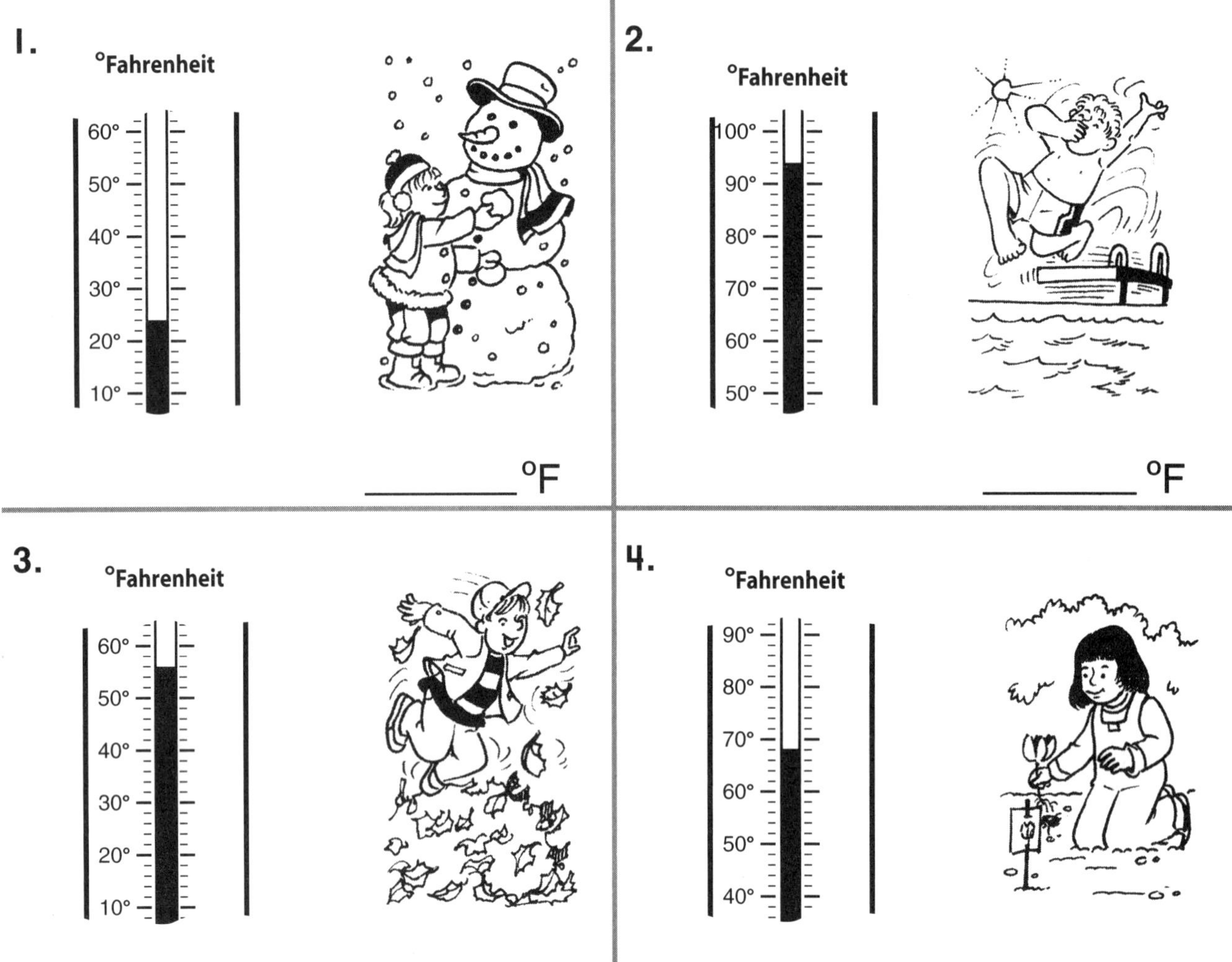

1. ________ °F

2. ________ °F

3. ________ °F

4. ________ °F

Writing and Reasoning Rico reads the temperature on his outside thermometer. He chooses a coat and mittens to wear to school. Which temperature does Rico's thermometer show, 37°F, 60°F, 75°F? Why do you think so?

____

Circle Time

Problem of the Day

TAKS Objective 1 TEKS 2.10A

Write the temperature.

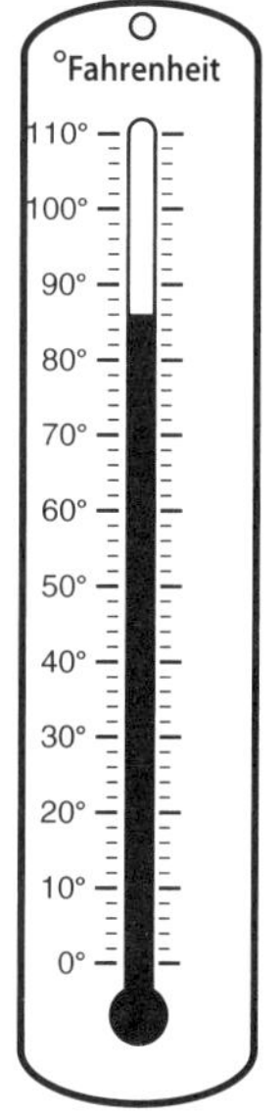

____

Data

TAKS Objective 1 TEKS 2.11B

Students in the School Bus	
Monday	☆☆☆☆☆☆☆
Tuesday	☆☆☆☆☆☆☆☆☆
Wednesday	☆☆☆☆☆☆☆☆
Key: Each ☆ stands for 2 students	

How many fewer students were in the bus on Monday than Tuesday?

Word of the Day

TAKS Objective 1 TEKS 2.11A

bar-type graph

Create a bar-type graph showing each month and the number of children in your class born in each month.

Numerical Fluency

TAKS Objective 1 TEKS 2.1C

Circle the choice that is true.

A 962 is greater than 962 **B** $962 < 962$ **C** $962 = 962$

Draw a Picture

TAKS Objectives 4, 6
TEKS 2.10A, 2.12A

Solve.

1. Mandy's popsicle™ is melting. The outside temperature is 98°F. Mark the temperature on the thermometer with a red line.

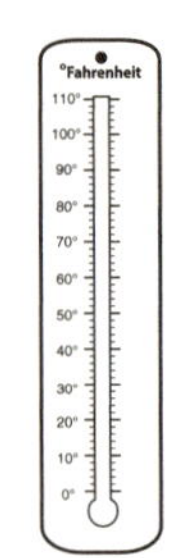

2. Mario is sledding with his family. The temperature outside is 46°F. Color in the thermometer up to the correct temperature.

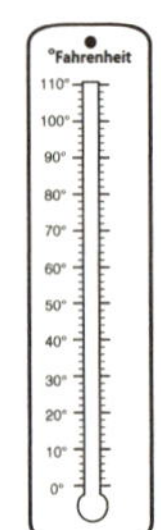

3. Angel is walking home from school. She sees a thermometer outside that reads 76°F. What type of clothes might Angel be wearing?

____

Color in the thermometer up to the correct temperature.

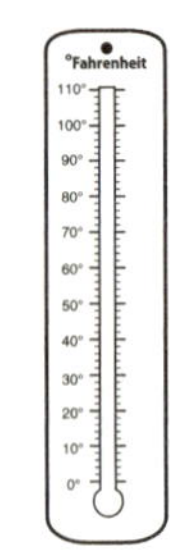

4. Tom is playing inside with friends. The inside thermometer reads 72°F. Color in the thermometer up to the correct temperature.

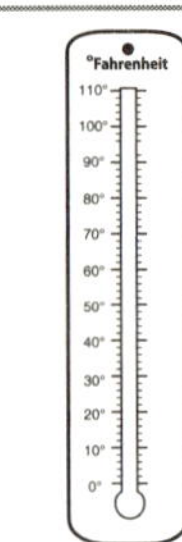

Writing and Reasoning Why do you want to know the outside temperature?

____

____

Name ______________________ Date ____________

Circle Time

Problem of the Day

TAKS Objective 1 TEKS 2.10A

Circle the thermometer that shows the temperature on a nice spring day.

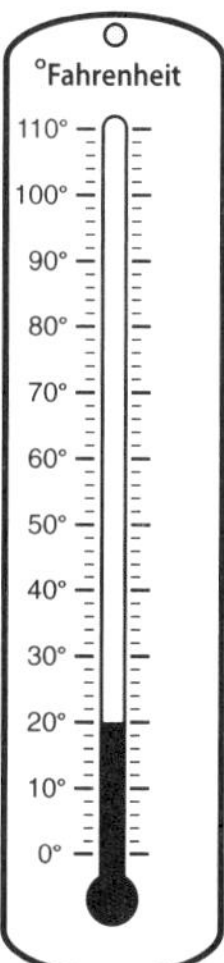

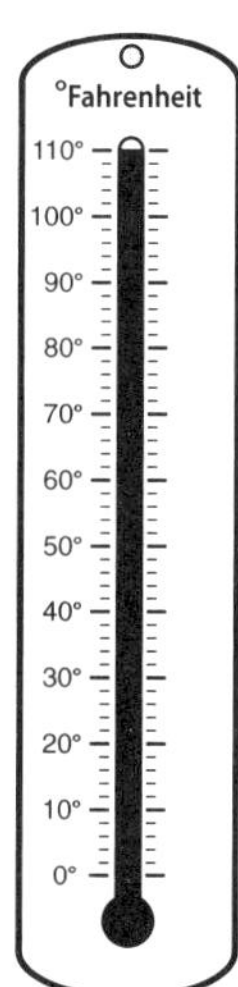

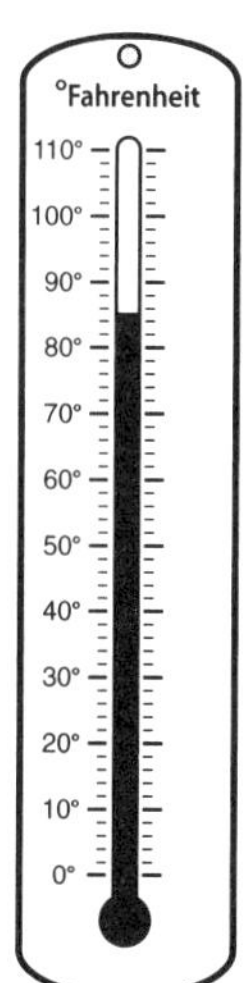

Operations

TAKS Objective 1 TEKS 2.3B

Add.

$$\begin{array}{r} 38 \\ +47 \\ \hline \end{array}$$

Number of the Day

TAKS Objective 1 TEKS 2.10C

5

Name 5 things that take more than 5 minutes to do.

Facts Practice

TAKS Objective 1 TEKS 2.3A

Write the facts family for 5, 8, and 13.

_____ + _____ = _____

_____ + _____ = _____

_____ − _____ = _____

_____ − _____ = _____

Compare Length

TAKS Objective 4
TEKS 2.9

Compare the length of the objects.

Write *shorter* or *longer* to complete each sentence.

1. Compare a tens rod and a paper clip.

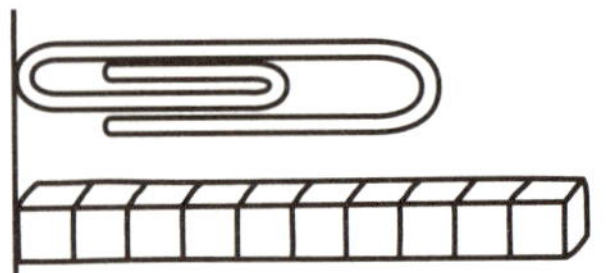

The tens rod is ______________ than the paper clip.

The paper clip is ______________ than the tens rod.

2. Compare a pencil and an eraser.

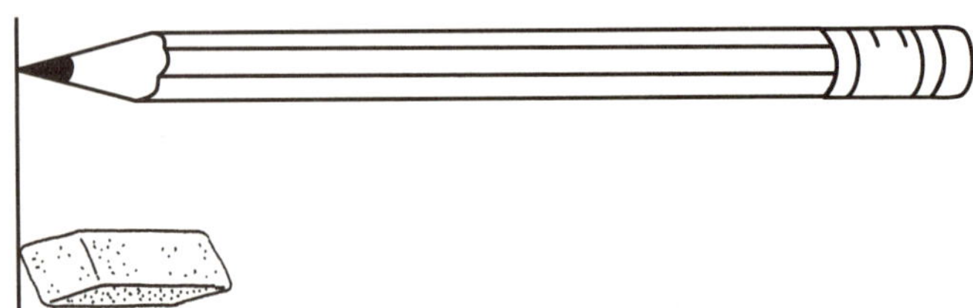

The pencil is ______________ than the eraser.

The eraser is ______________ than the pencil.

3. Choose two objects to draw. Compare the lengths.

The ______________ is ______________ than the ______________.

The ______________ is ______________ than the ______________.

Writing and Reasoning What item in your classroom is about the same length as a pencil? Find it and compare their lengths. Which one is longer?

____

Name ______________________ Date ____________

Circle Time

Problem of the Day

TAKS Objective 1 TEKS 2.9A

Gene wants to measure the length of the balance beam on the playground. Would it be better to use footprints or paper clips to measure?

Operations

TAKS Objective 1 TEKS 2.12C

Michele is distributing 5 colored sheets to each student. How many sheet does Michele need for 6 students?

Students	1	2	3	4	5	6
Sheets	5	10	15			

Word of the Day

TAKS Objective 1 TEKS 2.7A

face

Count the number of faces on these objects: a number cube, a box of pasta, a ball.

Facts Practice

TAKS Objective 1 TEKS 2.3A

Add.

1. ▢▢▢▢▢ ▢ + 1 = ______
2. ▢▢ + 5 = ______
3. ▢▢▢▢▢ ▢▢ + 5 = ______
4. ▢▢▢▢▢ + 9 = ______
5. ▭ ▢▢▢▢▢ + 1 = ______

Name ______________________ Date ____________

Measure With Paper Clips and Cubes

TAKS Objective 4
TEKS 2.9A

Find the real object.

Use [paper clip] and [cube] to measure.

	Object	Measurement
1.		about ________ [paper clip] about ________ [cube]
2.		about ________ [paper clip] about ________ [cube]
3.		about ________ [paper clip] about ________ [cube]
4.	Blue	about ________ [paper clip] about ________ [cube]

Math Journal **Writing and Reasoning** Hugh's mom asked him to take a quick measure of the length of the dining room table. He has a penny, a shoelace and a toothpick. Which would you tell him to use and why?

____

____

Name ______________________ Date ____________

Circle Time

Problem of the Day

TAKS Objective 1 TEKS 2.9A

Use [paper clip] to measure the length.

The spoon is about ______ [paper clip].

Number Sense

TAKS Objective 1 TEKS 2.3A

There are 17 girls and 9 boys in the music club. How many more girls are in the club than boys?

Calendar Activity

TAKS Objective 1 TEKS 2.12C

Guess and check to find the number of school days left in the month.

Facts Practice

TAKS Objective 1 TEKS 2.3A

Use connecting cubes. Write the facts family for 2, 9, 11.

_____ + _____ = _____

_____ + _____ = _____

_____ − _____ = _____

_____ − _____ = _____

Name ______________________ Date __________

Measure With Ones Blocks

TAKS Objective 4
TEKS 2.9

Find the real object. Use [ones block] to measure.

Write about how many.

	Object	Measurement
1.		about ________ [ones block]
2.		about ________ [ones block]
3.		about ________ [ones block]

Find an object to measure.

Use [ones block]. Write about how many.

4. ________ about ________ [ones block]

Compare. Circle the longer object.

5.

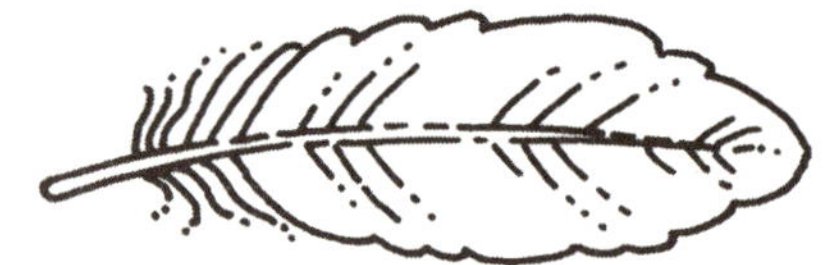

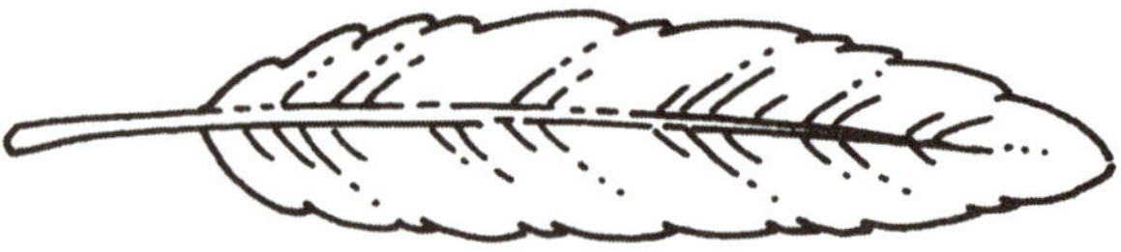

Writing and Reasoning Marge measures a stick to be longer than 9 [ones block] long but shorter than 12 [ones block]. What could the stick measure in [ones block]?

Name ____________________ Date __________

Circle Time

Problem of the Day

TAKS Objective 1 TEKS 2.9A

Use ☐ to measure.

about ______ ☐.

Number Sense

TAKS Objective 1 TEKS 2.1

Write the numbers in order from least to greatest.

475 480 491 9

______ ______ ______ ______

Number of the Day

TAKS Objective 1 TEKS 2.5C

13

Write 2 fact families using the number 13.

Numerical Fluency

TAKS Objective 1 TEKS 2.3B

$20 + 19 =$ ______

$30 + 3 =$ ______

$50 + 19 =$ ______

$12 + 60 =$ ______

Area

TAKS Objective 4
TEKS 2.9B

Use square units.

Find the area of each shape.

1. 

about __________ square units

2. 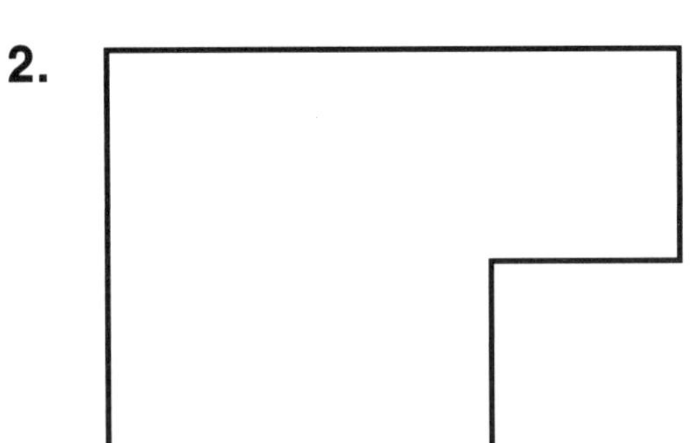

about __________ square units

Writing and Reasoning Kristen made a book cover. It is 9 square units long and 5 square units wide. What is the area of her book cover?

__________ square units

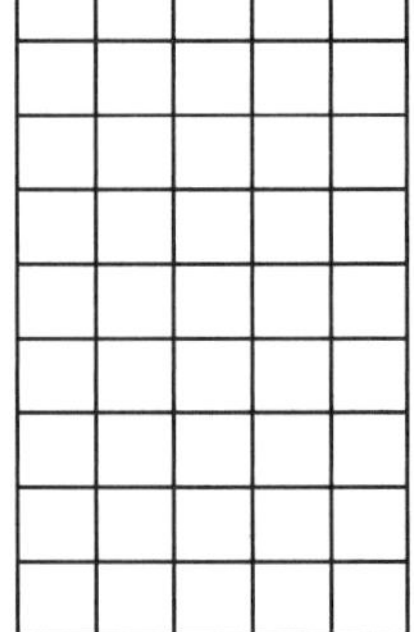

Circle Time

Problem of the Day

TAKS Objective 1 TEKS 2.9B

Use square units.

Find the area of the shape.

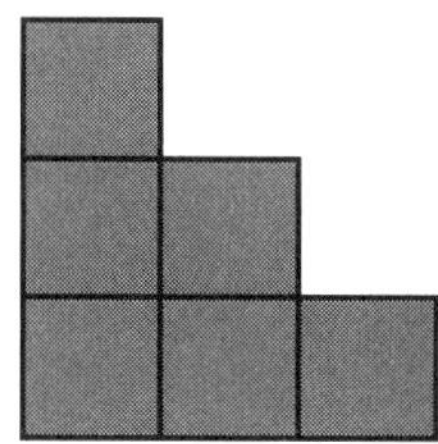

about ______ square units

Measurement

TAKS Objective 1 TEKS 2.10A

Write the temperature.

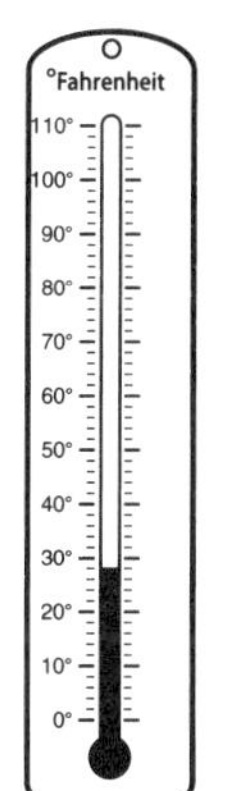

______ °F

Word of the Day

TAKS Objective 1 TEKS 2.9D

light

Use the word *light* to describe classroom objects.

Numerical Fluency

TAKS Objective 1 TEKS 2.3B

Add.

80 + 14 = ______

56 + 44 = ______

Guess and Check

TAKS Objective 4
TEKS 2.9B, 2.12B

Mr. Green wants to cover a board with pictures the size of this block.

1. How many pictures can Mr. Green put on this board?

   Guess: ________ pictures

   Check: ________ pictures

2. How many pictures can Mr. Green put on a board this shape?

   Guess: ________ pictures

   Check: ________ pictures

3. How many pictures can Mr. Green put on a board this shape?

   Guess: ________ pictures

   Check: ________ pictures

Math Journal **Writing and Reasoning** What do you need to remember when you are finding the area of a shape using a square unit?

____

____

Circle Time

Problem of the Day

TAKS Objective 1 TEKS 2.9B

Look at the stamp. 

About how many stamps can you put on a shape of this size?

______ stamps

Measurement

TAKS Objective 1 TEKS 2.9B

Use square units. 

Find the area of the shape.

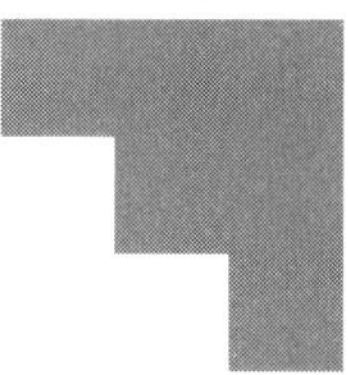

about ______ square units

Number of the Day

TAKS Objective 1 TEKS 2.3C

50

Write three number sentences where the difference is 50.

Numerical Fluency

TAKS Objective 1 TEKS 2.1C

Circle the choice that is true. Use base-ten blocks and Workmat 6 to help if you wish.

A. 498 is greater than 891

B. 498 < 891

C. 498 is equal to 891

How Much Can It Hold?

TAKS Objective 4
TEKS 2.9C

Find the capacity.

How many?	Measure
1. in a	about ______
2. in a	about ______
3. in a	about ______
4. in a	about ______

Circle the item with the greater capacity.

5.

6.

Writing and Reasoning What would you choose to measure the capacity of a water bottle? Explain.

____

____

Circle Time

Problem of the Day

TAKS Objective 1 TEKS 2.9C

Look at the cup. 

About how many cups of water will this jar hold?

about ______ 

Operations

TAKS Objective 1 TEKS 2.3A

Write the doubles and doubles plus-one sum.

5 + 5 = ______

5 + 6 = ______

6 + 5 = ______

Calendar Activity

TAKS Objective 1 TEKS 2.6B

Find today's date on the calendar. Starting at this date, count by twos as high as you can.

Numerical Fluency

TAKS Objective 1 TEKS 2.1B

Count how many. Write the tens and ones.

______ tens and

______ ones

Write the value.

______ + ______

Write the number. ______

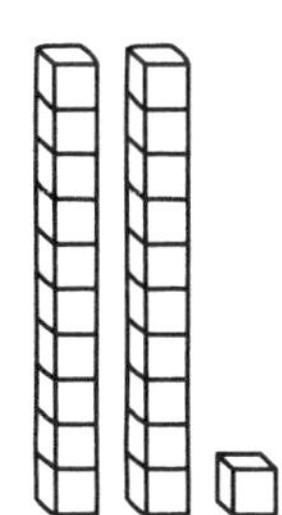

Hands On: How Heavy Is It?

TAKS Objective 4
TEKS 2.9D

Find objects in the classroom. List them or draw them in the table. Use a balance scale and marbles.

Object	How heavy?
1. ______	______ marbles
2. ______	______ marbles
3. ______	______ marbles

Circle the heavier object.

4.  

5.  

Circle the lighter object.

6.  

7. 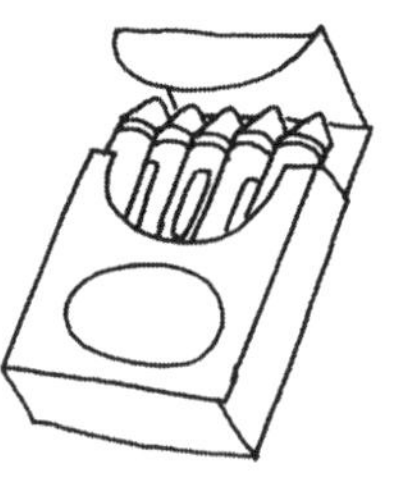 

Math Journal **Writing and Reasoning** Which object is heavier, the book or the notepad? How do you know?

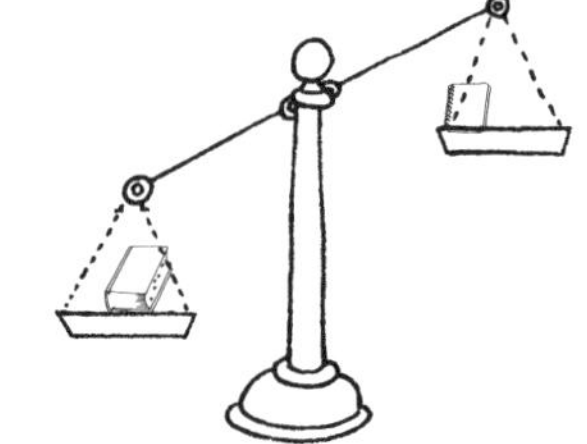

____

____

Circle Time

Problem of the Day

TAKS Objective 1 TEKS 2.9D

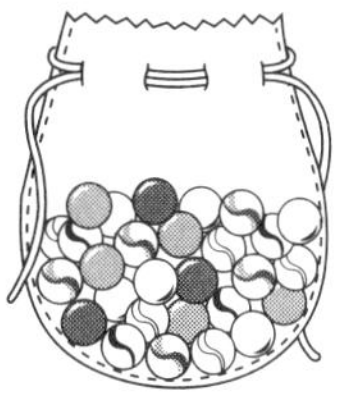

Circle which is heavier.

Data

TAKS Objective 1 TEKS 2.13A

This is the result of James's survey.

Favorite Type of Movies	
Action	𝍸 |
Comedy	𝍸 ||
Sci-Fi	||||

How many students took part in the survey?

Word of the Day

TAKS Objective 1 TEKS 2.7C

triangles

Cut two triangles from a sheet of paper.

Numerical Fluency

TAKS Objective 1 TEKS 2.1A

Circle a way to show the number 32.

A. 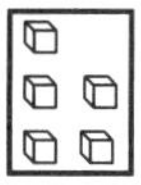

B. 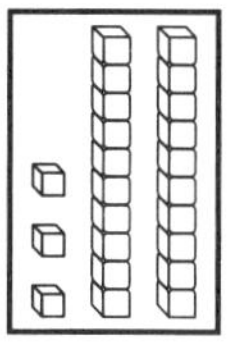

C. $3 + 2$

D. $30 + 2$

Compare Capacity and Weight

TAKS Objective 4
TEKS 2.9C, 2.9D

Compare capacity. Circle the correct answer.

1. 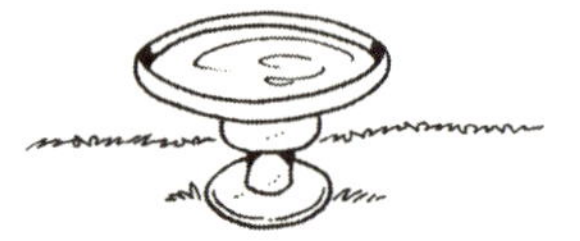 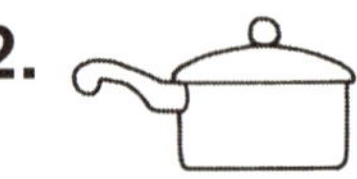

The birdbath holds ______ the flower pot.

more than   the same as   less than

2. 

The pan holds ______ the wastebasket.

more than   the same as   less than

3.  

The cup with milk holds ______ the cup with juice.

more than   the same as   less than

4.  

The paint can holds ______ the bathtub.

more than   the same as   less than

Compare weight. Circle the correct answer.

5.  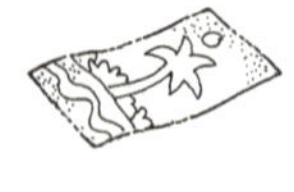

The chair is ______ the towel.

heavier than   lighter than

6.  

The ball is ______ the umbrella.

heavier than   lighter than

Writing and Reasoning How could you prove two containers have the same capacity?

____

____

____

Circle Time

Problem of the Day

TAKS Objective 1 TEKS 2.9C

Circle the object that holds the most.

Circle the object that is heaviest when filled.

Geometry

TAKS Objective 1 TEKS 2.7A

Circle the triangle.

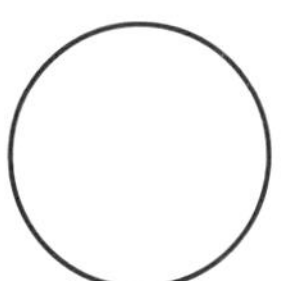
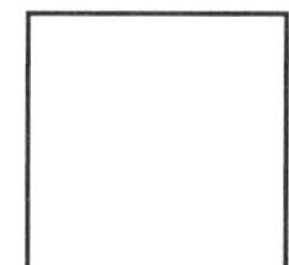

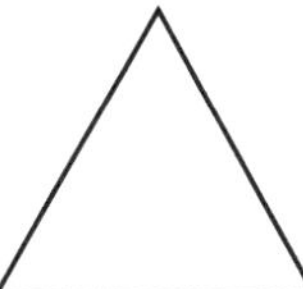

Number of the Day

TAKS Objective 1 TEKS 2.10C

1

Name things that take less than 1 minute to complete.

Facts Practice

TAKS Objective 1 TEKS 2.3A

Subtract.

1. 13 − 7 = ______
2. 7 − 4 = ______
3. 15 − 5 = ______
4. 13 − 4 = ______

Problem Solving: Guess and Check

TAKS Objective 4
TEKS 2.9D, 2.9B

Guess and check to solve.

1. An ice cream cone and an apple together weigh the same as 40 cubes. The ice cream cone and 8 cubes weigh the same as the apple. How much does the ice cream cone weigh?

   ______ cubes

2. John's comb and brush together weigh the same as 25 cubes. His comb and 9 cubes weigh the same as his brush. How much does his brush weigh?

   ______ cubes

3. A notepad and 2 pencils weigh 38 cubes altogether. The notepad weighs the same as 20 cubes. How much does each pencil weigh?

   ______ cubes

4. The watch and the belt together weigh the same as 30 cubes. The belt weighs the same as 2 watches. How much does the belt weigh?

   ______ cubes

Writing and Reasoning How did you find the weight of each pencil in Exercise 3?

____

____

Circle Time

Problem of the Day

TAKS Objective 1 TEKS 2.9D

A CD in its case weighs 25 paper clips. An empty CD case weighs 15 paper clips. How much does the CD weigh by itself?

Probability

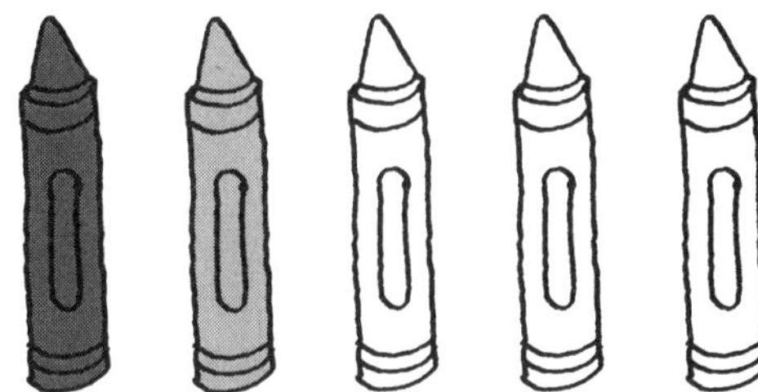

Pedro picks a crayon without looking. Which color crayon is Pedro most likely to pick?

Word of the Day

TAKS Objective 1 TEKS 2.10A

temperature

Draw a picture of a tool you can use to measure temperature.

Numerical Fluency

TAKS Objective 1 TEKS 2.3B

Add.

39	46	79	80
+ 11	+ 12	+ 13	+ 10

Hands On: Measuring My World

TAKS Objective 4
TEKS 2.9

Estimate.

1. About how many  will it take to fill a pitcher ?

about ______ 

2. What is the length of this piece of string?

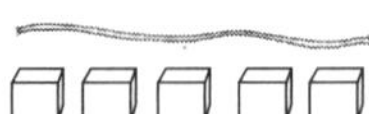

about ______ cubes long

3. Which is heavier, the watch or the ring?

The ______ is heavier.

4. What is the area?

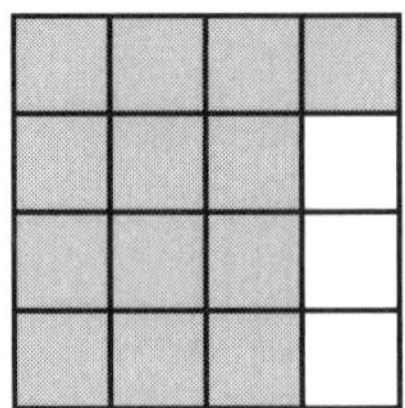

about ______ square units

Measure.

5. Use your pencil to find the length of your desk.

 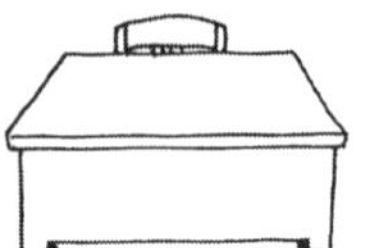

about ______ pencils long

6. Use a balance scale and marbles to find how heavy a stapler is.

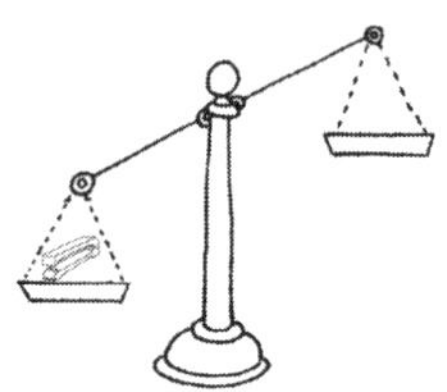

about ______ marbles

Math Journal **Writing and Reasoning** Mira and Jake want to find the capacity of a pail. Mira says to use a pencil to measure and Jake says to use a cup. Who is right and why?

____

Circle Time

Problem of the Day

TAKS Objective 1 TEKS 2.9

Circle the item with the lesser capacity.

Patterns

TAKS Objective 1 TEKS 2.12C

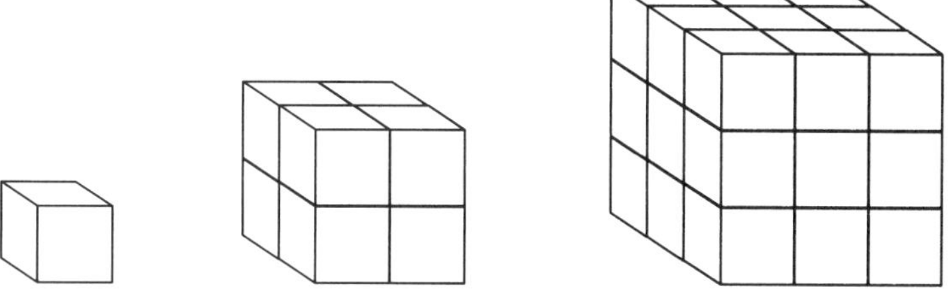

Show what comes next in the pattern.

Number of the Day

TAKS Objective 1 TEKS 2.3D

5

How much money do you have if you have 5 dimes?
5 nickels? 5 pennies?

Numerical Fluency

TAKS Objective 1 TEKS 2.1C

Write the numbers in order from greatest to least.

668 737 520 219

Name ______________________ Date ____________

Sides and Vertices

TAKS Objective 3
TEKS 2.7A, 2.7B

Look at the figures. Count the sides and vertices. Write the name of the figure.

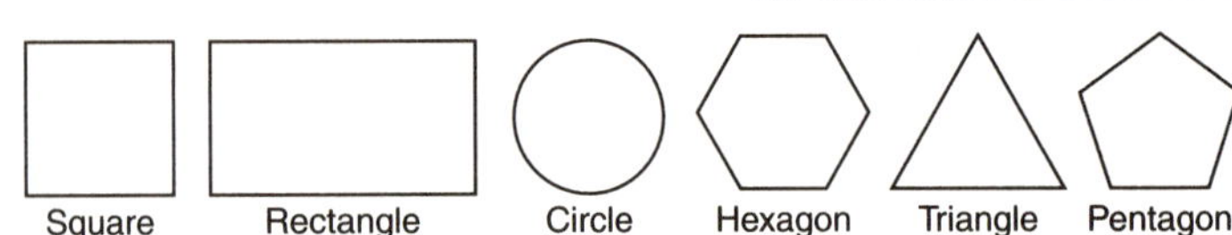

1. 6 sides, 6 vertices

____

2. 4 sides, 4 vertices

____

3. 0 sides, 0 vertices

____

4. 5 sides, 5 vertices

____

5. 4 sides, 4 vertices

____

6. 3 sides, 3 vertices

____

Look at the figure. Write the number of sides and vertices.

7. ______ sides

______ vertices

8. 

______ sides

______ vertices

Writing and Reasoning How are a square and a rectangle the same?

____

Name ______________________ Date ____________

Circle Time

Problem of the Day

Objective 1 TEKS 2.7A

How many sides does this shape have?

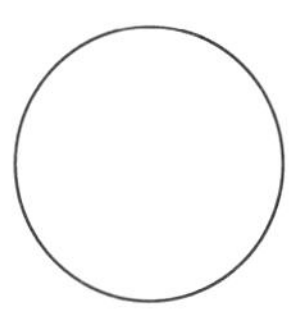

_____ Sides

Number Sense

Objective 1 TEKS 2.1B

Count how many.

Write the tens and ones.

_____ tens and _____ ones

Write the value.

_____ + _____

Write the number.

_____

Calendar Activity

Objective 1 TEKS 2.13B

Find a two digit number where both digits have numbers with curves ______________________

Numerical Fluency

Objective 1 TEKS 2.1B

Count how many.

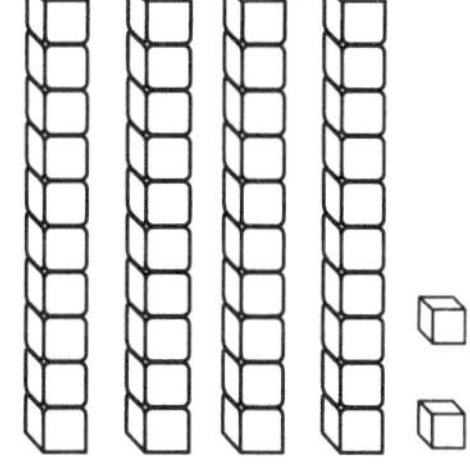

Write the tens and ones.

_____ tens and _____ ones

Write the value.

_____ + _____

Write the number.

_____

Compare Two-Dimensional Figures

TAKS Objective 3
TEKS 2.7A

Compare the figures.

1\.

Alike because ______________________

Different because ______________________

____

____

2\.

Alike because ______________________

____

Different because ______________________

____

3\.

Alike because ______________________

____

Different because ______________________

____

Writing and Reasoning How is a circle different from the other figures on this page?

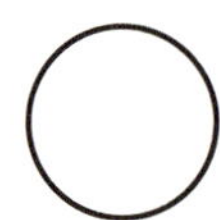

____

Circle Time

Problem of the Day

TAKS Objective 1 TEKS 2.7A

Compare the figures.

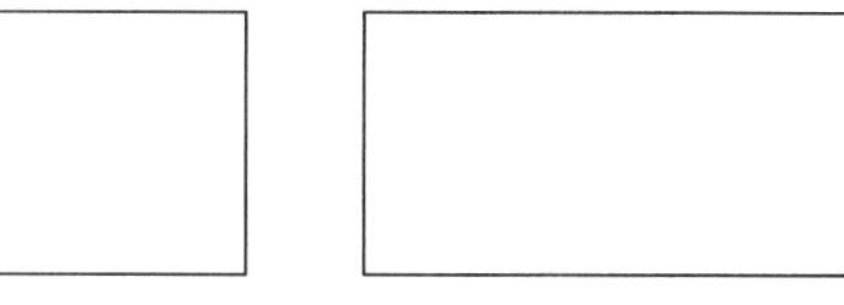

Alike because: ______________________________

Different because: ______________________________

Patterns

TAKS Objective 1 TEKS 2.6C

What comes next in this pattern?

43, 47, 51, 55, ______

Word of the Day

TAKS Objective 1 TEKS 2.3E

cent sign

Use the cent sign to write the values of the following coins: penny, quarter, nickel.

Numerical Fluency

TAKS Objective 1 TEKS 2.1A

Write the number shown by the model.

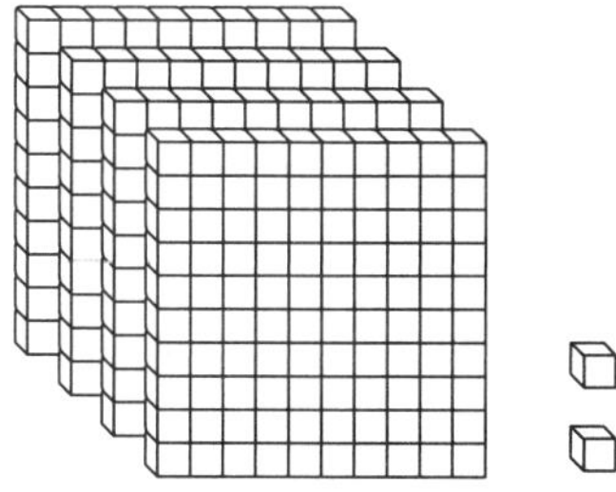

______

Polygons

TAKS Objective 3
TEKS 2.7A, 2.7B

1. Draw a circle around every figure with 4 sides.

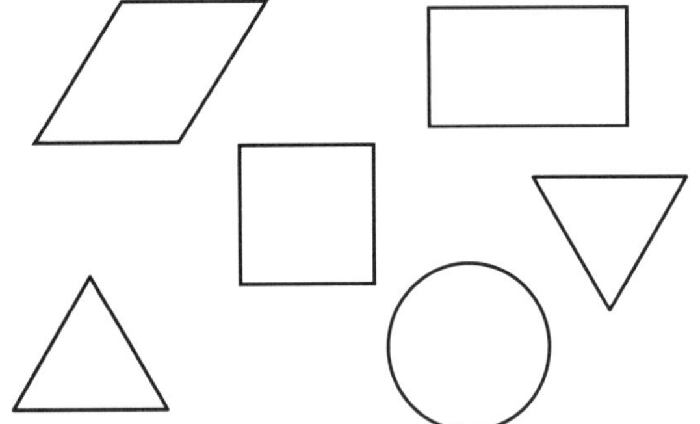

2. Draw a circle around every 6-sided figure.

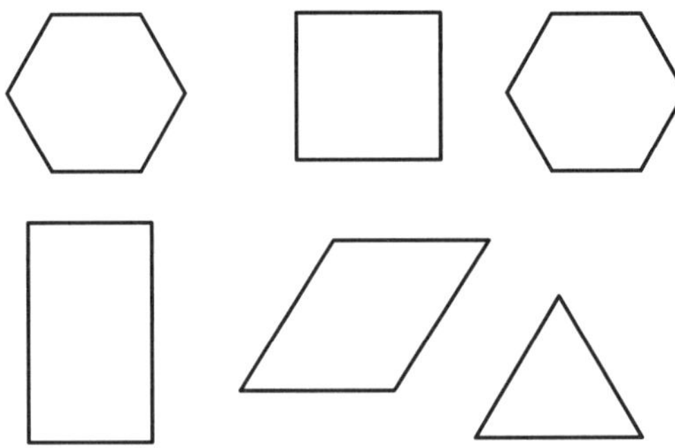

3. Circle all the figures that have 4 sides of equal length.

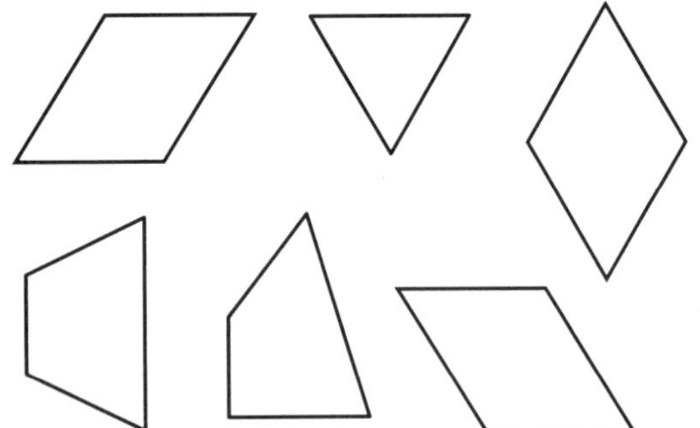

4. Draw a circle around every figure that has exactly 3 vertices.

Writing and Reasoning

Draw the polygon that matches the clues.
All its angles are the same.
It has the same number of sides as a rectangle.
All its sides are the same length.

Name ______________________ Date ____________

Circle Time

Problem of the Day

TAKS Objective 1 TEKS 2.7A

How many of the figures are polygons?

______

Probability

TAKS Objective 1 TEKS 2.11C

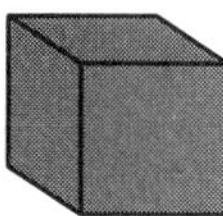 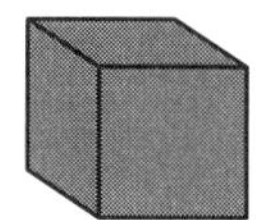 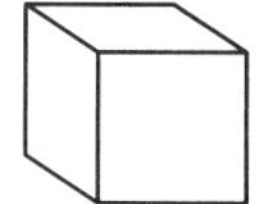

Pat picks a cube without looking. Which color cube is Pat more likely to pick?

Word of the Day

TAKS Objective 1 TEKS 2.13A

<, >, =

Name each of these symbols:
<, >, =.

Facts Practice

TAKS Objective 1 TEKS 2.3A

Model with connecting cubes.

Add.

9 + 1 + 7 = ______

$$\begin{array}{r} 9 \\ 1 \\ +\ 7 \\ \hline \end{array}$$

Name ______________________ Date ____________

Problem Solving: Use Models

TAKS Objective 3
TEKS 2.7C

Cut out the figures.

Use the figures to solve the problem.
Draw lines to show how you placed the figures

1. Frank has 2 △. He wants to make a figure with 4 sides. How can he do it?

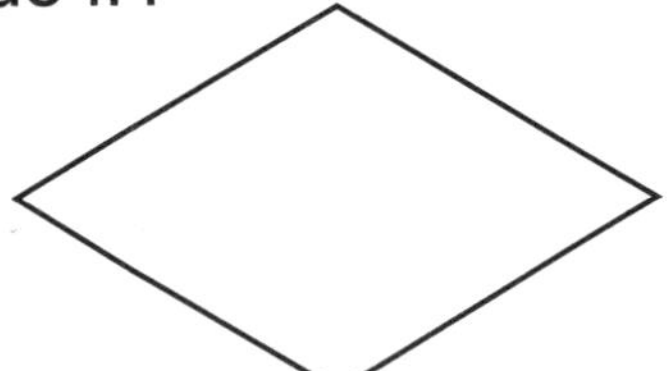

2. Eva has ⏢ and △. She wants to make a large △. How can she do it?

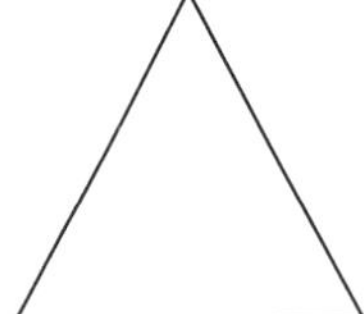

Writing and Reasoning Jack has 2 ⏢ figures. Amy has 6 △ figures. How can they each make the same 6-sided figure?

____

____

____

____

Circle Time

Problem of the Day

TAKS Objective 1 TEKS 2.7C

Look at the triangle.

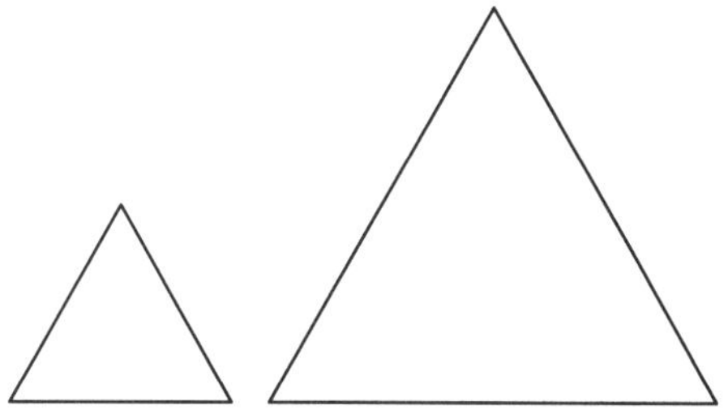

How many of the smaller triangles do you need

to make this larger triangle?______

Number Sense

TAKS Objective 1 TEKS 2.1C

Write >, <, or =.

45 ◯ 39

Number of the Day

TAKS Objective 1 TEKS 2.1B

136

Name the number 136 as many ways as you can.

Numerical Fluency

TAKS Objective 1 TEKS 2.3B

Use Workmat 3 and place value blocks.

Add.

53 + 47 = ______

Cutting Figures Apart

TAKS Objective 3
TEKS 2.7C

Draw lines to show how these shapes are made from other figures.

1.

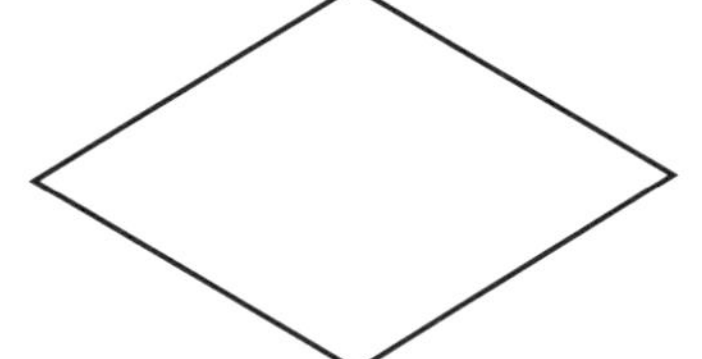

2.

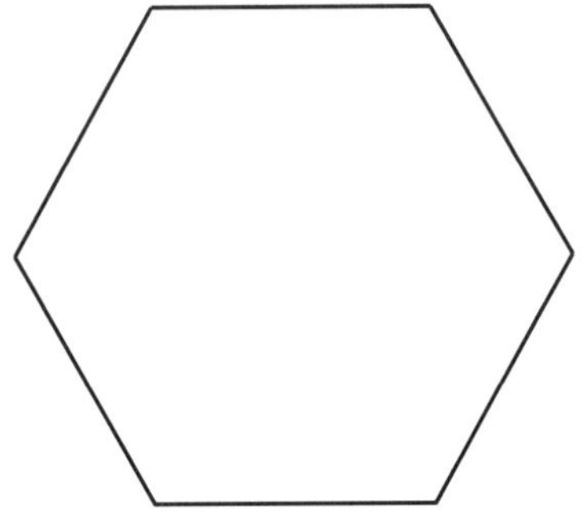

3.

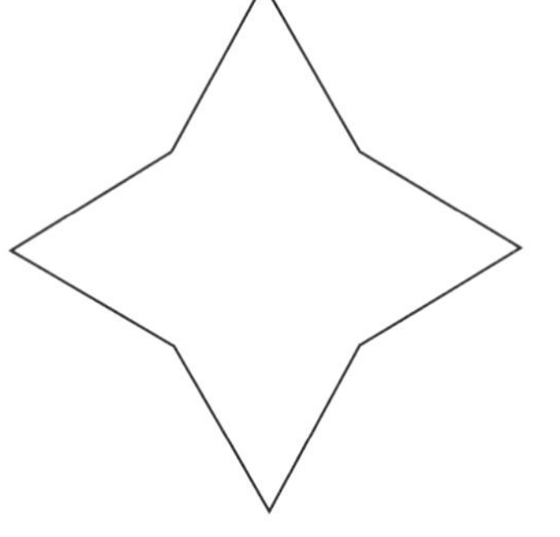

Math Journal **Writing and Reasoning** How can you cut this figure apart into triangles? How many triangles will you have? ______________

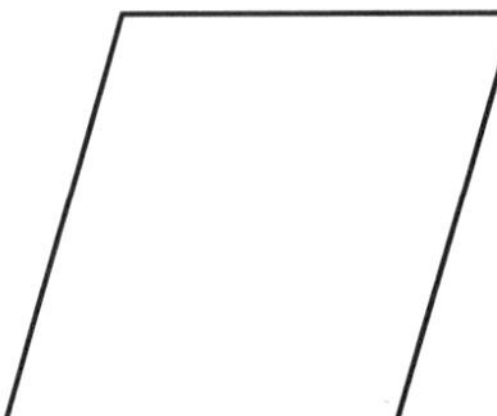

Name ______________________ Date ______________

Circle Time

Problem of the Day

TAKS Objective 1 TEKS 2.7C

How many of these triangles can you make by cutting this square?

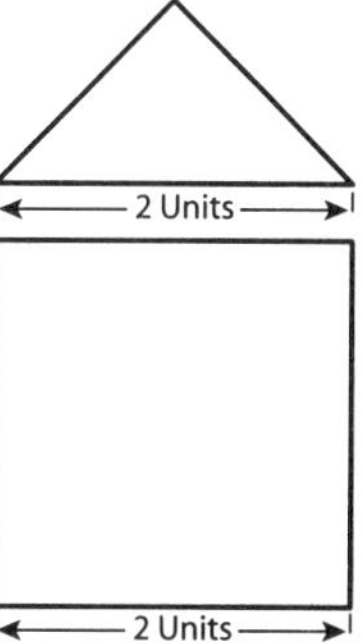

______

Measurement

TAKS Objective 1 TEKS 2.9A

Use  to measure the length.

The fork is about ______  .

Word of the Day

TAKS Objective 1 TEKS 2.7A

sides

Draw 2 shapes with 4 sides.

Facts Practice

TAKS Objective 1 TEKS 2.3A

Model with connecting cubes.

Add.

$3 + 4 + 1 =$

$$\begin{array}{r} 3 \\ 4 \\ +\ 1 \\ \hline \end{array}$$

Identify Figures

TAKS Objective 3
TEKS 2.7A

cube

sphere

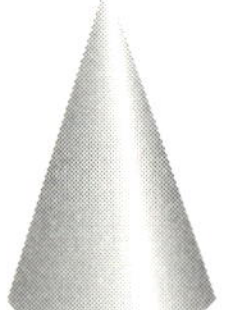
cone

square pyramid

rectangular prism

cylinder

Write the name of the two solid shapes in each picture.

1. 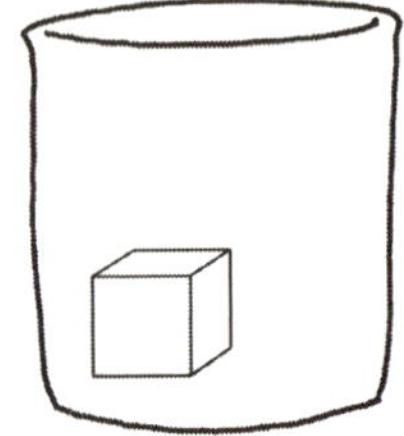

____

____

2. 

____

____

3. 

____

____

4. 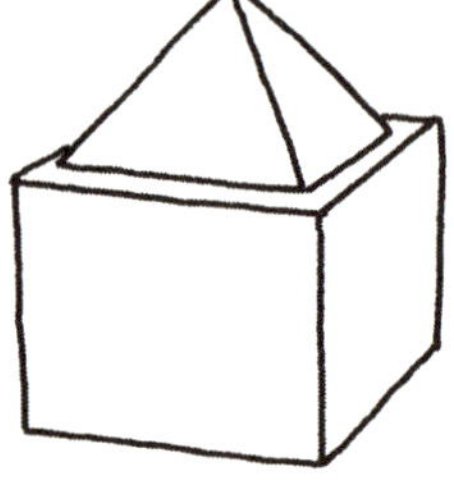

____

____

Math Journal **Writing and Reasoning** Which solid shape is most like a soup can?

____

Circle Time

Problem of the Day

TAKS Objective 1 TEKS 2.7A

What is the name of this figure?

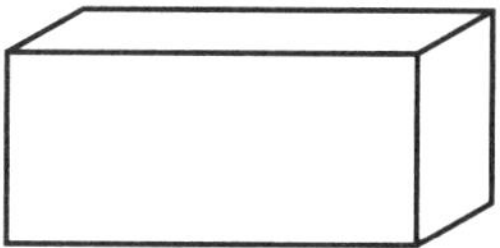

Measurement

TAKS Objective 1 TEKS 2.9A

Use ▢ to measure.

The crayon is about ____ ▢.

Number of the Day

TAKS Objective 1 TEKS 2.3C

25

What number is 1 more and 1 less than 25? 10 more?
10 Less?

Numerical Fluency

TAKS Objective 1 TEKS 2.3B

Use Workmat 3 and place value blocks.

Add.

$23 + 76 =$

Faces, Edges, and Vertices

TAKS Objective 3
TEKS 2.7A, 2.7B

Circle the shapes that match the description.

1. 6 faces, 12 edges, 8 vertices

2. 1 face, 0 edges, 1 vertex

3. 0 faces, 0 edges, 0 vertices

   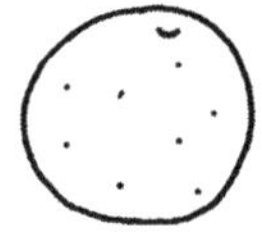

4. 6 faces, 12 edges, 8 vertices

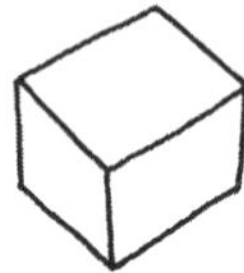   

5. 2 faces, 0 edges, 0 vertices

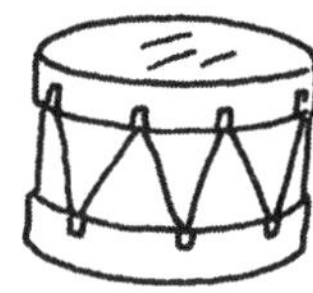  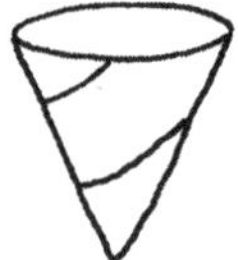 

Math Journal **Writing and Reasoning** Which solid figures both roll and slide?

____

How do you know?

____

Circle Time

Problem of the Day

TAKS Objective 1 TEKS 2.7A

Write the number of faces, edges, and vertices for this figure.

_____ faces

_____ edges

_____ vertices

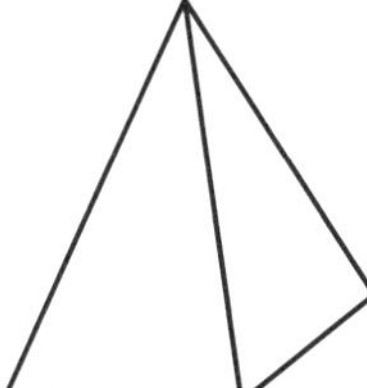

Operations

TAKS Objective 1 TEKS 2.12A

The shop at the zoo sold 45 lion puppets and 27 elephant puppets. How many puppets did the shop sell?

Calendar Activity

TAKS Objective 1 TEKS 2.3D

Adam's mom gives him a penny each day. How much money will he get this month?

Facts Practice

TAKS Objective 1 TEKS 2.3A

Model with connecting cubes.

Add.

$9 + 5 + 2 =$

$$\begin{array}{r} 9 \\ 5 \\ +2 \\ \hline \end{array}$$

Identify Faces

TAKS Objective 3
TEKS 2.7A, 2.7B

Draw the shapes you would make if you traced the faces of the object.

1. 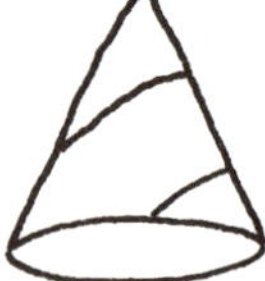

2. 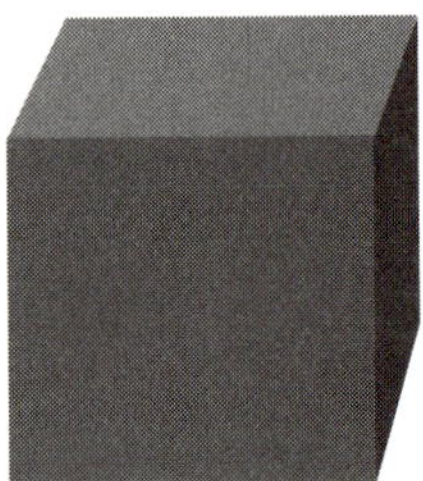

3. 

4. 

Writing and Reasoning What shape will you get if you trace the face of a soup can?

____

Circle Time

Problem of the Day

TAKS Objective 1 TEKS 2.7A

What shape would you get if you traced the faces of a cube?

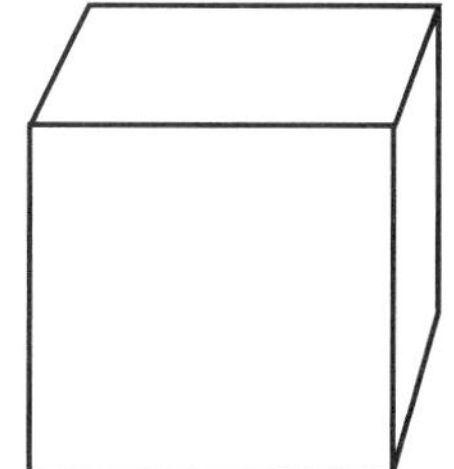

Operations

TAKS Objective 1 TEKS 2.3C

Choose a way to add. Add. Explain the way you found the sum.

$37 + 40 =$

Word of the Day

TAKS Objective 1 TEKS 2.7A

hexagon

Draw a hexagon.

Numerical Fluency

TAKS Objective 1 TEKS 2.3B

Use Workmat 3 and place value blocks.

Add.

$47 + 4 =$

Alike or Different

TAKS Objective 3
TEKS 2.7A

Write how the pair is alike or different.
Count the faces, edges, and vertices.

	Alike	Different
1.	______________ ______________ ______________	______________ ______________ ______________ ______________
2.	______________ ______________ ______________	______________ ______________ ______________
3.	______________ ______________ ______________	______________ ______________ ______________

Writing and Reasoning How is a cylinder like a cone?

How are they different?

____

____

Circle Time

Problem of the Day

TAKS Objective 1 TEKS 2.7A

Write how the pair is alike and different.

Alike because ______

Different because ______

Money

TAKS Objective 1 TEKS 2.3D

Count on to find the value of the coins.

Number of the Day

TAKS Objective 1 TEKS 2.1C

400

There are more than 400 ______ in our school.
There are less than 400 ______ in our library.

Numerical Fluency

TAKS Objective 1 TEKS 2.1A

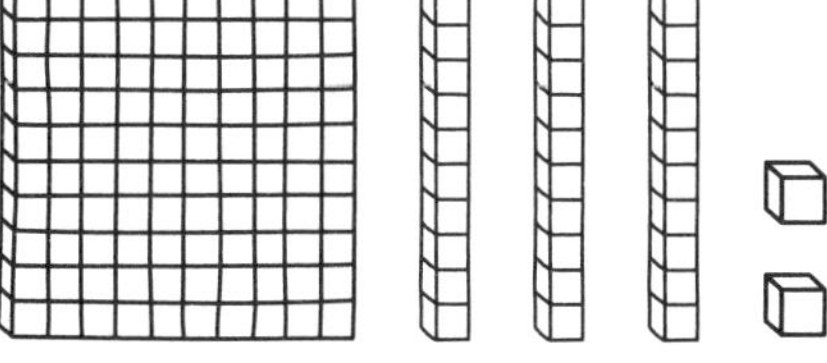

Write how many hundreds, tens, and ones.

______ hundreds ______ tens ______ ones

Write the number. ______

Name ______________________ Date ____________

Geometric Patterns

TAKS Objective 3
TEKS 2.6C

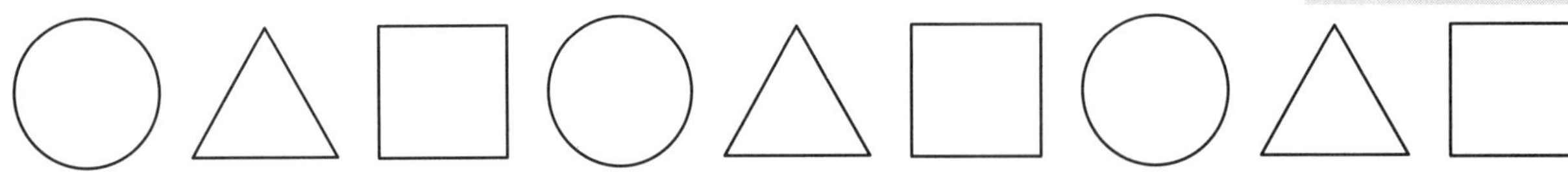

1. Rob makes this pattern on a folder.

What is the next shape in the pattern?

____

Is Rob's pattern repeating or growing?

____

2. Lisa draws this pattern for a rug.

Is she making a repeating or a growing pattern?

____

What is next?

____

3. Jane has this pattern on her quilt.     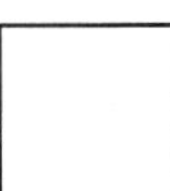

Is this a repeating pattern or a growing pattern?

____

Math Journal **Writing and Reasoning** Tell how you know the difference between a repeating pattern and a growing pattern.

____

____

____

Circle Time

Problem of the Day

TAKS Objective 1 TEKS 2.6C

What comes next in this pattern?

 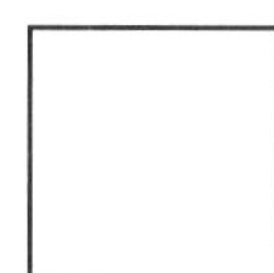 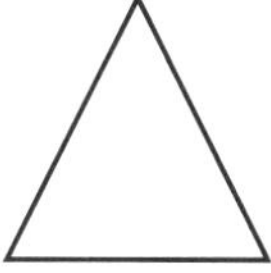    

Money

TAKS Objective 1 TEKS 2.3D

Use (Q) for quarter, (D) for dime, (N) for nickel, and (P) for penny.

Draw coins to show 37¢.

Word of the Day

TAKS Objective 1 TEKS 2.7B

alike

How are a square and a rectangle alike?

Numerical Fluency

TAKS Objective 1 TEKS 2.1A

Use >, <, or =.

382 ◯ 283

616 ◯ 661

812 ◯ 819

266 ◯ 200 + 60 + 6

Equal Parts

TAKS Objective 3
TEKS 2.2A

Draw to show how many equal parts.
Then fill in one equal part. Write the fraction.

1. 4 equal parts

____

2. 8 equal parts

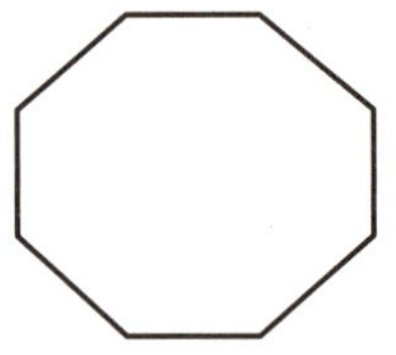

____

3. one whole

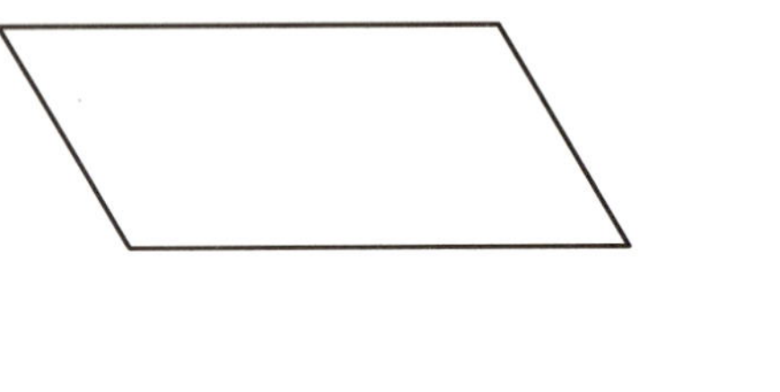

____

4. 2 equal parts

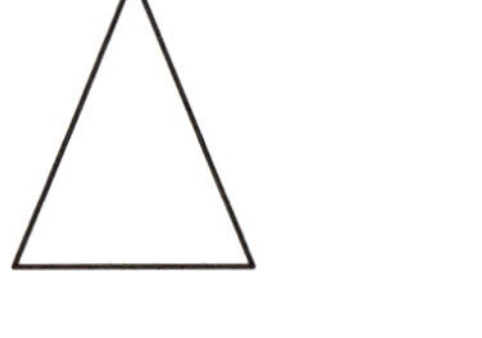

____

Fill in the fraction strip to show the fraction.

5. $\frac{1}{4}$

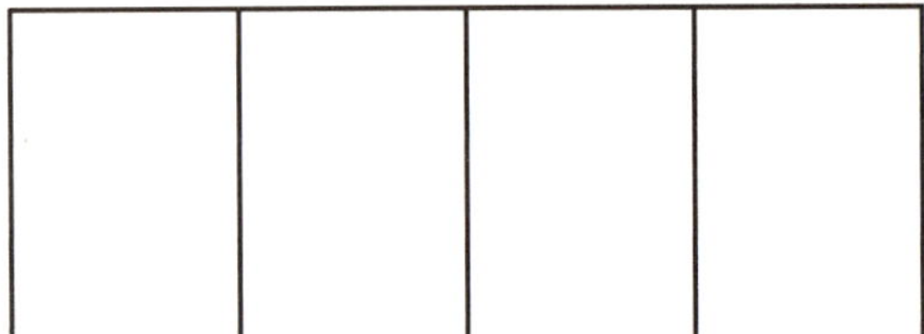

Writing and Reasoning Is this shape divided into fourths? Explain.

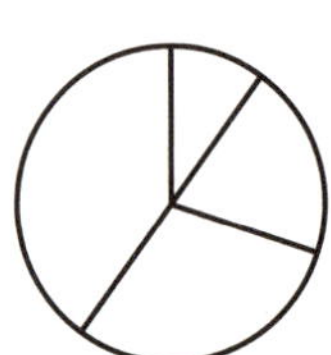

____

Circle Time

Problem of the Day

TAKS Objective 1 TEKS 2.2A

Claire cuts her pizza into six equal slices. She eats 1 slice. Fill in the fraction strip to show the fraction of the pizza that Claire eats.

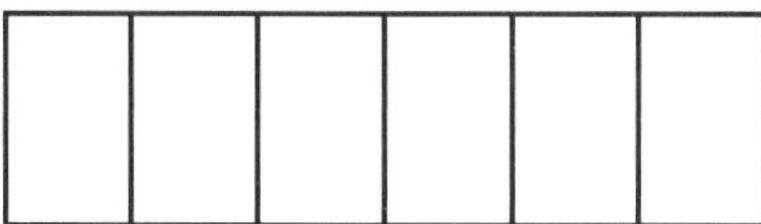

Geometry

TAKS Objective 1 TEKS 2.9B

Use square units.
Find the area of the shape.

about ________ square units

Number of the Day

TAKS Objective 1 TEKS 2.1B

9

What is the value of 9 in these numbers: 9; 493; 906?

Numerical Fluency

TAKS Objective 1 TEKS 2.2A

Write the fraction for the shaded part.

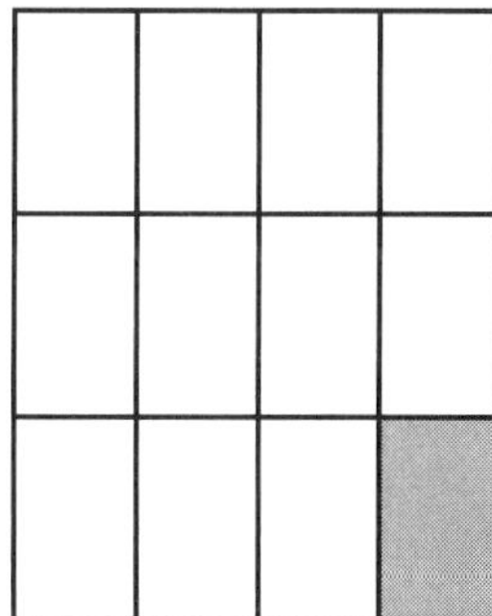

Name ______________________ Date ____________

Unit Fractions

TAKS Objective 3
TEKS 2.2A

Write the fraction for the shaded part.

1. 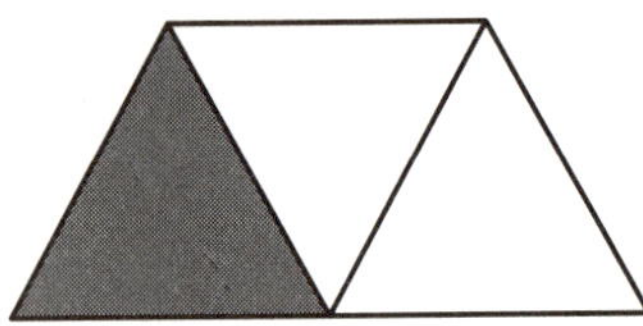

____

2. 

____

3. 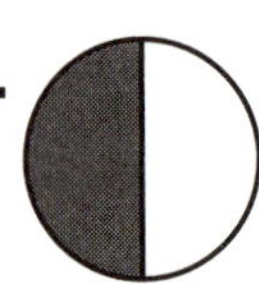

____

4. 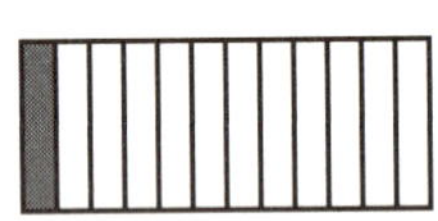

____

5. 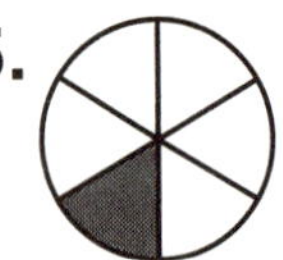

____

6. 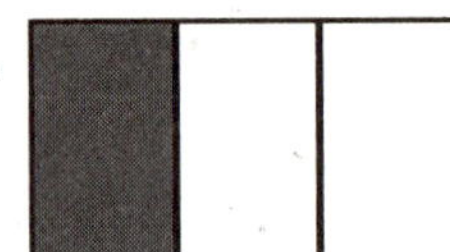

____

Color to show one shaded part.
Write the fraction.

7. 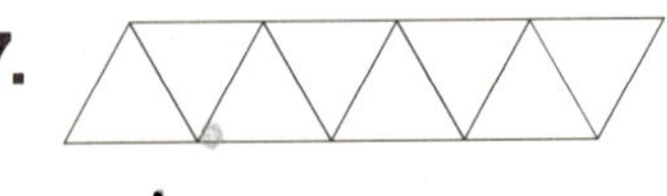

____

8. 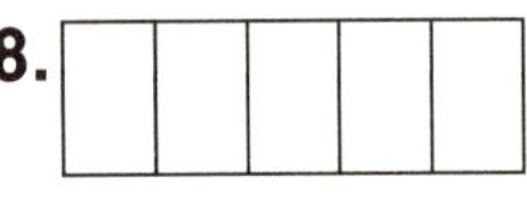

____

9. 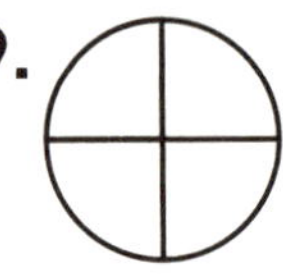

____

Math Journal **Writing and Reasoning** Shelley has a paper octagon. She cuts it into 8 equal shapes. What fraction names 1 piece?

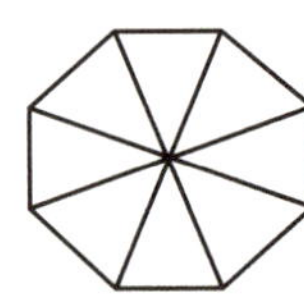

____

Circle Time

Problem of the Day

TAKS Objective 1 TEKS 2.2A

Write the fraction for the shaded part.

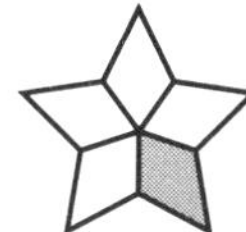

Time

TAKS Objective 1 TEKS 2.10C

About how long do you sleep at night?
Circle the best answer.

about 10 seconds

about 10 minutes

about 10 hours

Word of the Day

TAKS Objective 1 TEKS 2.10B

hour hand, minute hand

Clap once when the hour hand points at 11. Clap twice when the minute hand points at 11.

Numerical Fluency

TAKS Objective 1 TEKS 2.2A

Write the fraction for the shaded part.

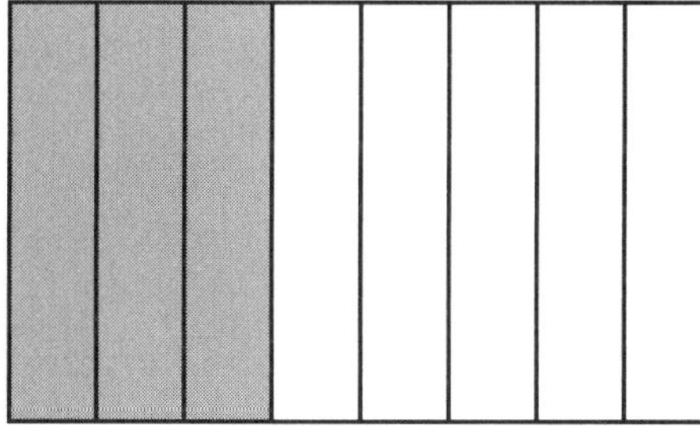

Name ______________________ Date ____________

Other Fractions

TAKS Objective 3
TEKS 2.2A

Write the fraction for the shaded part.

Remember
The fraction names part of a whole.

1. 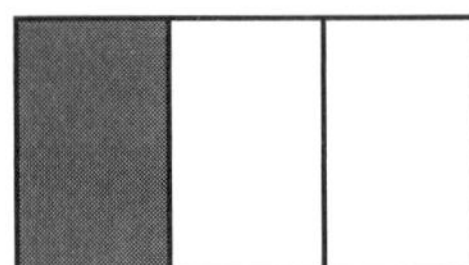 ______

2. 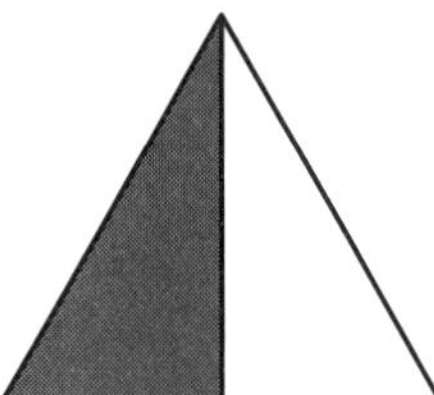 ______

3. 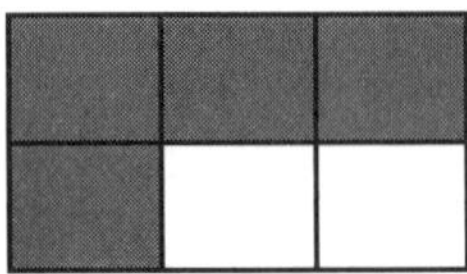 ______

4. 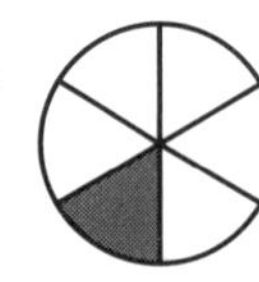 ______

5. 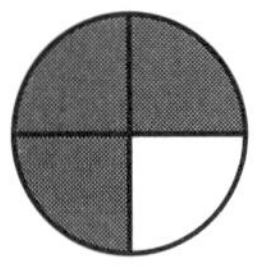 ______

6. 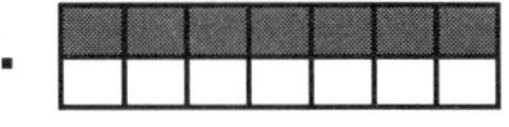 ______

7. 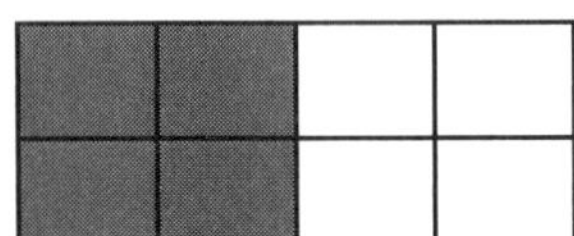 ______

8. 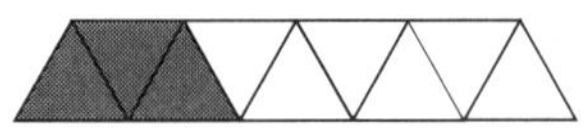 ______

Writing and Reasoning Draw a picture to show why $\frac{2}{4}$ is the same as $\frac{1}{2}$. Explain.

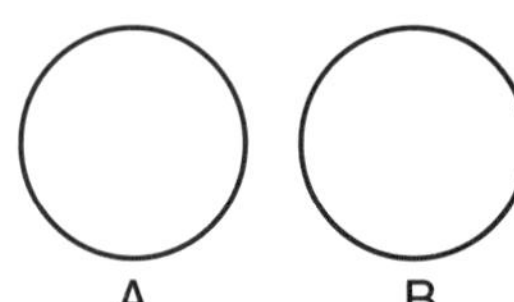

____

____

Name ______________________ Date ____________

Circle Time

Problem of the Day

TAKS Objective 1 TEKS 2.2A

Amina divides a circle into 4 equal parts. She colors 2 of the parts green. What fraction shows the green parts?

Data

TAKS Objective 1 TEKS 2.11B

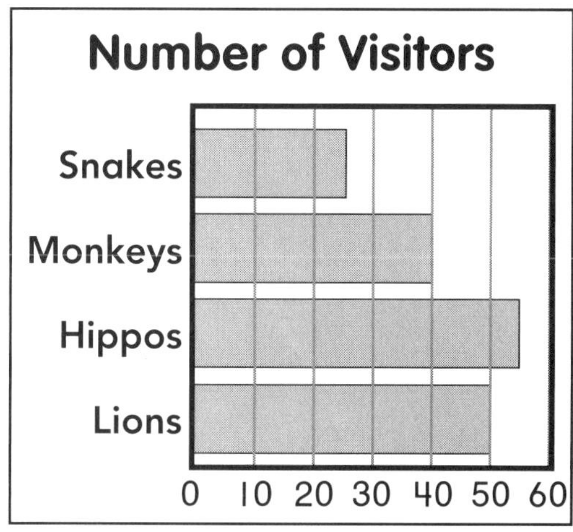

Which animal got the most visitors?

Calendar Activity

TAKS Objective 1 TEKS 2.3D

Use coins to show the amount of money that is the same as today's date.

Numerical Fluency

TAKS Objective 1 TEKS 2.2B

Write the fraction for the shaded part.

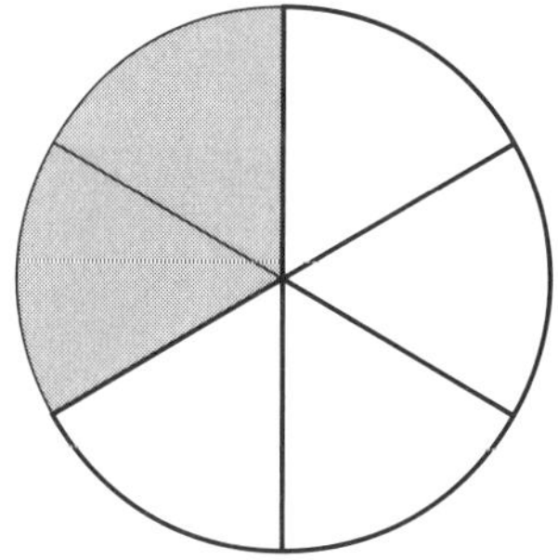

Fractions From Zero to One

TAKS Objective 3
TEKS 2.2C

Use the strips and number line. Show the fraction as close to 1, $\frac{1}{2}$, or 1.

1. 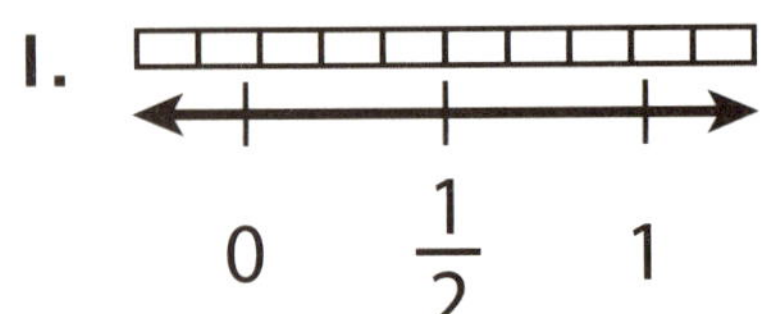

Color 5 parts.

Write the fraction. ________

0 $\frac{1}{2}$ 1

2.

0 $\frac{1}{2}$ 1

Color 2 parts.

Write the fraction. ________

0 $\frac{1}{2}$ 1

3. 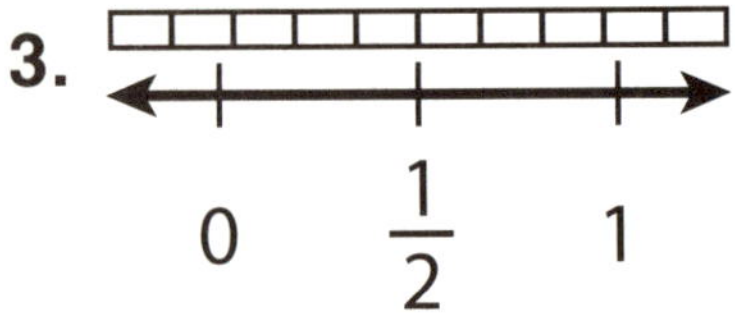

Color 7 parts.

Write the fraction. ________

0 $\frac{1}{2}$ 1

4.

0 $\frac{1}{2}$ 1

Color 4 parts.

Write the fraction. ________

0 $\frac{1}{2}$ 1

Writing and Reasoning How do you know that $\frac{7}{8}$ is greater than $\frac{3}{8}$ without using fraction strips or a number line?

____

____

Circle Time

Problem of the Day

TAKS Objective 1 TEKS 2.2C

Look at the model.

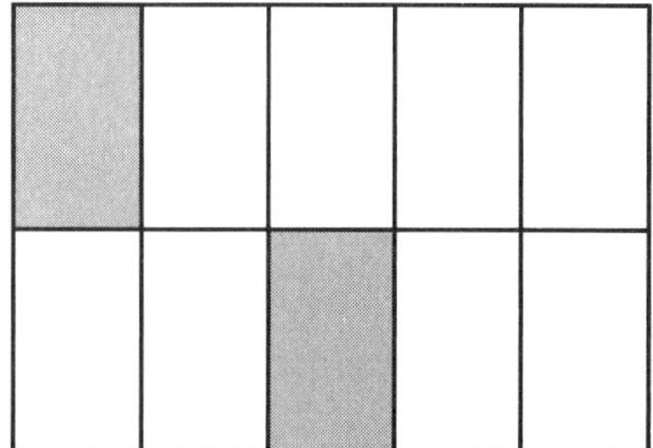

What fraction shows the shaded parts?

Is this fraction closer to 0, $\frac{1}{2}$, or 1?

Patterns

TAKS Objective 1 TEKS 2.5B

Show what comes next in this pattern.

659, 559, 459, ____, ____

Number of the Day

TAKS Objective 1 TEKS 2.7A

6

Name a classroom object that has at least 6 vertices.

Numerical Fluency

TAKS Objective 1 TEKS 2.1C

Use >, <, or = to compare.

$40 + 6 \bigcirc 60 + 4$

$600 + 20 \bigcirc 600 + 24$

$800 + 80 + 1 \bigcirc 800 + 10 + 8$

Problem Solving: Use a Picture

TAKS Objective 3
TEKS 2.2A, 2.12C

Use the picture. Color to solve the problem.

1. Max has 6 soccer cards. He gives 4 to Rosie. What fraction of the cards does Max give to Rosie?

_______ of the cards

2. Patsy has 4 shells. She gives 1 shell to Lewis. What fraction of the shells does Patsy have left?

_______ of the shells

3. Mrs. Wells cut an apple pie into 8 pieces. The children eat 6 pieces. What fraction of the pie is left?

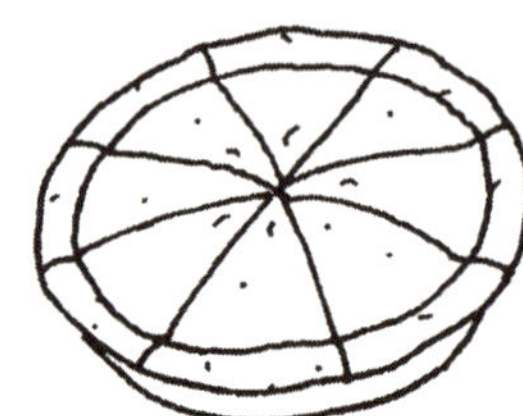

_______ of the pie

Math Journal **Writing and Reasoning** Write your problem about a sandwich cut into four pieces.

____

Circle Time

Problem of the Day

TAKS Objective 1 TEKS 2.2A

Fran ate 2 slices of the pizza.

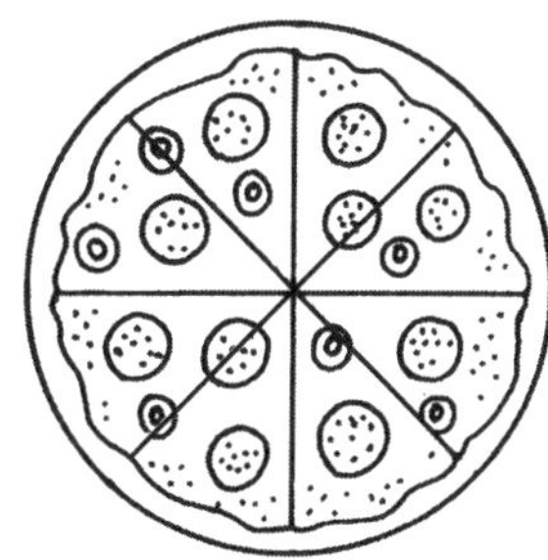

What fraction of the pizza did Fran eat?

Number Sense

TAKS Objective 1 TEKS 2.1A

Use base value blocks to show 342.

Word of the Day

TAKS Objective 1 TEKS 2.7B

cylinder

Find an object in your classroom that is shaped like a cylinder.

Numerical Fluency

TAKS Objective 1 TEKS 2.2C

What fraction shows the shaded part?

Is the fraction closer to 0, $\frac{1}{2}$ or 1?

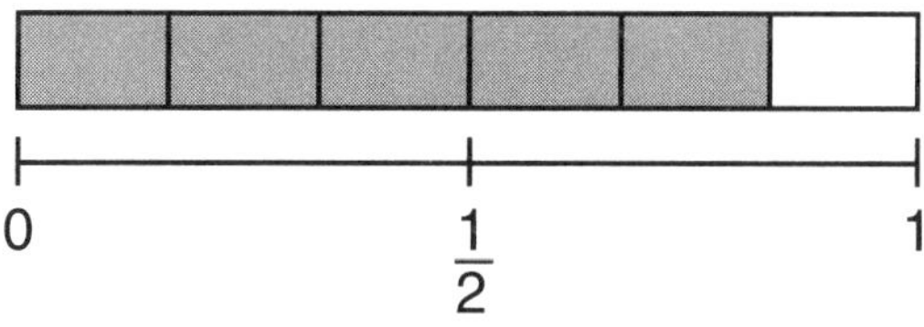

Model Fractions

TAKS Objective 1
TEKS 2.2B

Model with ◯. Write a fraction for each color.

1.

_____ black _____ gray

2.
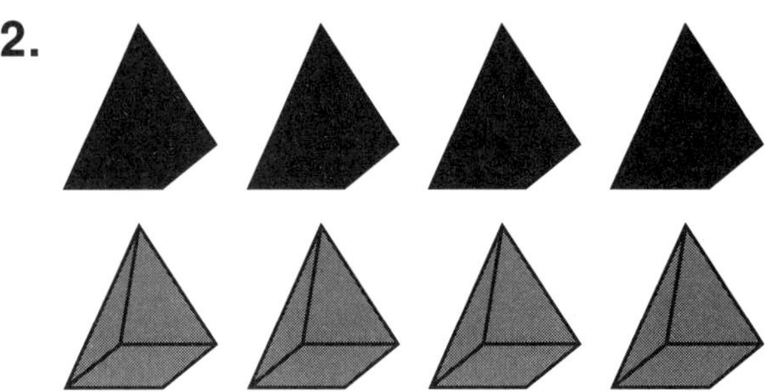

_____ black _____ gray

3.
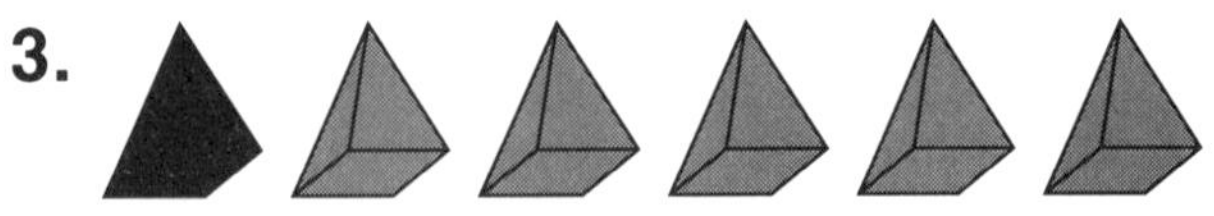

_____ black _____ gray

4.
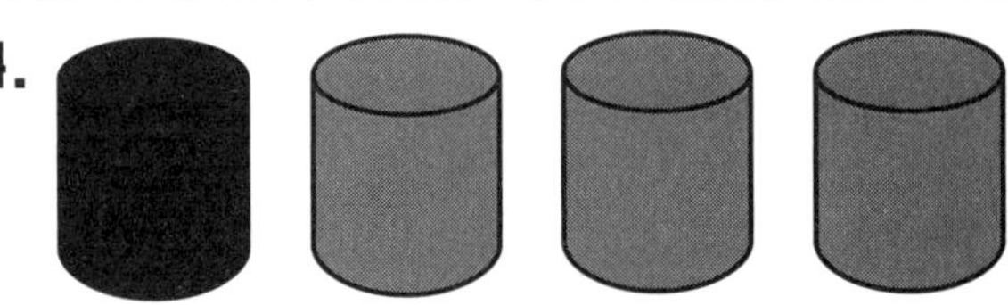

_____ black _____ gray

5.
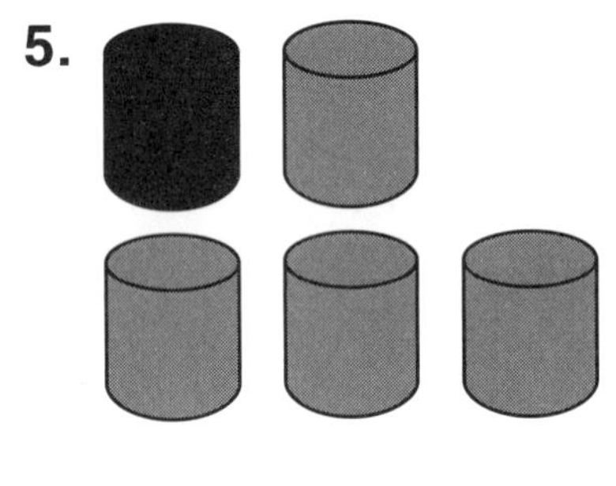

_____ black _____ gray

6.
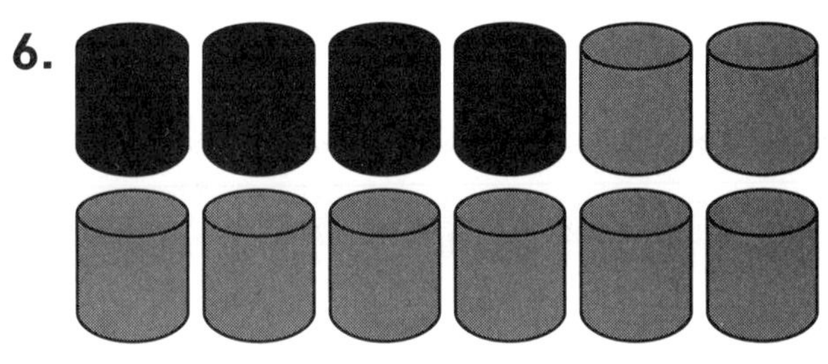

_____ black _____ gray

Writing and Reasoning There are 8 cylinders. $\frac{2}{8}$ of them are black. The rest are gray cylinders. What fraction of the set is gray? How do you know?

____

____

Name ______________________ Date ____________

Circle Time

Problem of the Day

TAKS Objective 1 TEKS 2.2B

Rebecca draws 6 apples. She colors 4 of them green and the reost red. Write the fraction that shows the number

of red apples. ________

Operations

TAKS Objective 1 TEKS 2.3A

Add. Then subtract.

7 + 5 = ______

13 − 5 = ______

13 − 7 = ______

Number of the Day

TAKS Objective 1 TEKS 2.1C

169

Find page 169 in your math book. Which pages come just before and just after page 169?

Numerical Fluency

TAKS Objective 1 TEKS 2.2A

Write the fraction for the shaded part.

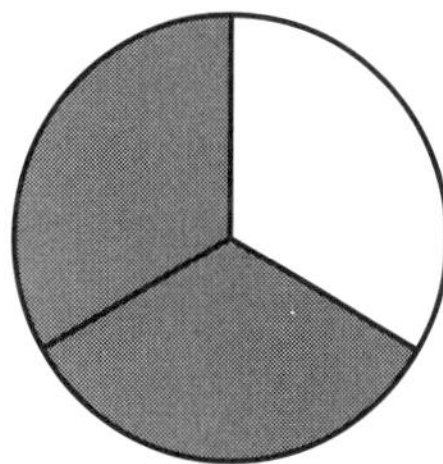

Name ______________________ Date ____________

Fractions of a Set

TAKS Objective 1
TEKS 2.2B

Write a fraction for each color.

1.	What fraction of the peppers is gray? What fraction of the peppers is black?	_____ gray peppers _____ black peppers
2.	What fraction of the beans is white? What fraction of the beans is black?	_____ white beans _____ black beans
3.	What fraction of the squash is gray? What fraction of the squash is white?	_____ gray squash _____ white squash
4.	What fraction of the pears is gray? What fraction of the pears is black?	_____ gray pears _____ black pears

Math Journal **Writing and Reasoning** How do you figure out the bottom number of each fraction?

____

Circle Time

Problem of the Day

TAKS Objective 1 TEKS 2.2B

Andrea has 5 marbles. 3 of the marbles are blue. The rest are green. Write a fraction for each color.

________ ________

Algebraic Thinking

TAKS Objective 1 TEKS 2.3A

Write the facts family for 11, 6, and 17.

Word of the Day

TAKS Objective 1 TEKS 2.13A

regrouping

Write an addition problem that requires regrouping.

Numerical Fluency

TAKS Objective 1 TEKS 2.2B

What fraction of the triangles is shaded?

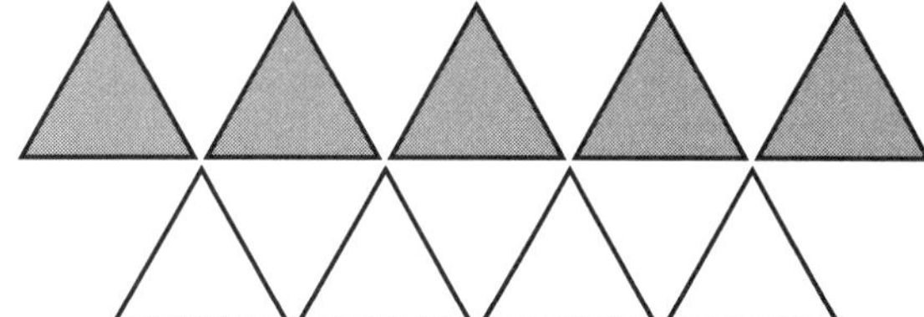

Name ______________________ Date ____________

Use Fractions

TAKS Objective 1
TEKS 2.2B

1. Color $\frac{2}{3}$ of the hats.

2. Color $\frac{5}{6}$ of the shoes.

3. Color $\frac{3}{8}$ of the socks.

4. Color $\frac{3}{4}$ of the shirts.

Math Journal **Writing and Reasoning** Draw 8 triangles. Then color in $\frac{1}{4}$, $\frac{1}{2}$, or $\frac{3}{4}$. Tell how many you colored, and how you know.

____

Circle Time

Problem of the Day

TAKS Objective 1 TEKS 2.2B

Color $\frac{3}{5}$ of the apples.

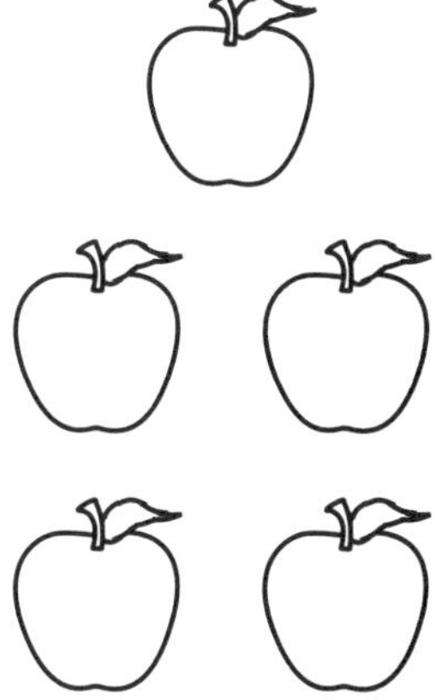

Operations

TAKS Objective 1 TEKS 2.12A

There are 28 students in the class. 15 are girls.
8 students wear glasses. Write a number sentence to show how many students are boys.

______ ◯ ______ ◯ ______

Calendar Activity

TAKS Objective 1 TEKS 2.3B

Subtract today's date from the last day of the month.
How many days are left in the month?

Numerical Fluency

TAKS Objective 1 TEKS 2.2B

What fraction of the squares is shaded?

Fractions of a Group

TAKS Objective 1
TEKS 2.2B

Color to show each fraction.
Write the number.

1. $\frac{1}{4}$

$\frac{1}{4}$ of 8 is ______.

2. $\frac{3}{5}$

$\frac{3}{5}$ of 10 is ______.

3. $\frac{1}{2}$

$\frac{1}{2}$ of 8 is ______.

4. $\frac{1}{3}$

$\frac{1}{3}$ of 12 is ______.

5. $\frac{1}{3}$

$\frac{1}{3}$ of 6 is ______.

6. $\frac{2}{3}$

$\frac{2}{3}$ of 6 is ______.

Math Journal **Writing and Reasoning** What does the bottom number of the fraction tell you when you are finding the fractional part of a group?

____

Circle Time

Problem of the Day

TAKS Objective 1 TEKS 2.2B

What is $\frac{3}{12}$ of 12?

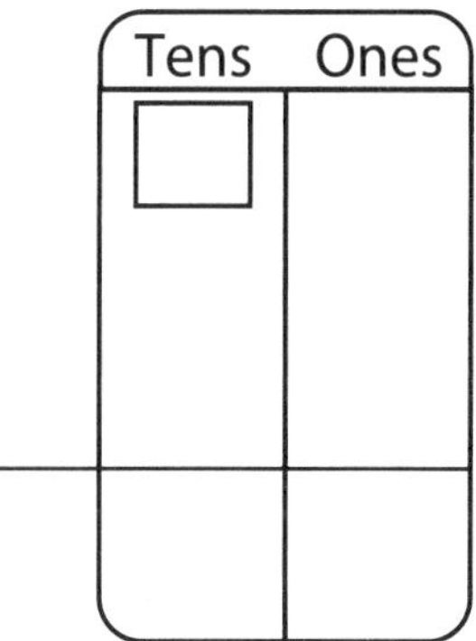

$\frac{3}{12}$ of 12 = ______

Operations

TAKS Objective 1 TEKS 2.3C

Rewrite the addends. Add.

74 + 18

Tens	Ones

Number of the Day

TAKS Objective 1 TEKS 2.1A, 2.1B

78

Show the number 78 using words and pictures.

Numerical Fluency

TAKS Objective 1 TEKS 2.2B

What fraction of the circles is shaded?

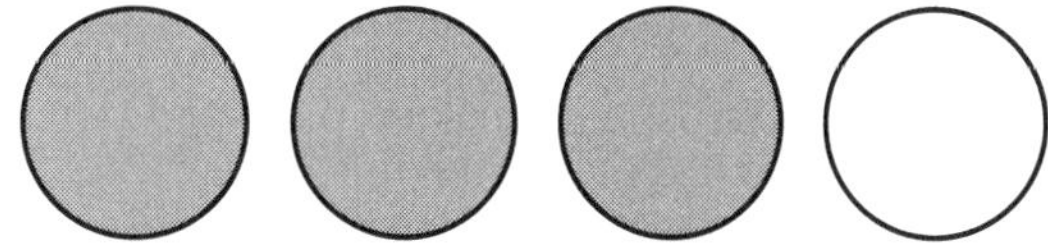

Problem Solving: Act it Out

TAKS Objective 1
TEKS 2.2B, 2.12C

You can use models or information in a picture to solve a problem.

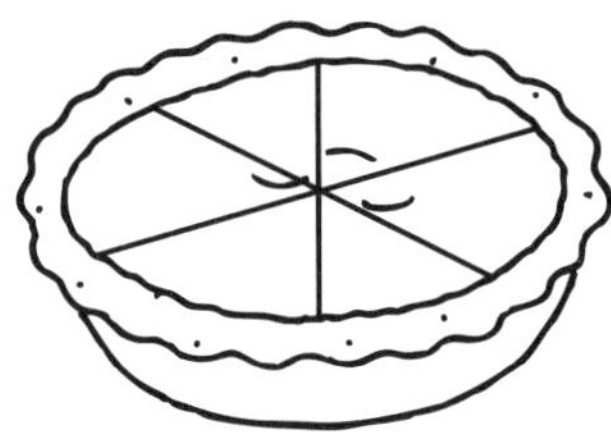

Use the picture to solve problems 1 and 2.

Draw or write to explain.

1. Nick gives 2 slices of pie to his sister. What fraction of the pie does he give her?

   ______ pie

2. Nick eats $\frac{2}{6}$ of a pie. Joe eats $\frac{3}{6}$ of that pie. Who eats more pie?

   ______ eats more

Writing and Reasoning Which is more, $\frac{1}{3}$ or $\frac{2}{6}$? Tell why.

____

____

____

Circle Time

Problem of the Day

TAKS Objective 1 TEKS 2.2B

Tim ate $\frac{6}{9}$ of the strawberries on the plate below.

How many strawberries did Tim eat?

Money

TAKS Objective 1 TEKS 2.3D

Count on to find the value of the coins.

Number of the Day

TAKS Objective 1 TEKS 2.3A

11

Write 5 number sentences using the number 11.

Facts Practice

TAKS Objective 1 TEKS 2.3A

Subtract.

12 − 6 = ______

13 − 6 = ______

18 − 8 = ______

18 − 9 = ______

Exploring Multiplication

TAKS Objectives 1, 2
TEKS 2.4A

Use Workmat I and counters.

Make equal groups with counters. Complete the addition sentence.

	Number of Equal Groups	Number in Each Group	How Many in All?
1.	3	2	____ + ____ + ____ = ____
2.	7	5	____ + ____ + ____ + ____ + ____ + ____ + ____ = ____
3.	5	4	____ + ____ + ____ + ____ + ____ = ____
4.	4	3	____ + ____ + ____ + ____ = ____

Writing and Reasoning

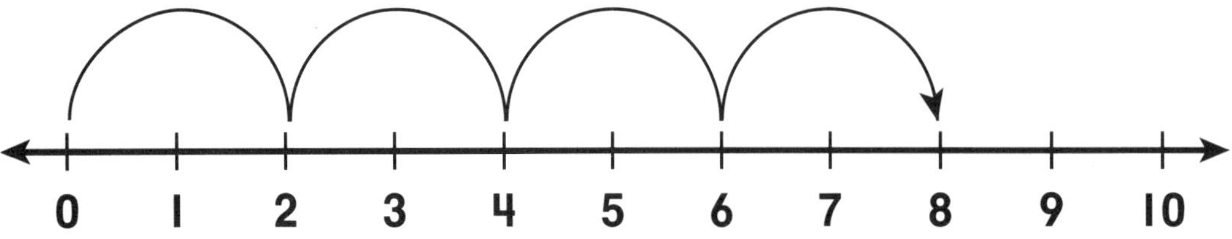

Describe the number sentence that the number line shows.

____

Circle Time

Problem of the Day

TAKS Objective 1 TEKS 2.4A

Ms. Wong has 3 bags of apples.
There are 5 apples in each bag.
How many equal groups?
How many in each group?
How many apples in all?

Operations

TAKS Objective 1 TEKS 2.3B

Add.

$$\begin{array}{r} 44 \\ +27 \\ \hline \end{array}$$

Word of the Day

TAKS Objective 1 TEKS 2.2A, 2.2B

fractions

Write 3 fractions and use drawings to show the fractions.

Facts Practice

TAKS Objective 1 TEKS 2.4A

Add.

$8 + 4 + 2 =$ _____

$9 + 6 + 1 =$ _____

$8 + 4 + 8 =$ _____

$7 + 3 + 7 =$ _____

Repeated Addition and Multiplication

TAKS Objective 1
TEKS 2.4A

Find the sum. Then find the product.

1. 4 groups of 2

$2 + 2 + 2 + 2 =$ ______

$4 \times 2 =$ ______

2. 2 groups of 2

$2 + 2 =$ ______

$2 \times 2 =$ ______

3. 3 groups of 5

$5 + 5 + 5 =$ ______

$3 \times 5 =$ ______

4. 4 groups of 5

$5 + 5 + 5 + 5 =$ ______

$4 \times 5 =$ ______

Multiply.

5. $4 \times 3 =$ ______
6. $1 \times 2 =$ ______
7. $4 \times 4 =$ ______
8. $0 \times 5 =$ ______
9. $2 \times 4 =$ ______
10. $5 \times 3 =$ ______

Math Journal **Writing and Reasoning** Write this number sentence in words. $0 \times 5 = 0$

____

Circle Time

Problem of the Day

TAKS Objective 1 TEKS 2.4A

Robin has 3 toy cars. Each toy car has 4 wheels.
How many wheels are there in all?

Algebraic Thinking

TAKS Objective 1 TEKS 2.3A

What way would you choose to add $48 + 36 + 2$?

What is the sum?

____

____

Calendar Activity

TAKS Objective 1 TEKS 2.4A

What days are on the weekend?
How many weekends are there in this month?

Facts Practice

TAKS Objective 1 TEKS 2.4A

Circle the picture that best represents
3×5 apples.

Skip Count to Multiply

TAKS Objective 1
TEKS 2.4A

Draw ants. Skip count. Then find the product.

1. 2 groups of 4 ants

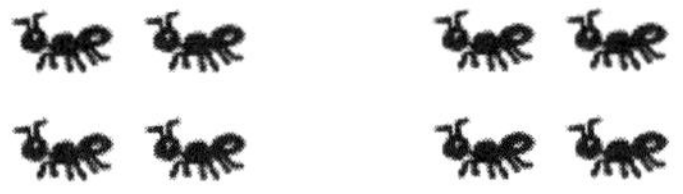

$2 \times 4 =$ ______ ants in all

2. 3 groups of 5 ants

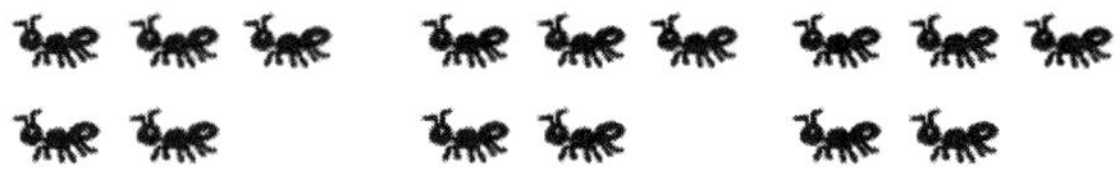

$3 \times 5 =$ ______ ants in all

3. 3 groups of 3

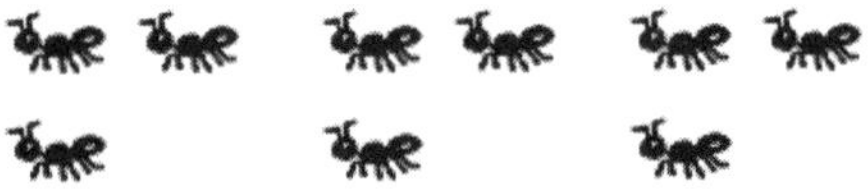

$3 \times 3 =$ ______ ants in all

4. 4 groups of 2

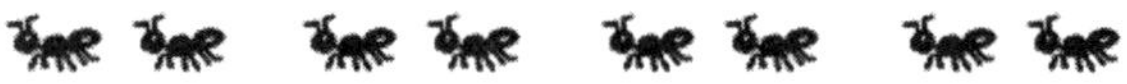

$4 \times 2 =$ ______ ants in all

5. 2 groups of 10 ants

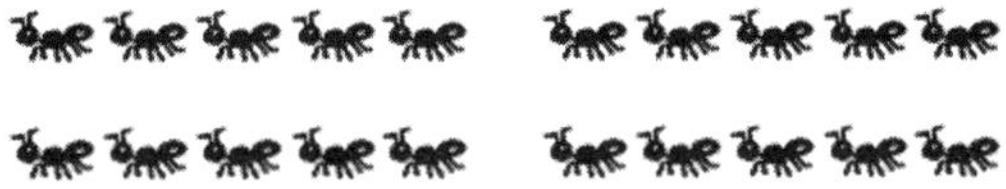

$2 \times 10 =$ ______ ants in all

6. 3 groups of 4 ants

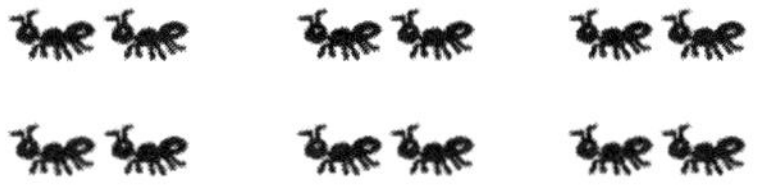

$3 \times 4 =$ ______ ants in all

Math Journal **Writing and Reasoning** Write the multiplication sentence that tells about this picture. Then write the information in words.

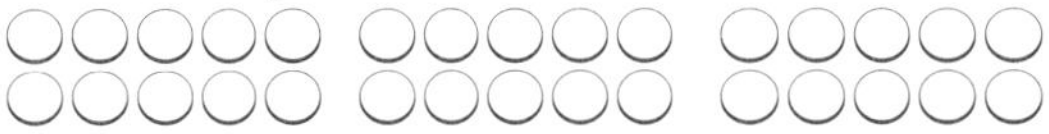

____

____

Name ______________________ Date ____________

Circle Time

Problem of the Day

TAKS Objective 1 TEKS 2.4A

Rosa has 6 dimes. How much money does she have?

Operations

TAKS Objective 1 TEKS 2.3C

Choose a way to add. Add. Explain the way you found the sum.

$$26 + 64 =$$

Number of the Day

TAKS Objective 1 TEKS 2.1A

233

Show the number 233 using place value blocks.

Facts Practice

TAKS Objective 1 TEKS 2.4A

Circle the picture that best represents 2 × 7 cherries.

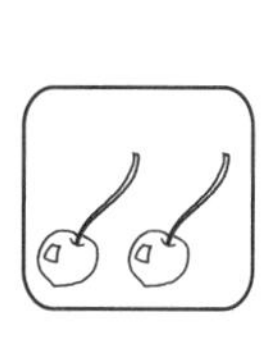
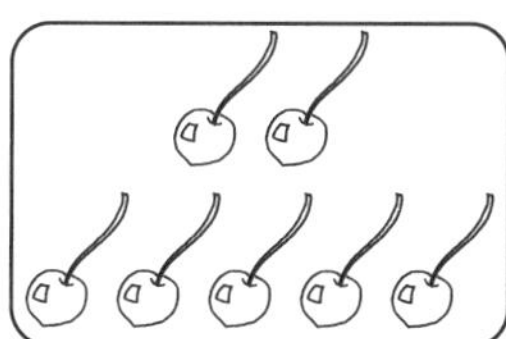

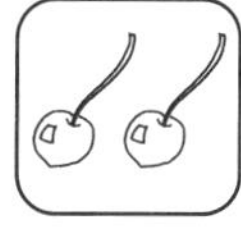
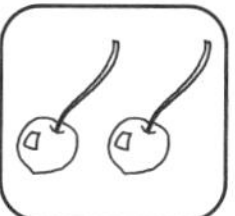

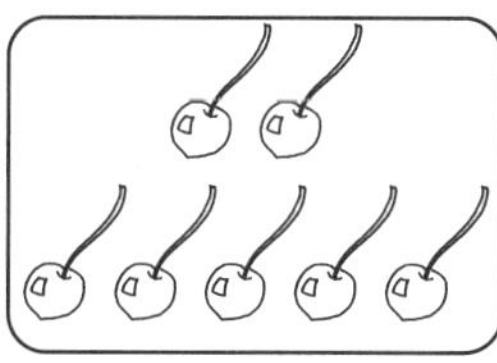
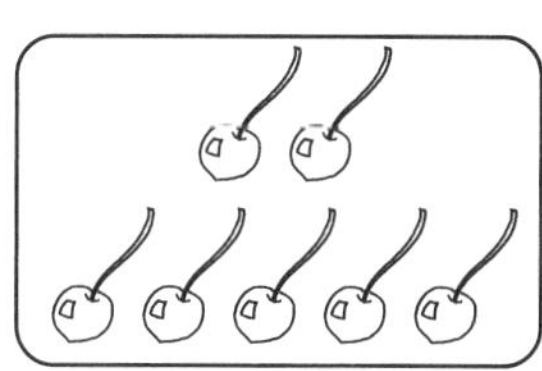

Draw a Picture

TAKS Objectives 1, 6
TEKS 2.4A, 2.12B

Sometimes you can draw a picture to solve a problem. Solve each problem. Draw a picture to help you.

Draw or write to explain.

1. Tanya has 3 friends at camp. Each friend sends her 3 letters. How many letters does she get?

Think
Should I draw friends or letters?

_______________ letters

2. Rashid did 10 math problems every day. How many math problems did he do in 3 days?

Think
How many problems did he do each day? How many days?

_______________ problems

3. There are 7 boats. Each boat has 2 sails. How many sails are there in all?

_______________ sails

Math Journal **Writing and Reasoning** Write a number sentence that shows 2 groups of 6. Explain.

____

____

Circle Time

Problem of the Day

TAKS Objective 1 TEKS 2.4A

Ethan puts 3 goldfish in each bowl. He has 2 bowls.
How many goldfish does he have in all?

Money

TAKS Objective 1 TEKS 2.4A

Skip count. Then find the product.

_____ _____ _____ _____ _____ _____

$6 \times 5 =$ _____

Word of the Day

TAKS Objective 1 TEKS 2.7A

faces

How many faces does a number cube have?

Facts Practice

TAKS Objective 1 TEKS 2.4A

Circle the picture that best represents 2×5 circles.

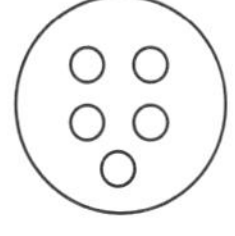
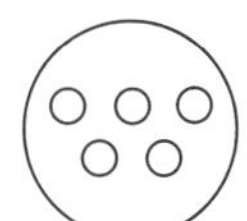

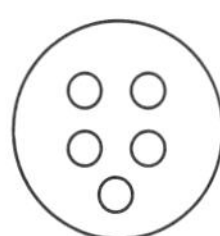

Name ______________________ Date ____________

Use a Pattern

TAKS Objective 2
TEKS 2.6A

Use a pattern to complete the table.
Write the multiplication sentence to solve.

Think
How many chapters each night?

1. Carmen reads 8 chapters every night. How many chapters does she read in 4 nights?

______ × ______ = ______

Night	1	2	3	4
	8	16		

2. The toy factory makes 20 teddy bears a day. How many teddy bears do they make in 3 days?

______ × ______ = ______

Day	1	2	3
Teddy Bears	20		

3. Everyone at the party ate 2 tacos. If there were 8 people at the party, how many tacos were eaten?

	1	2	3	4	5	6	7	8
Tacos	2							

______ × ______ = ______

Math Journal **Writing and Reasoning** How does making a table help you solve multiplication problems?

____

____

____

Name ______________________ Date ____________

Circle Time

Problem of the Day

Objective 1 TEKS 2.6A

Gina has seven pairs of gardening gloves.

Fill the table.

Pairs	1	2	3	4	5	6	7
Gloves	2	4	6				

How many is 7×2?

Number Sense

Objective 1 TEKS 2.1

Circle another way to show the number: two hundred eleven

20011   2011   211

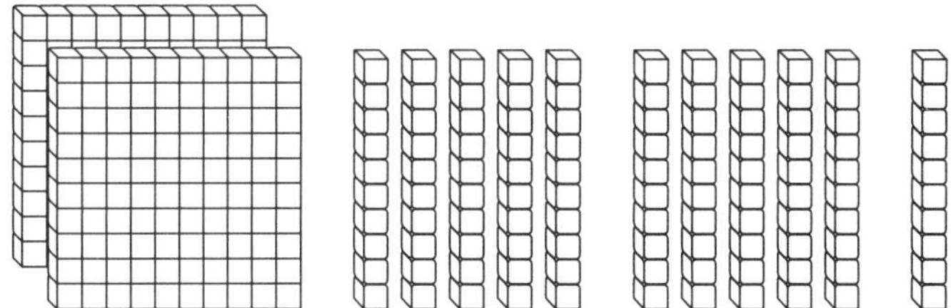

Number of the Day

Objective 1 TEKS 2.7A

5

Name a solid that has 5 faces.

Facts Practice

Objective 1 TEKS 2.4A

Circle the picture that best represents 1×9 circles.

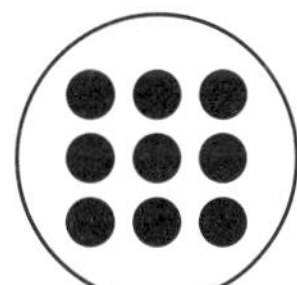

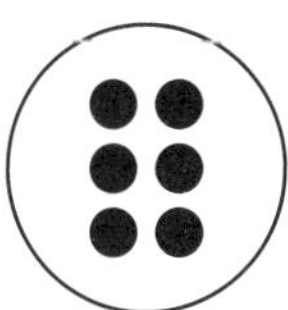

Share Equally

TAKS Objectives 1, 2
TEKS 2.4B

Use counters.
Draw dots to show the number in each group.
Write how many are in each group.

1. 6 counters 3 groups	●●	●●	●●	$6 \div 3 =$ ____ ____ in each group
2. 8 counters 2 groups		$8 \div 2 =$ ____ ____ in each group
3. 15 counters 5 groups		$15 \div 5 =$ ____ ____ in each group
4. 14 counters 7 groups		$14 \div 7 =$ ____ ____ in each group

Math Journal **Writing and Reasoning** There are 15 pencils to put in 3 boxes. Tell how Bob can put the same number in each box. How many pencils will be in each box?

____

____

____

____

Name ______________________ Date ____________

Circle Time

Problem of the Day

TAKS Objective 1 TEKS 2.4B

Nancy has 8 stamps. She divides them into 4 equal groups. How many stamps are in each group?

Geometry

TAKS Objective 1 TEKS 2.7A

How many faces, edges and vertices does a rectangular prism have?

_______ faces

_______ edges

_______ vertices

Word of the Day

TAKS Objective 1 TEKS 2.6C, 2.7A

squares, rectangles

Create a pattern using squares and rectangles.

Facts Practice

TAKS Objective 1 TEKS 2.3A

Add.

12 + 6 = ______

8 + 7 = ______

9 + 6 = ______

4 + 16 = ______

Equal Groups of 2

TAKS Objectives 1, 2
TEKS 2.4B

Circle equal groups of 2.
Divide. Write the number of groups.

1.
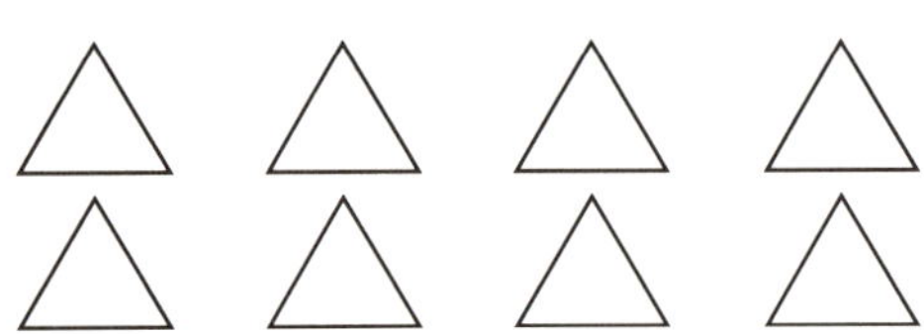

$8 \div 2 =$ _____ groups.

2.
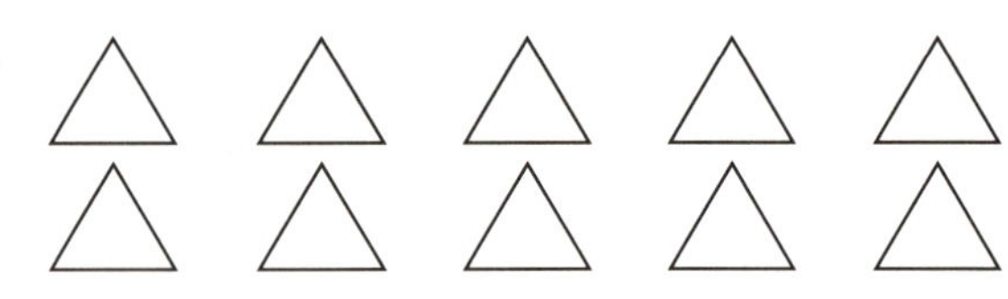

$10 \div 2 =$ _____ groups.

Use counters.

	Start with this many.	Number in each group.	Divide. How many groups?
3.	18	2	$18 \div 2 =$ _____ groups.
4.	30	2	$30 \div 2 =$ _____ groups.
5.	14	2	$14 \div 2 =$ _____ groups.
6.	22	2	$22 \div 2 =$ _____ groups.

Writing and Reasoning If Alex starts with 6 counters, can he make equal groups of 9? Why or why not?

____

____

____

Circle Time

Problem of the Day

TAKS Objective 1 TEKS 2.4B

Circle equal groups of 2.

Divide.

Write the number of groups.

$10 \div 2 =$ ______ groups

Measurement

TAKS Objective 1 TEKS 2.9C

Circle the object that holds the most.

a spoon

a glass

a big bottle of soda

a fish aquarium

Calendar Activity

TAKS Objective 1 TEKS 2.4B

A school week is made up of 5 days. How many full school weeks are there in this month?

Facts Practice

TAKS Objective 1 TEKS 2.3A

Subtract.

$16 - 7 =$ ______

$14 - 10 =$ ______

$18 - 9 =$ ______

$20 - 11 =$ ______

Name ____________________ Date ____________

Equal Groups of 5

TAKS Objectives 1, 2
TEKS 2.4B

You can subtract counters by groups of 5.
Use counters. Then write the division sentence.

	Start with this many.	Number in each group	Solve. How many groups?
1.	30	5	30 ÷ 5 = _____
2.	25	5	25 ÷ 5 = _____
3.	10	5	10 ÷ 5 = _____
4.	15	5	15 ÷ 5 = _____
5.	35	5	35 ÷ 5 = _____

Use counters to model.
Write the division sentence.

6. Start with 20 counters. Make 5 equal groups.

_____ ÷ _____ = _____

7. Start with 40 counters. Make 8 equal groups.

_____ ÷ _____ = _____

Math Journal **Writing and Reasoning** There are 20 flowers to plant in 4 rows. Stella plants the same number in each row. How many are in each row? _____ flowers. Explain.

____

____

Circle Time

Problem of the Day

Objective 1 TEKS 2.4B

There are 35 ants altogether. They are in groups of 5. How many groups are there?

Operations

Objective 1 TEKS 2.3A

Use Workmat 1 with counters.

Subtract.

$$\begin{array}{r} 17 \\ -17 \\ \hline \end{array}$$

$17 - 17 =$ ______

Word of the Day

Objective 1 TEKS 2.4A

multiplication sentence

Write 1 example of a multiplication sentence.

Facts Practice

Objective 1 TEKS 2.4B

There are 6 bees altogether. They are in groups of 2. How many groups are there?

$6 \div 2 =$ ______ groups

Name ______________________ Date ____________

Use Repeated Subtraction

TAKS Objectives 1, 2
TEKS 2.4A

Subtract by 5s to divide by 5. Use the number line on Workmat 4 to divide.

1. 25 ÷ 5 = 5
2. 15 ÷ 5 = ______
3. 45 ÷ 5 = ______
4. 5 ÷ 5 = ______
5. 30 ÷ 5 = ______
6. 20 ÷ 5 = ______
7. 40 ÷ 5 = ______
8. 10 ÷ 5 = ______
9. 35 ÷ 5 = ______
10. 50 ÷ 5 = ______

Subtract by 2s to divide by 2. Use the number line on Workmat 4 to divide.

11. 8 ÷ 2 = ______
12. 12 ÷ 2 = ______
13. 4 ÷ 2 = ______
14. 14 ÷ 2 = ______
15. 16 ÷ 2 = ______
16. 6 ÷ 2 = ______
17. 20 ÷ 2 = ______
18. 4 ÷ 2 = ______
19. 18 ÷ 2 = ______
20. 22 ÷ 2 = ______

Writing and Reasoning Tell how you would solve the division sentence 10 ÷ 5.

____

____

Name ______________________ Date __________

Circle Time

Problem of the Day

TAKS Objective 1 TEKS 2.4B

Nadine puts 10 muffins in boxes. She puts 2 muffins in each box. How many boxes does Nadine have?

Money

TAKS Objective 1 TEKS 2.3D

A toy train is 95¢. Shawn has 3 quarters, 4 nickels, and 3 pennies. Does Shawn has enough money to buy the toy train?

Number of the Day

TAKS Objective 1 TEKS 2.1A, 2.1B

89

Show the number 89 using words and pictures.

Facts Practice

TAKS Objective 1 TEKS 2.4B

Subtract by 5s to divide by 5. Use the number line on Workmat 4 to divide.

$35 \div 5 =$ ______

$40 \div 5 =$ ______

$15 \div 5 =$ ______

$25 \div 5 =$ ______

Choose the Operation

TAKS Objective
TEKS 2.4A, 2.4B

Add, subtract, or multiply to solve.

1. Jamal's team scored 17 points in the first game and 18 points in the second game. How many points did they score in all?

   Think: Am I finding how many in all or am I comparing?

   Draw or write to explain.

   ________ ◯ ________ = ________

2. Each tank has 8 dolphins. If there are 3 tanks, how many dolphins are there?

   Think: How many groups are there? Are the groups equal?

   Draw or write to explain.

   ________ ◯ ________ = ________

3. 25 second-graders brought peanut butter sandwiches for lunch. 9 second-graders brought tuna fish sandwiches. How many more peanut butter sandwiches were there than tuna fish sandwiches?

   Draw or write to explain.

   ________ more peanut butter sandwiches

Math Journal **Writing and Reasoning** What operation did you decide to use for Problem 3? What words made you choose this operation?

____

____

Looking Ahead Activities

These activities will help you get ready for math next year.

Addition Puzzles

TEKS 2.3C and 2.12B; prepares for 3.3B and 3.14B

By yourself

In each puzzle, a shape stands for the same number each time it is used.
Add the boxes across and down to find sums.
Find the missing numbers in each puzzle below.
Tell what number each shape stands for.

1.

triangle	triangle	24
circle	15	____
25	27	

2.

hexagon	24	____
hexagon	cross	49
64	____	

3.

35	octagon	74
diamond	____	____
61	81	

4.

trapezoid	circle	61
51	____	70
____	32	

5.

star	48	____
____	star	40
40	63	

6.

____	rounded shape	79
18	rounded shape	41
____	46	

Objective: Use addition and subtraction to solve problems with two-digit numbers to complete puzzles.

Name ______________________ Date __________

Highest Number

TEKS 2.1A; prepares for 3.1A

With your partner

Materials: number cube labeled 1–6

- Player 1 tosses the number cube and writes the number in any place on the place value chart. Player 2 then takes a turn.
- Each player tosses the number cube 3 times. Once a number is written in the chart, it cannot be moved.
- The player who writes the greatest number earns 1 point. Circle the winner.
- Play 5 times. The player with the most points wins!

Player 1: ______________________ Player 2: ______________________

Round 1

Hundreds	Tens	Ones

Hundreds	Tens	Ones

Round 2

Hundreds	Tens	Ones

Hundreds	Tens	Ones

Round 3

Hundreds	Tens	Ones

Hundreds	Tens	Ones

Round 4

Hundreds	Tens	Ones

Hundreds	Tens	Ones

Round 5

Hundreds	Tens	Ones

Hundreds	Tens	Ones

Objective: Find the greatest 3-digit number using a number cube.

Name ______________________ Date ____________

Show Fractions

TEKS 2.2B; prepares for 3.2A

With your partner

Materials: two-color counters, crayons

You can write fractions to name parts of a set.

Use counters to model the fraction.
Draw to show the counters.

1. 2 out of 3 counters are red.
2. $\frac{3}{4}$ counters are yellow.
3. 5 out of 5 counters are yellow.
4. $\frac{1}{2}$ counters are red.
5. 4 out of 6 counters are red.
6. $\frac{5}{8}$ counters are yellow.

Work with your partner to show fractions of a set. Show a fraction of a set with counters. Draw to show the counters. Complete each sentence.

5. ________ out of ________ counters are red.
6. $\frac{\square}{\square}$ counters are yellow.

Objective: Use two-color counters to show fractions of a set.

Name ______________________ Date ____________

Looking Ahead
Activity 4

Patterns on a Hundred Chart

TEKS 2.5A; prepares for 3.6B

Use counting chips on the hundred chart to show each pattern.

With a small group

Materials: small counting chips

1	2	3	4	5	6	7	8	9	10
11	12	13	14	15	16	17	18	19	20
21	22	23	24	25	26	27	28	29	30
31	32	33	34	35	36	37	38	39	40
41	42	43	44	45	46	47	48	49	50
51	52	53	54	55	56	57	58	59	60
61	62	63	64	65	66	67	68	69	70
71	72	73	74	75	76	77	78	79	80
81	82	83	84	85	86	87	88	89	90
91	92	93	94	95	96	97	98	99	100

1. Skip count by 3. What pattern do you see?

____

____

2. Skip count by 4. What pattern do you see?

____

____

3. Skip count by 5. What pattern do you see?

____

____

4. Find another number with a skip counting pattern that is the same as the pattern for 2.

____

____

Objective: Find patterns in numbers on a hundred chart.

Name ______________________ Date ____________

Looking Ahead
Activity 5

Model Multiplication

TEKS 2.4A; prepares for 3.4A

With your partner

Materials: two-color counters, graph paper

You can use counters to make arrays.

Use counters and graph paper to show each array. Write the multiplication sentence.

1. 2 rows of 4

   ______ × ______ = ______

   4 rows of 2

   ______ × ______ = ______

2. 3 rows of 5

   ______ × ______ = ______

   ______ × ______ = ______

3. 3 rows of 2

   ______ × ______ = ______

   2 rows of 3

   ______ × ______ = ______

4. 5 rows of 4

   ______ × ______ = ______

   ______ × ______ = ______

5. Make an array with 12 counters. Can you make more than one array?

   ____

   ____

Objective: Model multiplication situations with arrays.

Name ______________________ Date ____________

Measure Length

TEKS 2.9A; prepares for 3.11A

You can estimate and measure length using paper clips.

With your partner
Materials: small paper clips

I inch is about I paper clip.
Estimate the length of the object in paper clips.
Then measure using paper clips.

	Object	Estimate	Measurement
I.	crayons	about ______ paper clips	about ______ paper clips
2.		about ______ paper clips	about ______ paper clips

Choose three objects. Estimate their lengths in inches.
Then measure.

	Object	Estimate	Measurement
3.		about ______ paper clips	about ______ paper clips
4.		about ______ paper clips	about ______ paper clips
5.		about ______ paper clips	about ______ paper clips

6. Which object is shortest? ______________________

Objective: Estimate and measure length in inches using concrete objects.

Name ______________________ Date ____________

Looking Ahead Activity 7

Measure Height

TEKS 2.9A; prepares for 3.11A

With your partner

You can estimate and measure length using your arm.

1 foot is about 1 

Estimate the length of the object in feet. Then measure using your .

	Object	Estimate	Measurement
1.		about ______ feet	about ______ feet
2.		about ______ feet	about ______ feet

Choose three objects. Estimate their lengths in feet. Then measure using your .

	Object	Estimate	Measurement
3.		about ______ feet	about ______ feet
4.		about ______ feet	about ______ feet
5.		about ______ feet	about ______ feet

6. Which object is shortest? ______________________

Objective: Estimate and measure length in feet using your forearm length.

Name ______________________ Date ____________

Finding the Area

TEKS 2.9B; prepares for 3.11C

You can find the area of a figure by covering it with square units.

With a small group

Materials: unit cubes

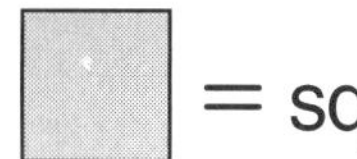

Cover each figure with square units.
Count how many square units.

1. Estimate: about ______ square units	2. Estimate: about ______ square units
3. Estimate: about ______ square units	4. Estimate: about ______ square units

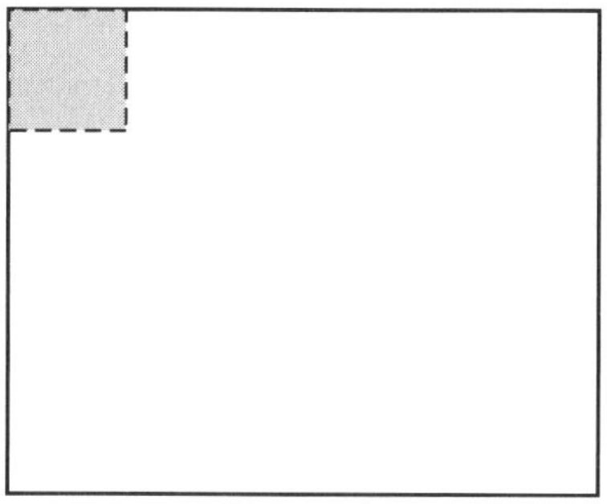

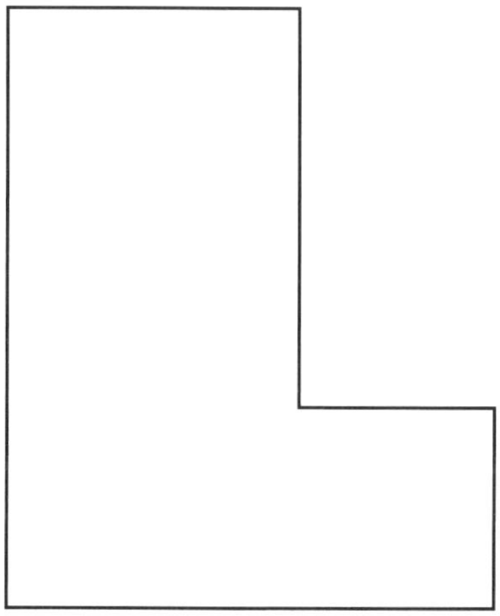

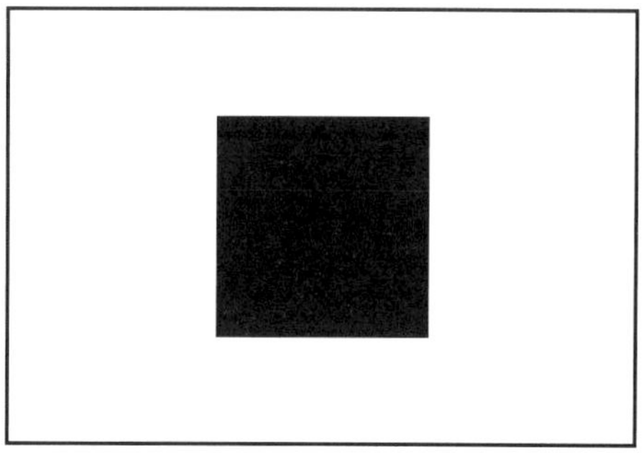

Objective: Use unit cubes to estimate the area of a figure.

Name ______________________ Date ____________

How Much Time?

TEKS 2.10C; prepares for 3.12B

With a partner

It takes about one second to raise your hand.	It takes about one minute to count slowly from 1 to 60.	It takes about one hour to go to the grocery store.
	1...2...3...4	

Think about the length of time.

Draw or write at least 3 things you do that take that long.

1. about one second

2. about one minute

3. about one hour

Objective: Name activities that take about one second, one minute, or one hour.

Name ______________________ Date __________

Describe with Measurements

TEKS 2.9A and 2.9D; prepares for 3.11A

You can use measurments to describe objects.
Choose four classroom objects.
Complete the chart for each object.
Trade descriptions with another pair and try to guess the object.

With a partner

Materials: classroom objects, paper clips

Object	How long is it?	How wide is it?	How tall is it?	Describe its weight
1.				
2.				
3.				
4.				

Objective: Describe classroom objects using length.

Name ______________________ Date ____________

Sort Two-Dimensional Figures

TEKS 2.7A; prepares for 3.9A

With your partner

Two-dimensional figures can be sorted by the number of sides and vertices they have.

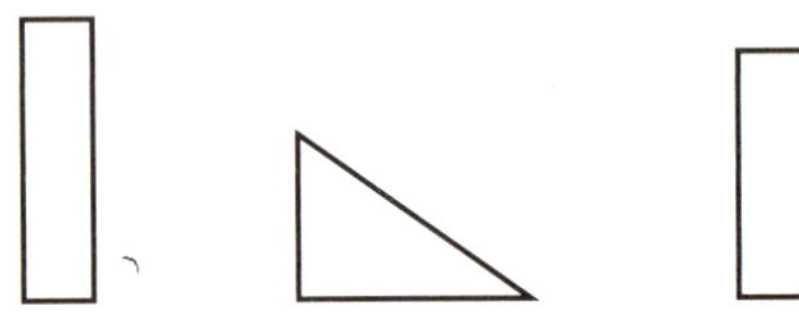
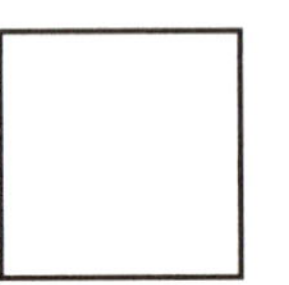

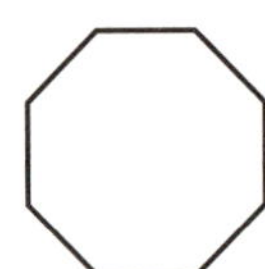

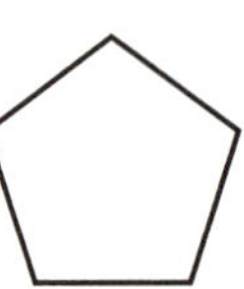

1. Sort the two-dimensional figures by the number of sides. Draw each figure in the Venn diagram.

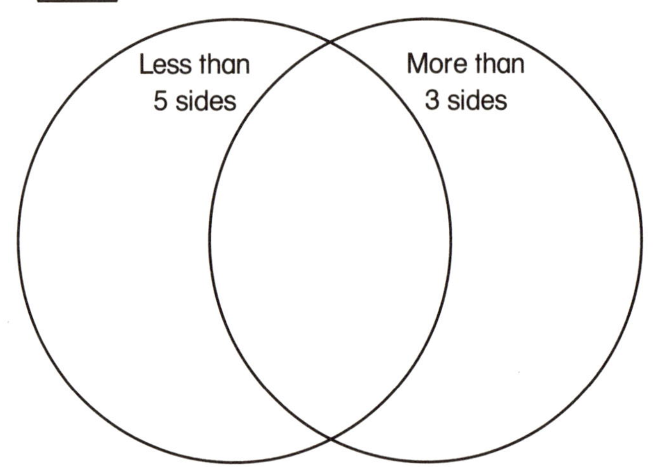

2. How many sides do the figures in the center part have?

____

3. Sort the two-dimensional figures by the number of vertices. Draw each figure in the Venn diagram.

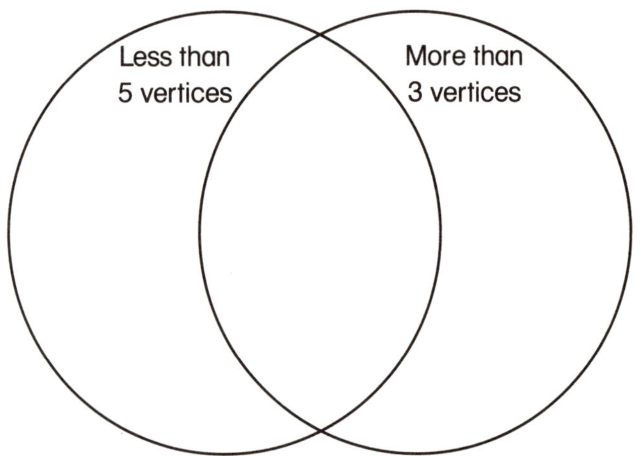

4. How many vertices do the figures in the center part have?

____

Objective: Sort two-dimensional figures using attributes.

Name ______________________ Date ____________

Build Two-Dimensional Figures

TEKS 2.7A; prepares for 3.9B and 3.9C

You can put pattern blocks together to make new figures.

With your group

Materials: pattern blocks

1. Outline the hexagon pattern block. Use other pattern blocks to make the hexagon. Draw as many different ways as you can find.

2. What other pattern blocks can be made from smaller pattern blocks? Find as many as you can and draw them in the space below.

Objective: Use pattern blocks to build two-dimensional figures.

Name ________________________ Date ______________

Tangrams

TEKS 2.7A; prepares for 3.9A

With your partner
Materials: tangram pieces

A tangram is a square cut into seven pieces.
Each piece is a two-dimensional figure.
Use all seven tangram pieces to make each figure below.
Draw lines in the figure to show how you solved the puzzle.

1.	2.

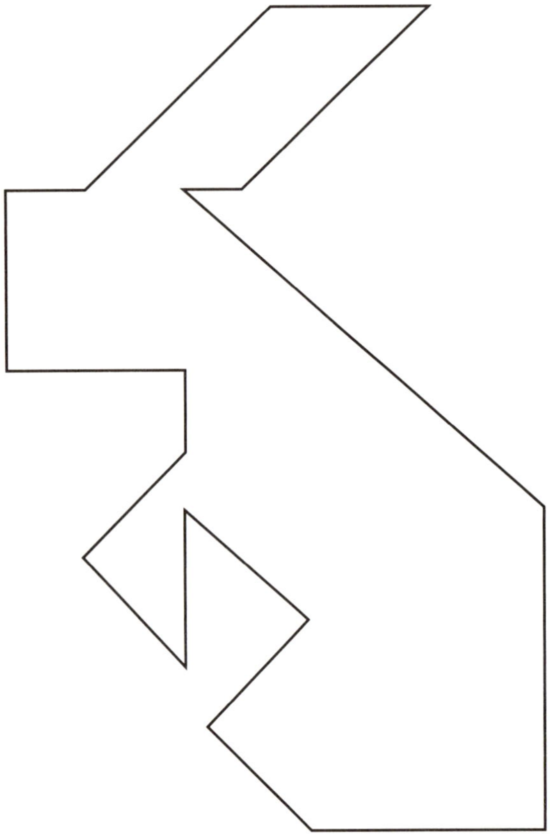

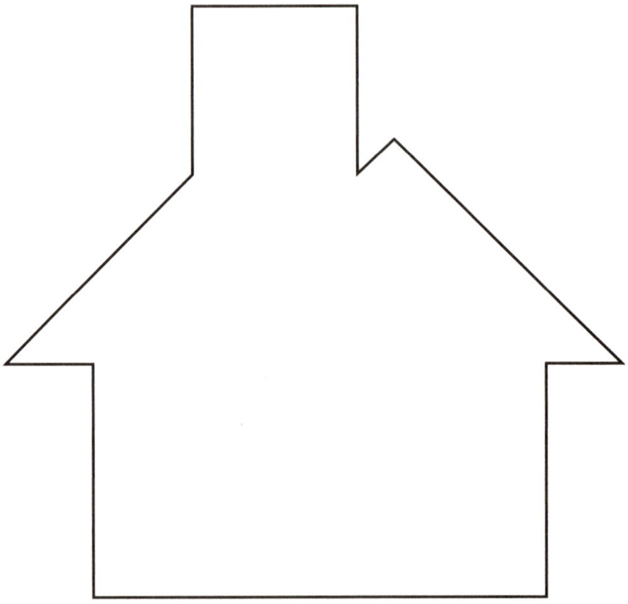

Objective: Use tangrams to build shapes.

Name ______________________ Date ____________

Mirror Designs

TEKS 2.7A; prepares for 3.9B and 3.9C

With your partner
Materials: pattern blocks

Some figures have two sides that match exactly.

Use pattern blocks to finish the design so both sides match exactly.

Trace the image.

1.	**2.**
3.	**4.**

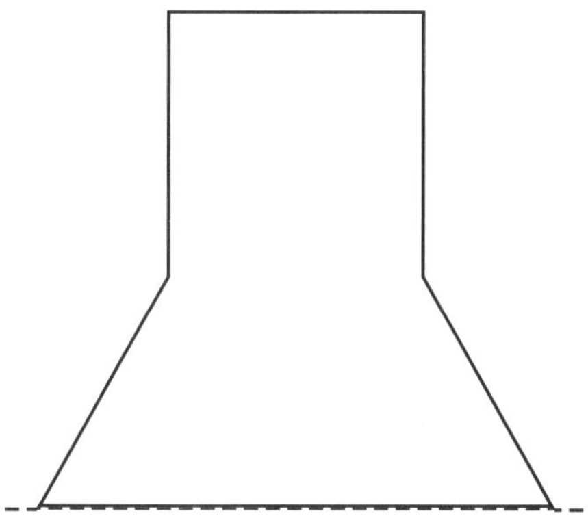

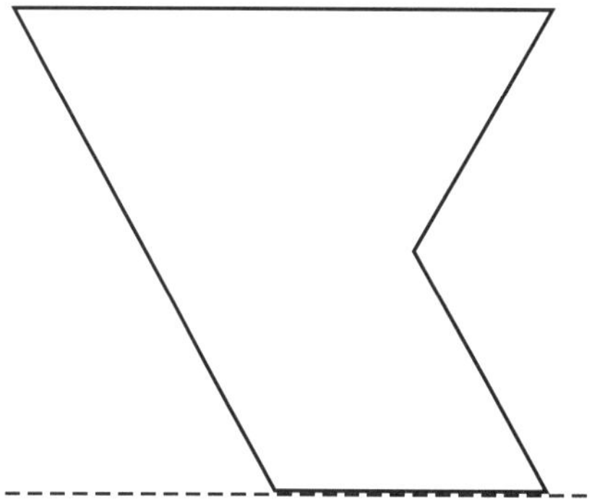

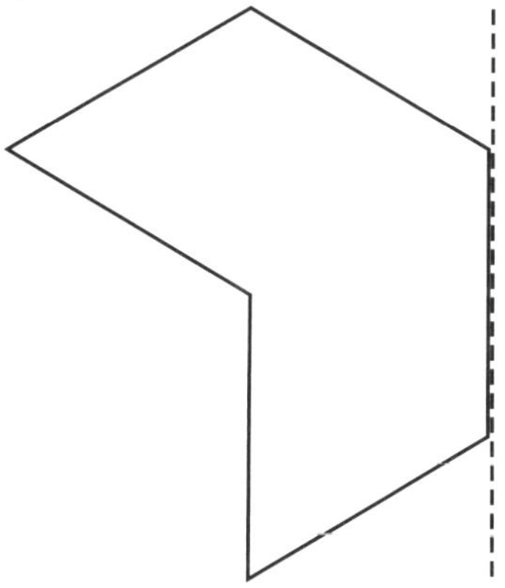

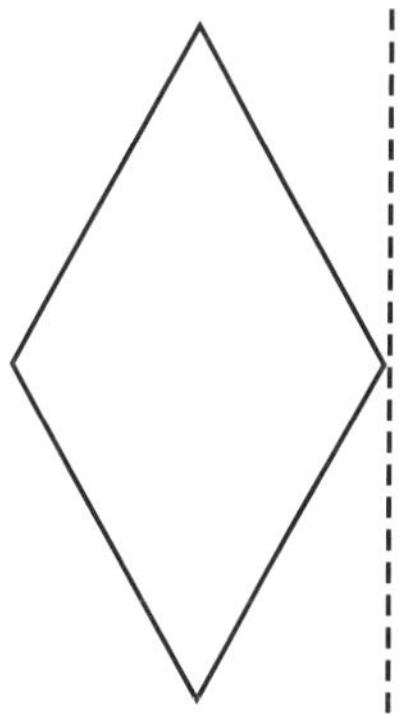

Objective: Use pattern blocks to make a mirror image of a design.

Name ______________________ Date ____________

Looking Ahead
Activity 15

More Mirror Designs

TEKS 2.7A; prepares for 3.9B and 3.9C

By yourself

Figures in real life can have line symmetry. Each of these objects has been folded in half. Do your best to draw the mirror image of the objects below to complete the drawings. The dashed line is a line of symmetry.

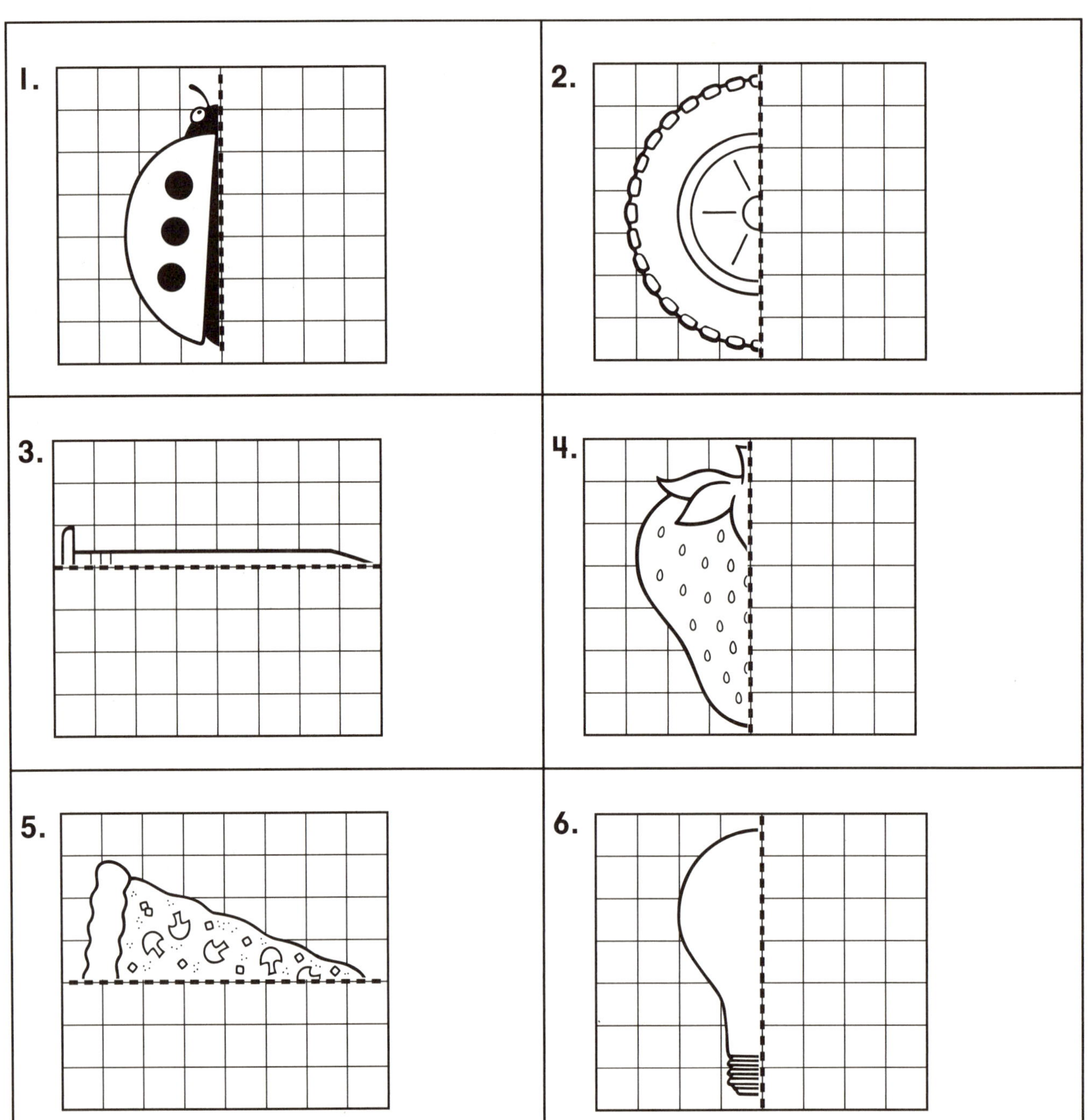

Objective: Draw a mirror design of an image on grid paper.

Name ______________________ Date ____________

Looking Ahead
Activity 16

Geometric Patterns

TEKS 2.6C; prepares for 3.6A

By yourself

A **repeating pattern** is one that repeats again and again.

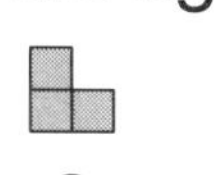
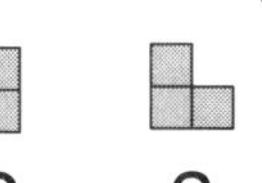
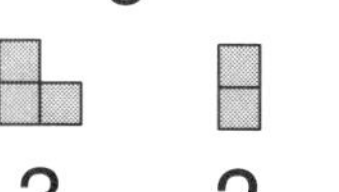
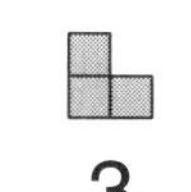

2 3 2 3 2 3

An **additive pattern** gets bigger in the same way again and again.

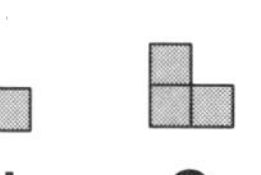
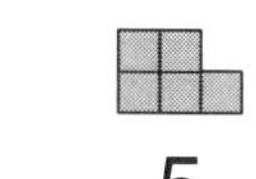
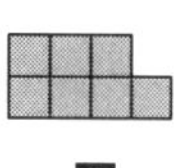

1 3 5 7

Draw the next picture to continue the pattern.
Write the numbers.
Tell if it is an additive or repeating pattern.

1.
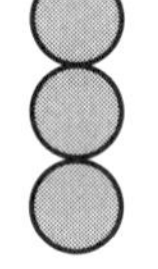
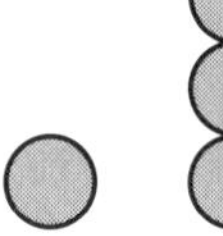
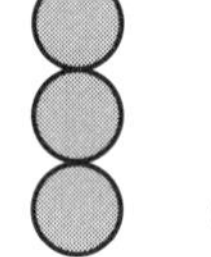
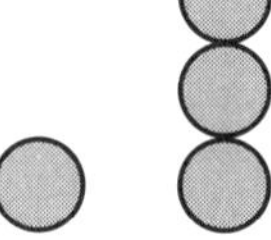
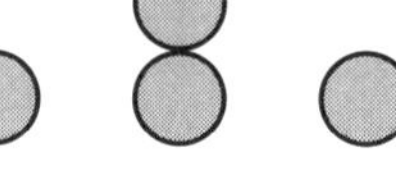

3 1 ___ ___ ___ ___ ______________ pattern

2.
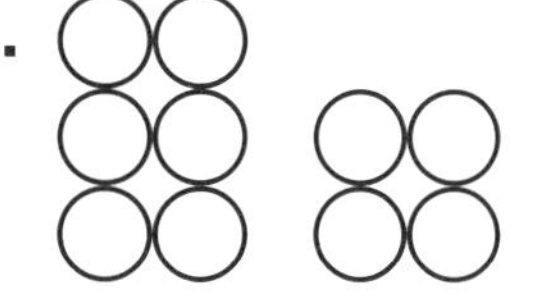

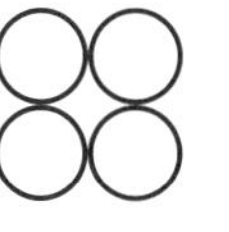

6 4 2 ___ ___ ___ ______________ pattern

3.
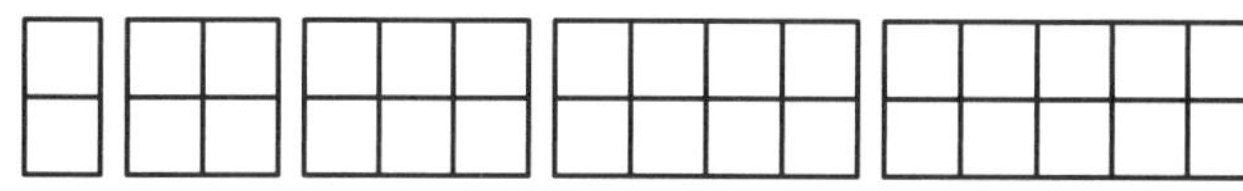

2 4 ___ ___ ___ ______________ pattern

Draw your own pattern.

4.

Objective: Create and extend geometric patterns.

Name ______________________ Date ____________

Looking Ahead Activity 17

Patterns on a Hundred Chart

TEKS 2.5A; prepares for 3.16A

By yourself

Write a rule from the board for each hundred chart. Color the numbers to show the rule.

1. Rule: ______________________

1	2	3	4	5	6	7	8	9	10
11	12	13	14	15	16	17	18	19	20
21	22	23	24	25	26	27	28	29	30
31	32	33	34	35	36	37	38	39	40
41	42	43	44	45	46	47	48	49	50
51	52	53	54	55	56	57	58	59	60
61	62	63	64	65	66	67	68	69	70
71	72	73	74	75	76	77	78	79	80
81	82	83	84	85	86	87	88	89	90
91	92	93	94	95	96	97	98	99	100

2. Rule: ______________________

1	2	3	4	5	6	7	8	9	10
11	12	13	14	15	16	17	18	19	20
21	22	23	24	25	26	27	28	29	30
31	32	33	34	35	36	37	38	39	40
41	42	43	44	45	46	47	48	49	50
51	52	53	54	55	56	57	58	59	60
61	62	63	64	65	66	67	68	69	70
71	72	73	74	75	76	77	78	79	80
81	82	83	84	85	86	87	88	89	90
91	92	93	94	95	96	97	98	99	100

Objective: Identify and show a rule on a hundred chart.

Name ______________________ Date ____________

Looking Ahead
Activity 18

Paired Numbers

TEKS 2.6A; prepares for 3.7A

By yourself

Write a table of paired numbers for each problem. The first one is started for you.

1. A tricycle has 3 wheels. How many wheels do 5 tricycles have?

Number of Tricycles	1	2	3	4	5
Number of Wheels	3	6			

__________ wheels

2. Each snowflake has 6 sides. How many sides do 5 snowflakes have?

Number of Snowflakes	1	2	3	4	5
Number of Sides					

__________ sides

3. A dragonfly has 4 wings. How many wings do 6 dragonflies have?

Number of Dragonflies	1	2	3	4	5	6
Number of Wings						

__________ wings

4. Pens are sold in packages of 5. How many pens are in 6 packages?

Number of Packages	1	2	3	4	5	6
Number of Pens						

__________ pens

Objective: Write a list of paired numbers based on real-life situations.

Name ____________________ Date ____________

Read a Graph

TEKS 2.11B; prepares for 3.13B

With your class

Rory makes a bar-type graph to show the number of drinks sold at his lemonade stand.

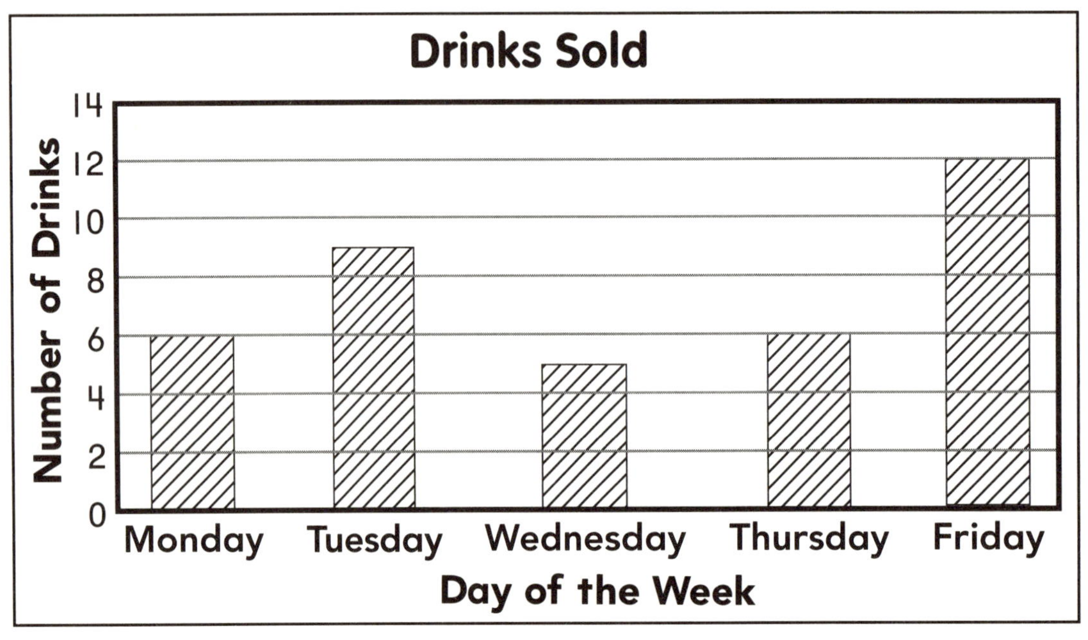

1. On which day is the least number of drinks sold?

____

2. How many drinks were sold on Tuesday?

____

3. How many drinks were sold on Monday and Tuesday in all?

____

4. How many more drinks were sold on Friday than on Wednesday?

____

5. Write your own question that can be answered using the graph.

____

____

Objective: Draw conclusions and answer questions using a bar-type graph.

Name ______________________ Date ____________

Looking Ahead
Activity 20

Make a Graph

TEKS 2.11A; prepares for 3.13A

With your partner

Take a survey using one of the questions on the board.
Ask 10 classmates to take the survey.

1. Make a tally chart.

Topic:	

2. Use the tally chart to make a picture graph or a bar-type graph.

Objective: Construct a bar-type graph showing information about your classmates.